The Queer Parent

Everything You Need to Know From Gay to Ze

Lotte Jeffs and Stu Oakley

bluebird
books for life

First published 2023 by Bluebird

This paperback edition first published 2024 by Bluebird
an imprint of Pan Macmillan
The Smithson, 6 Briset Street, London EC1M 5NR
EU representative: Macmillan Publishers Ireland Ltd, 1st Floor,
The Liffey Trust Centre, 117–126 Sheriff Street Upper,
Dublin 1, D01 YC43
Associated companies throughout the world
www.panmacmillan.com

ISBN 978-1-0350-0183-5

1 3 5 7 9 8 6 4 2

A CIP catalogue record for this book is available from the British Library.

Illustrations by Katie Lukes, 2023

Typeset in Charter ITC Std by Palimpsest Book Production Ltd, Falkirk, Stirlingshire
Printed and bound by CPI Group (UK) Ltd, Croydon, CR0 4YY

Visit www.panmacmillan.com/bluebird to read more about all our books
and to buy them. You will also find features, author interviews and
news of any author events, and you can sign up for e-newsletters
so that you're always first to hear about our new releases.

CONTENTS

FOREWORD BY SANDI TOKSVIG

Hello, I'm Sandi Toksvig and I wanted to share a few words on why I think *The Queer Parent* is such an important book.

When my then partner and I set out to have kids, it was back in 1987. We were two women so isolated that we had never even heard of lesbians having children. Apart from understanding the mechanics of needing to find a donor, we had no idea about the social, legal, or any other implications. We were not even certain that if we had a child, social services might not come and take the baby away. Now, more than thirty-five years later, I am introducing a book in which my grown-up son Theo has written a section. When he was born, the beacon of kindness *The Daily Mail* took it upon itself to be appalled. So appalled that it was on the front page and we had to take our newborn son and his two older sisters into hiding to escape the death threats that followed. Today, that precious baby is a man who has the word 'Mums' tattooed inside a heart on his shoulder. He boasts of his lesbian parents on his body. The world has changed.

How comforting it would have been if, back at the beginning, we could have had a book like this to turn to with all our many questions. There were so many unknowns, from how to deal with heterosexual presumptions with schools, doctors and so on and trying our best to keep some less-than-welcoming members of our family calm. We had to cobble together our own agreement with the donor father and find our own way to negotiate matters which only arise for the LGBTQ+ parent. Some of it was very tough indeed and we often felt alone in our endeavors. Fortunately, all three of our fabulous kids have grown into even more fabulous adults and now we are grandparents. We must have got something right. But what heartache we might have been saved along the way if there had been others to guide us.

Hard to believe but this is the first ever UK mainstream LGBTQ+ parenting book. I am so glad it is here and only sorry it didn't arrive sooner. This book speaks to the more than 1.3 million people in the UK who identify as LGBTQ+ and to those around them, friends and family, who want to support any of the queer community who have, or want to have, families. It might even be a book to hand over to a teacher, health provider or anyone else who has contact with queer parents and their kids. It is that rare thing: an essential publication. I hope it brings you calm, I know it will bring you good sense and there's also a few laughs along the way.

INTRODUCTION

News flash! Ninety per cent of queer parenting is simply parenting. We're not unfurling Pride flags as we try and change our screaming baby's dirty nappy in the disabled loo at a restaurant, nor are we discussing gender binaries while trying to extract a toddler from a bouncy castle, and we are certainly not thinking about the heteronormative injustice of crippling fertility costs for lesbians while desperately trying to download the latest episode of *Hey Duggee* for a small person on the verge of an Elton-sized tantrum. No, in these everyday moments we are so focused on keeping our kids safe and happy that we'd probably not even notice if RuPaul was standing next to us, serving serious side-eye.

'What, then, is the point of this book?' we hear you cry. Well, before you close it and decide that your mum was right, routine and a good swaddle is all you need after all – listen. Being queer when you're a parent or a parent-to-be brings with it a whole host of conundrums that heterosexual parenting gurus couldn't even begin to fathom. And while it's true that raising kids is a great democratizer and we might actually be able to find something in common with School Gates Suze, it's this other layer of being a minority and dealing with everything that entails that means we seek comfort and reassurance from a community of LGBTQ+ people with children. And if you are School Gates Suze, or an ally, or just a curious cis heterosexual person, then welcome to our queer world; we can't wait for you to discover more and enjoy the educational ride you may go on.

Hello and welcome, then, to this informative, inspiring, funny, emotional and wildly entertaining A-to-Z of being a family when you aren't cis or straight.

Firstly, congratulations. Whether you're just starting to think that you'd like to welcome children into your life, are knee-deep in nappies or have waved your firstborn off to university already, this journey takes bravery, resilience and a good sense of humour, and being on it at any stage deserves, we think, a standing ovation. But maybe that's just because we're still annoyed that *we* don't get a 'Well Done' sticker at the end of every day.

We've decided to write the book as an A–Z because a) knowing the alphabet can help massively when you become a parent, and b) it makes it hopefully easier to read and connect with, particularly if you're sleep-deprived or generally feeling too frazzled for anything more arduous. But before we delve any deeper into what you can expect over the following pages, allow us to introduce ourselves.

I'll go first (Lotte). My wife Jenny and I decided that we wanted to start trying for a baby shortly after we got married (tragically hetero, I know). It's something we had talked about throughout our six-year courtship (please allow me to imagine I'm in a Jane Austen novel for a moment longer). I had always known I wanted to have children, and it took some years for Jenny to get to the same page as me. I was patient and relentlessly positive about it and each conversation we had, normally after a bottle of

Malbec at a nice restaurant, brought us a step closer to making the decision to go for it. Our first instinct was to use one of our dashing Darcy-like male friends as our donor. We never asked anyone outright, but over the course of a few years, during which we made it known it was something we were thinking about, three different men very seriously offered to donate their sperm so that we could start a family. We had long, earnest conversations with each of these potential suitors (okay, now I'm in *Mamma Mia!*) and they each got as far as getting their motility checked before deciding it wasn't something they were ready for, particularly as we were asking that they wouldn't be involved in the child's life. I am so grateful to these friends, not just for offering to help us create the family we wanted but for realizing that it wasn't right for them and being honest with us. The process made Jenny and I realize that an anonymous donor was the right route for us to take, so we set about reading the countless profiles on sperm bank websites in search of The One (more on these in 'D is for Donors', page 60). We were very, very lucky and Jenny became pregnant after one round of IUI (intrauterine insemination – more on this process in 'I is for IVF', page 145). Flash-forward three years and I decided, after much soul searching, that I'd like to try and carry too, and it hasn't been as easy. After three rounds of IVF (in vitro fertilization), I've decided to call an end to my adventures in trying to conceive. But what this means for you, dear reader, is that I can offer the unique insight of my experience as the 'other' mother and also as someone who has been on a long and winding fertility rollercoaster of their own.

In 2019 I was asked to host a podcast called *Some Families*, which celebrates all the different non-straight paths to parenthood. I enlisted my friend Stu, who had at that point adopted two children with his husband John (I'll let Stu tell you how they became parents to *three* kids himself!). It's been so mind-opening to speak to people outside of my own little bubble of the same-sex female experience of motherhood. Through

Some Families I've met trans dads, people who foster disabled kids, single parents through adoption, parents through surrogacy and so many other kinds of parents or carers. Speaking to these people over lockdown as we recorded the show really made us feel connected to a powerful community, and I'm so pleased that many of our *Some Families* guests have contributed to this book.

Oh, and who am I when I'm not presenting our (award-winning) podcast or being a parent to a beautiful and intelligent four-year-old? I can't remember (*sort of* joking – see 'Y is for You Do You', page 357, for the importance of maintaining individuality and a sense of self outside your role as a parent). I'm a journalist and I often write about LGBTQ+ parenting and relationships for the national press and magazines such as *ELLE* and *Grazia*. I've also written a self-help book for adults about harnessing soft power in hard times and my first picture book for kids is called *My Magic Family* and is about a little girl with a mama and a mum who learns more about her friends' wonderfully different families.

Finally – Lotte's passed the mic! I'm Stu, an adoptive cis gay dad to not one, not two, but three little people (please send help!). Even though my eldest is now seven, my husband and I have only been parents for four years, so, like Lotte, I'm also very new to this parenting malarkey and I am constantly learning and being inspired by other queer parents. Whether you are a parent, parent-to-be or just curious about the LGBTQ+ parenting experience, we hope you enjoy joining us on this exploration.

I am married to John and we've been together for almost seventeen years, which is surely classed as a diamond anniversary in gay couple years? I share our adoption story in the first chapter so won't delve into any spoilers here, but I will say that

I always wanted to be a dad. It wasn't till I met John, at the tender age of twenty-one, that I really gave any thought to the potential challenges involved in when and how we become parents. That part had never really crossed my mind. Like most people I've spoken to since, there didn't seem to be any clear info or a one-stop place for info, which is why I was so excited at the prospect of starting *Some Families* (which was the first EVER LGBTQ+ parenting podcast in the UK) with Lotte. Once we had done a little research, John and I decided surrogacy was not the path for us. Neither of us had the overwhelming desire to have our genes passed on and knowing that we couldn't create a child that was part him and part me just made it a moot point from the get-go. Therefore, for John and I, adoption was always the way.

Writing, podcasting and, dare I say, even parenting is not my full-time career and so I shall leave it to you, reader, to decide on if I should give up the 'day job' or not by the end of this book, and yes, I'll include parenting within that. I work in film publicity and, as Lotte once said to me, 'You thought you'd seen enough divas, then you had kids!', which is very, very true. Nothing compares to a toddler tantrum, even an A-list actress who doesn't have her five-star hotel suite at the right temperature. I've always been career-focused, and I knew that when we eventually had kids, I'd like to be the one to continue working. It helps that I love my job and have run publicity campaigns for films including *Star Wars*, *Frozen*, *Avengers* and *Jurassic World*. Let me tell you that during our adoption process I fully milked the 'I work for Disney' card. Forget what type of parent I was going to be, Mickey Mouse was my boss, so surely that trumped everything? So, it was fairly ironic that a year after having the kids I decided to pack up my suitcase of dreams and venture out into the wider world. Would the children ever forgive me for turning my back on the world of princesses and superheroes? Perhaps not, but they've since got to meet the real-life Barbie (well, Margot Robbie as Barbie, but they think it was the REAL Barbie), so I think I can be forgiven. The work vs parenting balance is a very real struggle but, as we discuss later in the book, being able to divvy up the emotional and physical division of labour as queer parents feels a lot more practical for us than our hetero friends. The joys of living outside the gender norms!

We adopted two children back in 2018 but our third came along as a 'surprise adoption' back in 2019. Throughout the book I'm open about my own mental health and struggles to keep it all together. The addition of a new child, the pressures of being a queer parent, my gay body insecurities, work, life, and a touch of a global pandemic with its subsequent lockdowns, all really tested the limits of my now-diagnosed anxiety, depression and body issues (the latter greatly impacted by truck loads of chicken nuggets). However, I know from this book, and the fact we've connected with countless other LGBTQ+ parents, that I am not alone. If you have struggled too, hopefully you will find comfort in mine and Lotte's honesty and that of the people with whom we have spoken.

OUR VIEW:
Using the Term 'Queer'

Before we continue, a note about the use of the word 'queer' throughout this book. We truly understand that this is not a term everybody is comfortable with, particularly if it was shouted at you in the playground by bullies. While Gen Z are claiming 'queer' to express a whole spectrum of the LGBTQIA+ experience, older generations remember it as a slur. We really hope that if you fall into the latter camp, our use of this word doesn't put you off reading this book. For us, it's a useful shorthand that encompasses the many gender and sexual identities we include in the book. We feel comfortable that we have wrenched the word back from homophobes and can redefine it as something wholly positive and inclusive. If it triggers unpleasant memories or doesn't sit well with you, we totally understand, but hope you can find a way to accept its use within these pages.

We/Us

Throughout this book the royal 'we' is Lotte and Stu, but there will be some areas where we write as ourselves, not in *Alvin and the Chipmunks*-style unison. We hope that you get to know us through the course of reading and find a sense of belonging in the stories we tell. We're still learning, and we are not in any way experts. But, you'll be pleased to hear, we are acutely aware of our own limitations and have invited people who know way more than we do on subjects to share their expertise in this book. From leading fertility experts, heads of adoption agencies and family lawyers to academics and psychologists, we've tracked down people with the answers to the questions you'll have. We know this because we have those questions too! We have also handed over to fellow parents with lived experience that we don't have. So, expect to hear from Black queer parents, trans parents, bisexual and queer disabled parents who offer a view that all of us will benefit from understanding more about.

We're learning from each other, too. When we first started talking all things queer parenting, we'd make mistakes. Stu kept referring to Lotte as a surrogate and was in a right old muddle about how IVF and IUI worked and what Lotte's role was as an 'other' mother, while Lotte wasn't even sure if gay people were allowed to adopt and had all sorts of preconceived ideas about adopted children being damaged and unlovable. She thought it was only people who couldn't have children of their 'own' who would adopt and, even then, they'd see it as a last resort. How wrong we both were! It took trust to admit the gaps in our knowledge and create a safe space where no question was a stupid question and nothing was off limits between us. Now I, Lotte, know all about adoption panels and therapeutic parenting, and I, Stu, know about egg collections and embryo transfers. And we are both better people and parents for broadening our perspective in this way.

So why did we decide to write this book, and why now? Well, since our kids are sleeping through the night, we were looking for another reason to stay up till the early hours again, and sitting hunched over a laptop, its blue glow barely illuminating the half-drunk bottle of wine beside us, seemed like a better idea than clubbing (which does actually still have its place as a parent – see 'Y is for You Do You', page 357!). Seriously though, when we first started thinking about having kids there was very little information out there. A lot of our research was through word of mouth, joining random Facebook groups, and reading the small print. *Wouldn't it have been great if we could have found not just answers to our many questions, but real-life experiences, all in one place*, we thought. *Some Families*, our podcast, was a start, but we wanted to create some-

thing you could keep on your shelf or your coffee table and share with friends and family. And so our book was born (4lb 3oz; Mum and Dad are both thrilled).

We hope more than anything that you don't just read the chapters that apply to you but that you delve into the worlds of queer parents who are nothing like you and that we all learn from each other in this way. The gay community can be very cliquey – you only need to sashay down Old Compton or Canal Street to see that, but as our forebears who fought for the rights that we now enjoy proved, coming together as a community that welcomes people of all genders, races and abilities is really how change happens. And there is still a lot of change needed for queer parents to be treated equally to straight parents – from the limiting binaries of mother and father demanded by birth certificates to the eye-watering costs of IVF for some queer couples and the outdated laws surrounding surrogacy and intended parenthood. We are relatively lucky in the UK compared to other places around the world where gay people cannot marry, adopt or have children of their own. This book is a small drop in the ocean in our global fight for LGBTQ+ rights.

And if you're coming to us not as a queer parent yourself but as a parent-to-be, a friend, grandparent or sibling who wants to understand what their loved one is going through on their journey to starting a family, we extend a warm welcome to you too. There's really something for everyone here and, as we explore in our final chapter on Gen Z (see page 367), so much to look forward to as a new, more evolved era of queer parenting takes over in the decades to come. Today's queer fifteen-year-olds, who care so much about identity and expression, who are less ashamed than we millennials ever were about their sexuality and are joyfully themselves, are the brilliant queer parents of tomorrow. So however we get there, let's unite in our desire to raise children who are strong, who are kind, who have open hearts and minds (and who will take care of their queer parents in their dotage! Those OAP Gay Cruises won't pay for themselves!).

Who Is This Book For?

Every day a member of the LGBTQ+ community, which numbers more than 1.2 million in the UK alone, will start to think about their future family. A few will decide parenthood is not the path they wish to take. However, many will start dreaming and questioning how to make it work for them. Today there are so many options for queer people to have kids, yet so few books and guides on the subject of LGBTQ+ parenting exist.

The Queer Parent is firstly for any LGBTQ+ person or family who is starting their own non-straight path to parenthood, since it covers the wide-ranging subjects that starting a queer family throws up. This book is a helpful light in the dark for anyone taking those first steps, questioning and trying to make sense of the options they have, including adoption, donor conception, co-parenting, surrogacy and more.

Additionally, the curvy, queer parenting path is not easy to navigate, and many LGBTQ+ parents travel forward without learning and listening to those outside their own sexual and gender identity. This book is for all queer parents who want to have their story reflected back at them, but, just as important, it is also for gay parents to learn from lesbian parents, for cis parents to learn from trans parents and for all of us to recognize how we can stand together as one queer parenting community and understand and support each other's stories.

Lastly, many of us are not alone on this path, and our many friends and family want to know more about the options ahead for their loved ones so they can support and understand their journey. The classic 'I will never be a grandmother' line is now a thing of the past, but for a lot of grandparents this book will offer a comforting and safe space to explore the adventures and challenges ahead for their extended family.

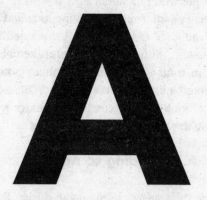

IS FOR ADOPTION

 For the average cishet couple, their parenting journey begins with a sensual embrace, perhaps after a bottle of wine and a romantic meal. The bedsheets brush their naked skin as they begin the process that ultimately leads to pregnancy . . . you don't need us to spell it out. However, for me (Stu) and my husband (John), our parenting journey began in a cold church hall off Pimlico Road in London. I assure you, though, we were not getting our rocks off on a Formica table while posters claiming 'Jesus Loves You' beamed down at us. No, we were sitting with thirty other wide-eyed people at our first ever toe-dip into the world of adopting at an information evening. Chances are that if you are reading this you've either been to one of these meetings, know someone who has, or are thinking about attending one. The meeting, which for some reason seems to be required by law to take place in a dusty church hall (honestly, queers deserve better), normally involves an agency or local authority giving a rough overview of the process along with some 'case studies' – people who talk about how it worked for them. We chose this agency's information evening as it had a good track record with 'the gays' (an advert in *Attitude* led us to believe this at least). And, hurrah, there was an actual real-life gay standing up in front of us telling us about how he and his husband adopted a little boy. We sat in a YO! Sushi in London Victoria Rail Station after discussing the things we had heard. We both knew this was the right path for us.

Deciding to Adopt

John and I met in a sweaty lesbian club during Brighton Pride in 2006 and, honestly, if we'd had the right bits, we probably would have started our parenting journey that night (sorry, too much info). Fast-forward eleven years and, following a wedding, gorgeous holidays, two dogs and plenty of lazy weekends, we decided to throw some chaos into our carefree life and adopt. I never exactly remember the first conversation, but we always had adoption in our mind rather than surrogacy or any other option. Adoption appealed to us as it meant we were going into parenting on an equal footing. Neither of us would have a biological link to our children. The legalities and costs of surrogacy, plus the knowledge that there were children out there needing a home, cemented adoption as the only route for us.

At the information evening we were told to be as honest as possible throughout the process to ensure nothing came to bite you on the ass that might delay or interrupt things. Great advice, I thought. The agency arranged to call me to have a quick chat and gather some basic info about John and me before our first official meeting took place. It was going great, and the questions were fine. I was excited to have taken a big adoption leap for us . . . and then, 'And do you smoke?' asked the lady on the other end of the phone. 'No . . . well, I used to.' 'When?' 'I gave up back in 2007.' 'Great!' she said . . . But with 'be honest' bubbling around in my head, I decided to admit, 'I do occasionally social smoke.' The words just tumbled out. 'Oh . . .' Her tone had changed. Maybe that was a bit too honest . . . time to back-pedal! 'Well, very rarely,' I explained. 'The last time was just one at a Christmas party in December'; it was now March. It was too late, and the hole had been dug. She paused before finally saying, 'I need to check with my manager. We don't usually move forward with applications if there is evidence of smoking within the last six months.' SHIT! Ten minutes into our first adoption step and I'd already majorly fucked up. We had to put our application on hold till the summer to allow for me to be six months 'clean'. So, lesson learned. Be honest, but perhaps not *too* honest.

Starting the Process

After my smoking faux-pax I can *honestly* say the process was fairly plain sailing for us. That's not to say it's the same for everyone, and everyone's journey is incredibly individual, but I like to think our version of events can give hope and dispel the myth that the process is as arduous as many people may think it is.

I recently came across a letter we had been sent by our adoption agency inviting us for our first formal interview (post ciggie-gate!). The date of the interview was 28 June 2017. Our children's first night in their new home was 28 June 2018, a year to the date. We didn't hang about!

As you can imagine, that year was quite the whirlwind. We were heading into the unknown and anxieties were high. Aside from the utterly brilliant social worker from our agency, for the first part of our adoption we were on our own with no one to really share our concerns or questions with.

We had only 'come out' as potential adopters to our immediate family and close-knit group of friends. It was an exciting time but daunting to be just us. About three months into the process came our first group training session. Taking place at our agency's HQ over four days, we were about to have a crash course in how to 'be adopters'. What did that even mean? What did it entail? As an introverted extrovert there was part of me dreading the whole process knowing that I might be forced to make small talk with a bunch of strangers. There is nothing worse than small talk in my opinion. My fears were realized as there were group exercises, games and, the worst . . . the dreaded breakout groups. In any other situation it would be my idea of hell. So, we sat there at 9 a.m. on the first morning (actually it might have been more like 9:15 a.m. because I'm sure John and I were late as we tend to be late for everything and I recall that morning being particularly stressful as the weight of trying to be 'perfect' was already creeping in and the fact we were going to be late had sent me into a spiral). So, there we were at 9:15 a.m. in a room filled with strangers all united by one common theme: future adoptees. Even though our agency was known for supporting LGBTQ+ adopters, part of us still expected to be the only gays in the room. But there was another gay couple and a single lesbian adopter in the room. My usual inner conflict kicked in . . . 'Yay, other gays' mixed with 'Oh God, I need to somehow prove myself to them'. The latter, a lifelong issue I've had, was heightened by the fact that this other gay couple, Andy and Mark, were the toned, smart and groomed breed of gays. Gay anxieties aside, something quite wonderful happened in that room. By lunchtime, we suddenly felt part of a community. Other people were asking the questions we had been thinking, there were shared knowing nods and nervous laughter. The breakout groups became more like group confessionals in which we all deeply exhaled as we no longer felt alone in the fears we had. To help explain it to friends, I often compared the group to NCT classes and the friendships that are formed pre-birth.

It was here I started to draw parallels between adopters and queer groups. As an adopter, you are an outsider from the traditional norms. You are in a minority. Like John and me, you may not have 'come out' as adopters yet, and sometimes things don't quite make sense till you find 'your people' and discover a sense of belonging. Walking into the training room was the equivalent of being seventeen and heading into the bright lights of my first gay bar with my then best gay mate Tommy, with just a little less nipple on show and no rum and cokes sadly. Over the days we formed a close bond with Andy and Mark and another couple. The community was sealed by the forming of a WhatsApp group so we could continue to keep each other updated as we all went forward in the process.

Being part of the group that formed at our adoption training was special; we felt less alone and part of a bigger picture. The training also allowed us to delve into deeper questions about the process, managing behaviours, self-care and much more. Our friends and family were also offered the opportunity to take part in a similar training group, which I believe a number of different adoption agencies offer, to help them understand what we were venturing into, which was fabulous as it really prepared some of our closest support network for what was potentially ahead of us.

INSIGHT:
LGBTQ+ Adopters

It's no coincidence that RuPaul, queen of all the drag queens, is often coined 'Mother Ru', as the sense of family and belonging is so strong within the LGBTQ+ community (for more about drag families, see 'N is for Nurture', page 212). For decades, groups of chosen families have formed when birth families became inaccessible due to good old-fashioned queerphobia and rejection. Perhaps, therefore, the notion that you can choose your own family via adoption has become such a natural fit for us gays. One in six adoptions[1] within the UK are now by LGBTQ+ folk, although according to New Family Social, an organization that supports LGBTQ+ adopters, this number may actually be higher.

Government data shows that one in six adoptions in England in 2022 were to same-sex couples[2] and in Wales it was one in four.[3] In Scotland in 2021 it was one in eleven.[4] There's no comparative data published by the Northern Ireland administration.

All of the data released by each government under-counts how many LGBTQ+ people adopt. This is because the data focuses on the family composition that a child is adopted into – whether it's a male/female couple, a male couple, a female couple or a single person. There's no data on sexual orientation or gender identity beyond those household types. As a result, it's impossible to calculate how many single adopters are LGBTQ+. Similarly, you can't identify the number of bi·people in different gender relationships who adopt. Trans and non-binary adopters are invisible in the released data, which only allows for a person to be described as male or female.

Adoption Myth-Busting

There are countless myths about the modern adoption system, especially as people do get confused around how things used to be (thanks to shows like *Long Lost Family* and general histor-ical horror stories) vs how they are now. Here are some of the most common misconceptions and the truth behind them:

'Could I/we be discriminated against for being LGBTQ+?'

The law in the UK means that you can't be discriminated against for being LGBTQ+ during the adoption process.[5] However, we all know that what the law says vs what ordinary folk say, do and feel can be very different. John and I were on our guard from the outset. We knew what the law said but we were prepared to face off with Homophobic Henry, the gay-hating foster carer, or even Bigot Barbara, the ignorant social worker. We never met Henry or Barbara. That's not to say they don't exist, but in our experience, no one really cared if we were gay or straight and it was wonderfully refreshing. In some ways we felt we almost had an easier ride because we were a gay couple. 'LGBTQ+ people have lived experience of navigating their identity and place in the world, which can be a real advantage when parenting a child who experienced trauma in their early life,' says New Family Social. 'Unlike most opposite-gender couples, for LGBTQ+ people adoption is often the first route to parenthood. An increased visibility of LGBTQ+ people adopting has inspired more people to do so; when New Family Social (an agency that supports LGBTQ+ adopters) launched its annual recruitment campaign to encourage more LGBTQ+ people to consider adoption or fostering, one in thirty-one adoptions in England were to same-sex couples. It's now one in six. Many agencies have worked hard to encourage more engagement with their local queer community but it's also the case that if LGBTQ+ people see their friends successfully adopt that it becomes a more achievable goal for them.'

'Do all children available for adoption have severe behavioural problems?'

Most social workers will tell you that 99.9 per cent of all children in the care system awaiting adoption have suffered some form of trauma. This can be a sliding scale, and depending on the trauma involved there might very well be behavioural problems. However, with the right approach, namely therapeutic parenting (a highly nurturing parenting approach, with empathy at its core, which uses firm but fair boundaries and routines to aid the development of new neural pathways in the brain so children may gain trust in adults), behavioural problems can be managed. One of the exercises I found most enlightening during the training process to help understand what a child goes through in the process was the scissor exercise. Fourteen of us stood around someone who was nominated to represent the child. We each had a role – school, house, pets, friends, smells, environment noises, and so on – that factored in this child's life. We each held a string that led to the 'child' in the middle. One by one the training lead cut each string representing the loss and change happening in that child's life. Simple things such as moving from the countryside to a busy town and the noises involved affect that child's trauma. Every child is different and there is every chance behavioural issues may appear, but don't pass up adoption because you think that it's not something you can handle. These children have been through a lot and just need your support. There could be the child for you out there and you are just who they need to match the needs they have. You could be the person to offer that empathy, understanding and love that they desperately need.

A social worker from PACT, the adoption agency John and I used, adds:

> The short answer is NO, not all adopted children have severe behavioural issues. However, all children come from a background of neglect and abuse of varying degrees where, through significant neglect, their basic needs were not met, e.g., having regular mealtimes or even enough food, being kept clean, being played with, living in a very dirty home, etc. Or their emotional needs were not met e.g., not being shown any love or affection, or distorted love and affection (this can be seen in respect of children who are sexually abused).

With these backgrounds children do find it difficult to manage feelings, so when feeling confused, afraid, sad or angry then can erupt, as seen in their behaviours, such as hitting out or being defiant. Although as said, it does not apply to all children that move on to adoption. But a truism I think is all children are having to manage mixed and confused emotional feelings which can be expressed in many different ways.

Adoptive parents need to help a child feel safe, help them to understand and regulate their emotions. Help them to accept love and feel wanted. It all takes time. Adoptive parents receive help post placement to manage this.

To finish off this myth I want to reflect on how I described trauma as a sliding scale. I recently read Ben Fergusson's book *Tales from the Fatherland*, in which he reflects on the adoption of his son. It's a great read, especially as it opened my eyes to how adoption may work in another country – in his case Germany – but I really related to his views on trauma. Like us, Ben adopted his son while he was still an infant (the baby, that is; not Ben!). He questions the very notion of trauma being present in, or forced upon, every adopted child. We adopted both our boys at the age of six months, and they had been in care since the day they were born. I very quickly got sick of people saying, 'Oh, he was only a baby so thankfully he won't remember anything.'

Yes, their age at the time of going into care does mean that their experiences did not directly relate to the same trauma that other older children go through, but, without going into detail for their own privacy, there are still factors that we need to address and monitor throughout their lives. But how much trauma will they really have?

'My issue,' says Ben, 'is that I look at my perfect little son toddling around our flat and I feel like the trauma of his adoption is something we have to gift him. He does not wake up screaming in the night. His weight and height are completely average. He speaks well. He has reached all of his developmental milestones. He is like any of his friends in his nursery – except for this sad fact about his birth that we slowly have to make him aware of. I worry that, in focusing on our son's adoption as his trauma, we are simply replacing one highly emotive narrative about how he is meant to feel about being adopted with another one.' It's a highly nuanced topic: like most things in adoption, it's not black or white. I find the notion of the potential trauma in our sons' lives as completely grey and we just have to be prepared for what may happen, or indeed what may not.

'You must take any child you are offered'

Linked to this is another myth: that you must take any child you are offered. Not true. The selection process is complex, and you are in complete control. In fact, you are encouraged to be as descriptive as you can in terms of deciding the child or children you want. I found the whole adoption process incredibly therapeutic. Not only are you reflecting on your own life story, but you have to really work out what you want. The most interesting part of this was the discussions between John and I in discovering what we each felt we could manage. The selection process goes deep and led to us having conversations that we never imagined, such as whether we would take a child who had HIV. Some may feel it's like a shopping list, and trust me the comparisons to dating websites are true, but you've got to be sure of what you can take on and what type of child you have in your mind, because otherwise it could lead to a lot of time wasted and potential upset on both sides. The process helps you with this, though, and we came to the end of our selection process with a completely different outcome of what I had expected us to go with, especially post training, where our eyes and minds had been opened.

This is explored further by the social worker from PACT:

From the beginning of someone being interested in adoption, we will ask them about the age of the child, the gender, whether they want one, two, three children, as well as background considerations. As someone progresses through their assessment, this is discussed in depth, so not only covering age and gender, but also could they consider a child that came from certain types of backgrounds, e.g., has been physically hurt or sexually abused. Could they consider a child whose birth mother abused alcohol or drugs during pregnancy (both abuses can impact upon brain development), or parents with mental health or learning difficulties? There are many matching considerations that are discussed. This matching is captured in the person's (or couple's) Prospective Adopters Report, which local authorities and family-finding social workers from regional adoption agencies will read. Depending on their matching criteria the person, or couple, would be approached via our family-finding team with a child or children that reflect that criteria.

'Will I/we only have the option to adopt an older child?'

False. While it's a truth that there are far more older children in the care system awaiting adoption, that doesn't mean that there are no babies awaiting a home. During our matching process we were surprised at the number of young babies whose profiles we were sent. However, these babies have not been given up by young teens who didn't feel ready for a child; that is indeed a falsehood. I think any social worker would agree that is incredibly rare. If you want a baby, then it's possible, but you are dealing with a much greater unknown in terms of development and health. These are the things you've got to think about.

'Can the birth parents take them back?'

In the UK, once an adoption order goes through the court, it cannot be reversed by the birth family. I have heard of hideous stories in America where the birth family have discovered a queer couple has adopted the child taken from them and they've been able to appeal. This is not the case, thankfully, in the UK. To complete an adoption, the case is taken to a family court so an independent judge can review the situation, including reading reports from all the social workers involved about you, your child and their birth family. During this hearing the birth parents can appeal, but if there are any objections based on sexuality this would be immediately thrown out by the judge. Plus, at this stage in proceedings, unless the family had a very strong case as to why they are now fit parents, it's incredibly unlikely even to be considered.

'Birth parents and their families are involved in court care proceedings, where there are assessments (as well as support given to families) to see if change can happen,' adds PACT. 'The Children Act 1989 and subsequent legislation is very clear a child should, if possible, grow up with their birth parents (and/or family), adoption is the very last resort. So when a Care Order and a Placement Order (a care order endorses a plan for adoption; then a placement order authorises the local authority to place a child for adoption) are granted, very intensive work has already occurred and there is confidence that a plan of adoption is the only outcome. The birth parents can appeal against the Care and Placement Orders but only in respect of the hearing not being fair: that they have not been represented properly. The Care Order (as do the Interim Care Orders that occur throughout court proceedings) gives the local authority the right to assume parental responsibility and make decisions on behalf of the child.'

When adoptive parents put their application into court to adopt their child or children (which can only occur from ten weeks following placement) the birth parents are notified as they still retain parental responsibility. The birth parents can represent themselves at court (or if able seek legal representation – this does not happen usually as while birth parents are given legal representation during care proceedings, they cannot have this during adoption proceedings so have to fund legal representation themselves). In most cases, birth parents, while not supporting adoption, are passive, often too caught up in their daily lives or it is too emotional for them to do so. In reality, when an adoptive parent puts an application into court to adopt it is usually a straightforward affair and is not contested.

If a birth parent does contest, the court will need to consider two things. What has changed in the birth parents' circumstances? You need to remember that court proceedings where Care and Placement Orders were granted, typically occurred only months previously, so the question would always be: 'Can such change really happen and is it sustainable?' Even if a birth parent can demonstrate change, then the second consideration is: what is best for the child? The court would be mindful how settled the child is in their adoptive placement, the loving attachments they have formed and whether they are thriving: what the damage to the child would be if they were removed from such an environment.

'Do you have to keep their name?'

It is highly recommended you don't change the child's name and highly frowned upon if you do wish to. This can be incredibly hard to get one's head round, especially if, like me, you'd always dreamed of and discussed the 'perfect name'. You've got to remember that your child's name is their identity. By changing it you are removing part of that identity. Early on in the process we embraced this, as it took away that feeling of responsibility of choosing a name. One less thing for us to worry about! And I love our children's names. They are their names, their identity and are beautiful. Best thing to do is to build a bridge and get over this one as quickly as you can. They will have your surname and if you have your heart set on a name you can always add it as a lovely middle name. In fact, my family has a tradition of giving the eldest boy the middle name 'Ernest' (don't get me started, I hated it for years but grew to embrace and love it!), so we gave our son that middle name and it was a perfect way of continuing the family legacy which he is now part of.

'Anyone who adopts is a saint'

Obviously not, but get ready to become one in the eyes of many. People will start praising you from the moment they hear you've adopted like you are some modern-day Mother Theresa of the gays. It can make you feel deeply uncomfortable and if you are reading this and have recognized yourself doing it, then please stop. John and I selfishly wanted to be parents. We wanted kids like most other people on the planet and it just so happened that we chose this route. The kids are not 'lucky' to have us; we are lucky to have them. We are not perfect parents, nor are we saints, so don't treat us that way . . . unless there is a free drink involved then pass it over. Amen.

'Adopting is for rich gays'

The world would like to believe that all gays have vast amounts of disposable income. But, much like the real pound, perhaps the pink pound is not as strong as it used to be. After all, isn't the notion that queers have loads of money to spend on Tom Ford fragrance, designer clobber and long days in the Mykonos sun based on the idea that they don't have to spend money on kids? With the rise of the queer parent, perhaps this stereotype will change, I think to myself as I shuffle along in my local Aldi throwing bargains into my large trolley. I hate to break it to anyone who thinks that upon coming out we get some form of financial gift from Dolly Parton as a thanks for being gay, but financial concerns can hit us just like anyone else. In fact, with issues around employment, discrimination and inaccessible healthcare, the LGBTQ+ community faces many financial complications.

INSIGHTS:

The Costs Involved in Adoption

So what expenses are involved in the adoption process? Are we looking at the same eye-watering costs that surrogacy can sometimes incur? 'Many are surprised to hear that there is no cost of adoption charged by agencies for applicants who wish to adopt a child, or children, from the UK,' says PACT.

This is the same whether you choose to adopt through an independent or voluntary adoption agency, a local authority or a regional adoption agency. While there is no cost for adopting a child, there are a couple of things that prospective adopters should be aware of that they may have to pay for as part of the adoption process. This can include:

- *medical checks from your GP, which many surgeries do charge for.*
- *an overseas Disclosure and Barring Service (DBS) check if an applicant has ever lived or worked abroad.*
- *a potential cost if there is a need for an interpreter and/or translator for any referees who are unable to speak or write in English.*

When assessing a family to become adoptive parents, we are not looking for people with high incomes or vast savings. Being on a low income or receiving benefits does not mean you can't adopt a child. We are looking for people to demonstrate they can manage their finances and are able to be at home with a child or children for at least twelve months. If you work, this will mean taking adoption leave. As anyone who has ever parented a child will know, having children can be expensive, but the adoption process is designed so that income is not a barrier for someone choosing to become a parent to a child, or children, in need of a permanent family.

'You can only adopt once'

This is one that from experience I can tell you is a complete load of bullshit. John and I adopted two children in 2018. We never had any intention of adopting more, but we always knew that the birth family's situation meant there could be additional children born in the future who might go straight into the care system. We discussed it with the panel and the authorities at the time, and we said it would be something we would consider depending on our circumstances. Once our kids came home, we didn't give it much further thought. Fast-forward to late October 2019. I was heading into work and as I stepped out the lift, I received an email from my social worker with the subject line 'News'. My heart stopped. Without opening it I knew what it was going to say, and I was right. There was another baby, and would we consider adopting. I immediately phoned John. There was no other information. We didn't know the baby's health status, their sex, their age and, rather unhelpfully, our social worker was in meetings until 2:30 p.m., so we had a hideous waiting game ahead of us. I travelled home and John and I sat and waited. In our minds it was a newborn baby that might need care in hospital, so one of us best get prepared to travel to be with them if needed. However, the situation was a bit different and allows me to address another fact. The UK care system is incredibly unfunded, understaffed and not running at full potential. It turns out the baby was in fact five months old. A little boy who was perfectly healthy but had been in care since the moment he was born. Earlier that year, while we had been in the final days of a family holiday to Disney World in Florida, he was left alone for two weeks in a hospital, only being cared for by the kind nurses. A fact that will always haunt me and anger us both forever. The services had failed to inform us for five whole months that he had been born, even though various independent officers had flagged that we should be the first point of contact and considered for fostering while the adoption order was granted (often called fostering to adopt). It was only because his foster family had wanted to be considered for adoption that someone finally contacted us, which is when our social worker was notified. The moment we heard about him, he felt part of our family. There was no decision to be made; our hearts had already done that for us. Every social worker we then spoke to agreed that he should be given the chance to live with his two older siblings. Something his incredible foster family also agreed with, as much as it hurt them to say goodbye to the little boy they had fallen totally in love with. They too had been unaware that we had made it clear from the outset we would adopt a sibling. In fact, they had actually been told we were 'not interested', which is why they considered adopting him in the first place. The whole situation was a mess. We only had six weeks to get him home before Christmas and we were faced with an incredibly difficult and slow local authority who didn't seem to grasp the fuck-up they had made. Our social worker and the agency were amazing and helped us fight through the red tape, as technically we had to go through the whole approval system again. With everyone's support we were able to fast-track certain areas as everyone was passionate that he should spend his first Christmas at home with his sister and brother. And we did it. It took a lot of work, but our little boy moved home that December and it is safe to say we adore him and can't imagine a life without him.

So, yes, you can adopt after adoption. However, the most important thing is that you consider how a new child or children might affect your existing child/children, bearing in mind any trauma or behavioural issues they might already have.

MEET . . .

James (he/him) and his husband Jay (he/him)

James and Jay adopted a second child five years after their first adoption.

After we adopted our first son we were not initially sure if we would adopt again. It was never on the cards when we first adopted, but I was certain that one day I'd like another, while my husband Jay was a little more hesitant. Things went so well for us the first time, and our son is so settled, I think he was worried about rocking the boat. However, four years later life moved on, we had a new house which we renovated, and then, post Covid, we felt ready to go for it. We didn't want to start the adoption process totally from scratch, so we decided to wait until the social worker who worked with us the first time was available, so at least we had that shorthand and had someone that knew us and our son.

We adopted our second son in 2022. Due to the six-year age gap, we think our eldest was initially a little disappointed to not have the play mate he thought he was getting, which was a little frustrating for him. He has such a nurturing side though, which ultimately played to our advantage as he is now enjoying the role of big brother. If anyone is thinking of adopting again, then during the matching process, the priority must be your existing child/children. Be prepared for completely different personalities. Everything you knew from before has to be re-learned as not everything that worked last time will necessarily work this time round.

Adoption is not easy, but it's not as hard as you may think. At the end of the day any form of parenting is not bloody easy. John and I have an incredible family and the love we have for our children is just insane. We still have a long way to go but I know my love for my three monkeys will never end. I do get 'adoption broody', especially when Lotte and I talk to families at the start of their process or I see posts from those excited people going to training sessions or signing up to agencies. Would I do it again? Not likely, but I loved the process. It taught us so much about ourselves and strengthened our bond as a couple. I truly believe that going through the assessments and the training has made us better parents than we would have been just left to our own devices. And who knows what the future may hold!

Talking Points

▶ Has your opinion of adoption changed in any way after reading this chapter?

▶ Is it something you would consider?

▶ Have you thought about what you feel you could 'take on', including children with any disabilities, medical conditions or life-limiting health issues?

▶ Do you feel prepared to help a child through trauma?

B

IS FOR BETTER LATE THAN NEVER

Buckle up, kids, it's time for our coming-out stories!

 My best friend Will came out when we were in Year 8 at school. I remember, we were sitting at my kitchen table cutting out pictures from magazines to cover our diaries with when he told me he liked boys. *Smash Hits* was open on a story about Take That and he pointed at Gary Barlow and said he was his favourite. Being a nascent lesbian, I was more of a Mark Owen gal myself. Will's coming out opened a fabulous door into the LGBTQ+ community for me from a very early age. A year later and I'd told him I was gay too, and so began our out-and-proud teenage life in London. We went to gay youth groups, snuck into club nights in Soho and squirmed our way through awkward dates at First Out Cafe. My first kiss was with a girl on the dance floor at the iconic gay club Pop Stars – I had never been surer of anything. It felt so right. I'm aware that my story is quite rare. There was no angst or shame or trying to hide – I was lucky that homophobia didn't factor into my early life at all.

 A shocking fact for you: I have never come out. Perhaps this is the time? Mum, if you are reading this, 'I'm gay.' Although I'd imagine you might have an idea after attending my wedding and being a wonderful nanny to our three children. I feel an immense privilege that I never had to sit my parents down and say those two words. I think it's down to two things: the first being that I have wonderful, open and fabulous parents who would have accepted me whatever I was; the second that I am so incredibly camp and gay that really there was no other option for me. Aged thirteen, I took part in my local amateur dramatics society's variety performance. My vision for my moment in the spotlight? Me, four backup dancers, Candi Staton's 'Young Hearts Run Free', a big Dolly Parton-style wig, a pink feather boa, fishnet stockings and my mum's red velvet split-leg dress (which I think she must have got in the early 1990s and which I took without her knowledge). My mum had no idea what I was doing till the curtain opened and she sat open-mouthed as her son lip-synched for his life on stage in front of her. As I took the time in the music interlude to go into the audience, sit on a grown man's lap and blow glitter in his face, my mum turned to my best friend's mum and said, 'Oh, I do worry about him some-times.' I guess you could call that my coming-out moment. Fast-forward ten years and my mum asked me round for dinner as my aunty was visiting. I explained that I had someone staying and she said, 'Bring them.' That person was John, whom I had only just started 'courting'. He turned up and she welcomed him with open arms and made a 'mum' joke about washing. It was the first time I'd ever brought a boy home and she just took it in her stride with little conversation. This wasn't in an avoiding-the-subject way, just it was what it was and wasn't that fabulous. I'm very lucky.

Coming Out Later in Life

Excuse us a moment while we mourn the loss of all the fantastic gay bars, youth groups and IRL places for teenage queers to hang out that defined our young queer lives. Liking an Instagram post just isn't the same as having to order a jacket potato with coleslaw and sit opposite another queer sixteen-year-old in an LGBTQ+ vegetarian cafe.

Okay, we've dried our eyes and we're back to talk about how different our experiences as gaybies were from those of people who came out later in life. And, furthermore, how our personal journeys to being out and part of the LGBTQ+ community have informed our attitude to parenting as queer people.

> *Lotte:* I suppose for me, because I had such a privileged queer youth, it never occurred to me that I wouldn't be able to do something straight people could do. I always wanted children and I was confident that one day I'd be a parent, even if I only had a vague sense of how that might work.

> *Stu:* Same for me, I assumed I'd get married and have children one day. I never worried about how. With the blissful naivety of youth I figured it would just happen.

Now, compare that to the experience of someone who, for whatever reason (and there are so many), didn't come to terms with their sexuality until they were well into adulthood. Or someone who did come out young but didn't have the support or acceptance of their own family. These kinds of experiences can lead some people to believe that being queer would mean they'd never be able to have children, or perhaps their sexuality was so riddled with shame and self-loathing that they might have felt they didn't deserve to.

Many people start out in cis heterosexual relationships and have children before realizing they are LGBTQ+. Some of these relationships are good and happy and end well and some don't. In 'X is for Ex-Partners, Divorce, Separation and Step Parents' (see page 340) we'll discuss this more. But a huge number of people in our community were parents before they came out. Many have experienced the difference in raising children when the outside world reads you as cis and/or straight and then when you are perceived as 'other'. Parents have had to come out to their children and have had to navigate their identity as a queer person alongside their identity as a parent, and this can be a challenge.

We hate the term 'Gold Star Lesbian' for a woman who has never been with a man, not least because there doesn't seem to be a male equivalent but also because, just, yuck – it implies there's a hierarchy of queerness and it doesn't account for the fabulously fluid nature of sexuality. We know many of our queer parent community came out later in life, and many also identify as bisexual, or pansexual, and are currently in het-assumed relationships. Does being in a relationship and parenting with someone of a different sex make them any less queer? Of course not!

We wanted to share some stories with you in this chapter from LGBTQ+ people who started their parenting journey in hetero relationships, because our community is full of these often-overlooked experiences and as a reminder that there's no 'right' way to be a queer parent.

MEET . . .

Eavan (she/her)

Eavan is a single mother to two children via natural conception.

I got married at twenty-two to a man who was much older. He was keen to have a family while I hadn't really found myself yet. We rushed into having children. I acknowledge the privilege I had with the ease it took to bring my kids into the world compared to others in the queer community. I ended up as a young mum with lots of questions about myself. I thought I might be bi but hadn't really tested it out properly, having shied away from that identity. But as I got older it just became more and more urgent for me to work it out and I became quite unhappy. With agreement from my husband, I began to explore relationships with women and I discovered I was actually a lesbian. I then slowly picked my way out of my heterosexual family situation, which culminated when he got stuck abroad during Covid. When he returned to London after a year apart, we agreed to divorce.

We now live in two separate houses, close to each other. He's a very kind person and has always been respectful and supportive. We share parenting fifty/ fifty. We have dinner at each other's houses and go on holidays together. It's very amicable.

So I am now a single lesbian mother.

I really want to knit my identities as a mum and as a lesbian together. At the moment they are entirely separate. Half of the time I'm doing the school run and helping with homework and the other half, I'm going to [the club night] Butch Please, going on hot dates and travelling. I'm in a bunch of chats and community groups but a lot of the people I chat to don't know I'm a parent, or that I was married to a man. I feel a bit ashamed of that. Like I'm letting the side down because I'm not a Gold Star Lesbian. I wonder how much of that is internalized heterophobia, where, in finding this new identity, I don't want people to know about my past, or the other half of my life.

My kids were four and six when I told them about why their mum and dad had separated. I made it about differentiating between types of love and I said, 'There's the people you want to kiss, and there's people you want to hang out with. And I'm the type of person that wants to kiss women.' That was the beginning of the conversation. They're fine about it. They know about girlfriends and I increasingly try to use more grown-up language around it. As they're getting older, I also inject some of the challenges that face the queer community and why it's important to be proud of it.

When I was first coming out four years ago, there were absolutely no resources. There were some stories online about people who came out later in life – in their fifties – and it seemed the narrative was that you wait until your kids are grown up and then you've done your bit. But I'm thirty-two and I was twenty-eight or so when things started kicking off. There was nothing online that really helped me through this.

More recently I discovered a Canadian woman who started an Instagram account called Late to Lesbian, which gathered together people in my situation. Some of them were just coming out. And some of them were coming out with kids. Within four months, this page had 50,000 followers. So the fact is I'm far from alone. It was nice to feel that support because we've got a lot to handle when we are coming out: parenting, working out our own life, our new identity. And there are a lot of people in my position who are people pleasers and are really grief-stricken because they feel that they've let everybody down.

I wear my story a little more comfortably than that: I'm a better parent now I'm out. I'm lighter and happier and the kids pick up on that.

Eavan's Advice for Coming Out of a Heterosexual Relationship

Ask yourself what example you want to set for your kids. Do you want to be a person who shows that your happiness is important, that your needs and your identity are as valid as the people's around you? If you were giving advice to your own child, you'd want your child to be happy. So model that behaviour.

I know a lot of people who come out late who are kind of held hostage emotionally by husbands or wives who are really sad about how things have turned out. And therefore they feel guilt and then stick around longer than they should in the marriage. Don't prioritize your partner's needs above your own; they're certainly not doing the same thing back for you.

Maintain your boundaries: you don't owe anybody not connected to the experience explanations.

Do everything with as much kindness and generosity of spirit and love as you can.

MEET . . .

Sharon Davey (she/her)

Sharon is the illustrator of Lotte's picture book *My Magic Family*.[6] She lives with her partner Janet and her two teenage children, whom she had via natural conception with her male ex-partner.

Could you tell us a bit about the evolution of your sexuality and your decision to end your straight relationship?

When my marriage became a mess and broke down when I was twenty-nine, I didn't think I'd have to consider the evolution of my sexuality. Making sure the kids were fed and I had managed a shower was enough. When I met Janet and an instant solid friendship turned into 'I can't let this woman walk out of my life for anything', I was surprised. There was no 'I wonder if I'm gay', just Janet, and everything about her was perfect for me, and that included her being a woman.

How old were your children at the time and how did you talk to them about what was happening?

My kids were five and seven when I divorced their dad. They got to know Janet as my friend, and I talked about her being funny and wonderful. I think they suspected, for a variety of reasons, that it was something more before we 'talked' about her being my girlfriend. They were excited. My seven-year-old knew it was unusual and was reticent to tell her friends, but my five-year-old could barely get through the school gates without yelling, 'My mum's got a girlfriend!'

Whenever I talked to the kids about their own future partners, I always used any gender as a possibility. We had friends who were in same-sex couples and working in theatre meant the kids regularly met a varied group of people. They were very supportive.

Did the kids have lots of questions?

I've never shied away from their questions – whether they're about volcanoes or body parts, it often holds the same level of importance to them. My eldest wanted to know everything. My youngest wanted to be able to introduce Janet to the postie, his teacher, the electrician who came to fix the boiler. The novelty was so much fun for him. He holds the house record for outing me to strangers.

What advice would you give someone about coming out to your children?

Be positive and supportive. If they want to talk or tell their friends or pretend you don't exist for a while – it's all good. Just keep extending your hand. Being as solid and stable through any big changes to a kid's life is the best thing you can offer.

When did you first introduce your children to Janet and how did it go?

Our first big outing as a four was to see the musical *Charlie and the Chocolate Factory*. Janet excitedly surprised them with Curly Wurlys on the train. It was then that I realized she knew very little about kids and their ability to cover every surface in sludgy caramel chocolate. As the parent who has been there from the beginning, you don't realize how much of an expert you become in reading your kids, what they need, what they like. It's easy to forget how much the new person has to learn.

We worked on it and talked about parenting all the time. We read books, listened to suggestions from others, but in the end if there is love and kindness the rest can be worked on as they grow.

Now they are older, how have your children navigated being part of a queer family?

When the kids started secondary school, we were more settled as a family and spent most of our time as a unit of four. We were keen for them to decide what they chose to tell their new peers. Mostly the eldest chose to keep family talk to a few people and the youngest told everyone. It's their story to tell after all. Being a teenager is awkward enough as it is. We know they love us; we don't need their reassurance.

Now, we go to Pride events together, discuss queer culture round the dinner table and are open to anyone from their world coming into our house. If they need us, sometimes it's the one who's better at first aid, sometimes it's the one who can make a puppet out of an envelope. Whoever they happen to need in that moment is fine with us.

MEET . . .
Jeremy Langmead (he/him)

Jeremy has two children in their late twenties with his ex-wife. His husband Simon also has a baby which Simon co-parents separately with a female friend. You can read Simon's story on page 48.

I was married when I was twenty-five and had two children with [the writer] India Knight, but that's another story. Then, just before lockdown, my husband wanted a baby, and he had a child with a female friend. So, I've visited gay parenting in two different formats.

I'd been very happily gay when I was at college and even had a boyfriend just before I met India; there was no secret of that. I hadn't had to dive into the closet, even her parents knew, but I genuinely and very unexpectedly fell in love with her. We were both impulsive and thought, 'Wouldn't it be funny if we got married' almost as a joke, and then that turned into something rather lovely. Then we thought, 'God, we would literally be the worst parents ever, wouldn't it be hilarious if we had children?', because nobody else we knew had them, and so we did. It was a reckless approach to life, but it made me have experiences that I never would have had if I'd thought more carefully about it.

We were living together as husband and wife for around six and a half years and then we split up. Then I had boyfriends and she had partners, but we actually remained married for almost twenty years, and we only got divorced when I got remarried to a guy.

We stayed married because we were really good friends so there was never a horrible bust-up. We just thought that, weirdly, in our strange little world, it worked just as it was. It was quite nice that we were still married for the children's sake. And we made a deal when I left that we would always live no more than three or four doors away from each other so the children could walk from one house to the other in their pyjamas.

Archie was probably about two and a half and Oscar around five when I left. They didn't really notice because children are, in a nice way, innately selfish. As long as Mummy and Daddy are still there, still friends, all went on holiday as a family, were together on Christmas Day and Daddy was just around the corner, they didn't question it too much. I feel that children don't need to know too many things at that age. All they want to know is that there will be biscuits. They used to come and stay with me every weekend, until they were around fifteen or more. So for all those years, when all my friends were having weekend parties and exotic holidays, I was visiting the science museum with the children. I missed out on a couple of decades of partying, but obviously had other things that more than made up for it.

India and I discussed the 'Dad-is-gay' thing and we decided, I don't know whether it's right or wrong, that we wouldn't tell them until they asked. We never lied to the children, but until it was of interest to them, we didn't discuss it. In the same way we wouldn't sit down and say, 'Oh, Mummy and Daddy have sex and Daddy puts his penis into Mummy.' They don't want to know! So we thought, why would they want to know what Daddy does with someone else?

I had boyfriends at that time and one or two of them came on holiday with the children and they never asked a thing; they must have just thought, 'Oh, it's expensive, and we shared a bed, so Daddy and his friend must share a bed too.' I remember they saw one boyfriend for most weekends and holidays as we were together for a few years. Then when we split up, I thought, 'I wonder how long before they ask where "Mr Scruffy" is?' (that's what they called him). It was three years before they asked where he was – that's how selfish children are. Again, not in a horrible way, but they just didn't really notice.

Then when they were eventually around their mid-teens, my sister said that Oscar had asked if I was gay. So I thought, 'Okay, *now* I have to have the conversation with them.' So I brought the subject up with him and asked how he felt about it. He seemed very unfazed. I mean, we lived in London and so we were lucky because capital cities are far more embracing of these things. I then went around to talk to my younger son, Archie, and said, 'I know you and Oscar know that I'm gay, and so I really want to know if you want to ask me anything or if there's anything that worries you?' He thought for a moment and then said, 'Erm, should I get the tomato pizza or the one with pineapple?'

I thought that one of the many advantages of being gay was, 'Great, nobody's going to pester me to get married and have more children.' Lo and behold, as wonderful as it is, of course, all the rules and legislation changed, and now here I am, married, with my husband having a daughter. I didn't want another child. I had two that I loved very much and I dedicated my formative years to the children and so quite looked forward to, and have happily embraced, a selfish older life. The thing about having children is that you love them and you worry about them so much that it is quite stressful. I just didn't want to worry all over again about schools, their friendships, and them being happy. My sons are now at an age when they can make their own decisions; they're both settled with jobs and girlfriends. The thought of starting all over again with changing nappies, not having enough sleep, them hurting themselves . . .

I love my husband, but I didn't want to do it all again. But he really did, and so we had to find a compromise.

To be fair to Simon, he explored all different ways around it and he found a female friend of his who hadn't met a guy and hadn't had a child and was desperate to be a mother, and so they decided to have one together and she'd be the primary carer.

My husband's daughter is adorable and it is lovely when she comes and stays. I'm really happy for her mother, who is an amazing parent. I'm more like an uncle, let's say . . . or the grumpy man that lives upstairs.

Talking Points

▶ How would you feel about coming out to your teenage children?

▶ What can the LGBTQ+ parenting community do to be more welcoming of people who were parents before they came out?

IS FOR CO-PARENTING

In the early days of recording *Some Families* (our award-winning podcast . . . plug plug!), Lotte and I spoke to the actor Charlie Condou about his family setup. Charlie, a gay man, who is married to Cameron Laux, has two children with the actress Catherine Kantar, a straight woman. This is not a surrogacy situation. Catherine and Charlie and Cameron (the three Cs!) all share parental duties and live in a harmonious co-parenting setup. Before we spoke to Charlie, I was so wrapped up in my own adoption blanket, while Lotte was living in her own IUI bubble, that we had never really thought about what the notion of co-parenting was or how it might work. Meeting Charlie was a turning point for us as we learned the importance of opening our eyes and minds to discover the many ways queer people can be parents, which laid the foundation for the podcast and this very book. As a community we need to understand each other to be able to support one another.

So, what the hell is 'co-parenting'? It can be different for everyone, but the general idea is that you and another person (or persons), with whom you are not necessarily in a romantic relationship, raise a child together. Shared custody, if you want to put a crude term on it. The setup can be whatever works for you, including living together or not living together. This is not a nuclear family setup. There could be two mums, one dad or two dads and two mums, or even three mums and five dads, because why the hell not?!

In Charlie's case, he and Cameron live near Catherine. They split up the time equally, so the children spend time at both houses with their parents. When we were interviewing him for the podcast, Lotte and I looked at each other: if the children spend a few days at Catherine's house, that means Charlie and Cameron get a few days alone. Together! 'It's a dream for us,' Charlie said. 'You are never wishing for a break like other parents. We get time together; Catherine gets time alone and we can be the best parents we can.' Sign us up! It's perfect childcare! In fact, I've since

suggested that Lotte and her wife join forces with the Oakleys to be a super-queer co-parenting family. Sadly, Lotte did the maths and quickly realized that meant her taking on three additional children. She passed and I don't blame her. John and I would definitely be the winners in that situation!

But what is it really like living day-to-day life as a co-parent?

MEET . . .

Simon Rayner-Langmead (he/him)

You met Simon's husband Jeremy in the previous chapter (see page 40). He and his friend Victoria are co-parents, with Simon living in the Lake District and Victoria in Glasgow.

Matilda's mum, Victoria, is an old friend of mine who I also used to work with. Matilda lives with her three-quarters of the time and with us for a quarter. I am Dad and my husband Jeremy is 'Uncle Jeremy'. He already has two children of his own from a previous marriage.

I had always wanted to be a parent for as long as I can remember. As Jeremy's children had already grown up and left home, he didn't want to go back to being a full-time dad. Co-parenting seemed like a good plan and worked well for Victoria too.

I own a pub so I have unusual days off, but it also gives me flexibility to a certain degree. Victoria and I usually plan a month or so in advance but keep things as flexible as possible for all of us rather than having set times. As she lives in Glasgow we usually meet about half way to swap over. Sometimes Victoria uses Matilda's time with us to have a couple of nights away.

Parenting is amazing but it's also extremely tiring. Our solution means that we all get to be 100 per cent with Matilda when we see her but between that we can live our own lives, work hard and see friends without having to constantly think about childcare. As Victoria and I are great friends we are always working for Matilda's best interests, unlike what you might get with divorced parents who have the potential added challenge of dealing with their own issues as an ex-couple as well as parenting.

The biggest challenge is not always being with Matilda. We miss milestones, and as she was born during lockdown, the first year was extremely hard as we were unable to spend proper time together. Right now, Matilda is very focused on ownership of things – her house, bed, car, Mummy, Daddy, etc., so she tends to want the thing that isn't in front of her, but I think that's more a two-year-old thing than being related specifically to co-parenting. I also think scheduling will become harder once she's at school and has set dates of where to be and when, especially being so far away.

Simon's Advice for Potential Co-Parents

For anyone wanting to explore co-parenting as an option for growing their family, you need to be totally honest with each other from the start. Share and discuss what you want to get out of it and what you expect from each other. It's much easier to have those conversations before the baby arrives than after. We did a very simple agreement based on the answers to a list of questions about topics like education, roles and responsibilities, our respective partners, etc. This was more to make sure we'd discussed things up front than to have a set agreement. Then once the baby arrives it all goes out the window and you must go with the flow. Nothing will be like you expect it to be so the best you can do is be supportive of each other and as flexible as possible with each other's needs. The most important thing is that the child's best interests are always the focus and just try your best to accommodate each other's needs.

Some great advice there to someone about to explore co-parenting. Someone like Eleanor Margolis, who has started thinking about co-parenting with her partner Leo.

MEET . . .
Eleanor (she/her) and Leo (she/her), a prospective co-parenting couple

Eleanor (who identifies as a lesbian) and Leo (who is bisexual) are a couple that are looking at the options around co-parenting. Eleanor wrote an article in *The Guardian* about their desire to become a co-parenting family and trying to find another queer couple to share joint parental responsibility. We wanted to chat to them about why they are considering co-parenting and what the start of that journey looks like.

Where did the idea of co-parenting come from?
We listened to an episode of Freddy McConnell's podcast, *Pride and Joy*, about co-parenting. It really spelled out to us that there can be a wide spectrum of parenting and there is no one set way. Seeing Freddy as a trans man and

having a baby opened our eyes to all the alternative ways to being a family. As opposed to straight parents, where things can happen by accident, we like the luxury of being able to plan. I was the result of an accidental pregnancy (explains Eleanor), so there is a great irony in that I am now planning to have a child in a very systematic way.

You've gone public in your desires to start co-parenting. What response did you expect?

With the political climate being quite toxic towards LGBTQ+ people, I find that when I publish articles related to queer content, I will usually get at least a couple of people screaming at me on Twitter. I thought putting something out about queer families, while protests about Drag Queen story times are happening at libraries, would result in death threats. But the response has been really lovely. I spoke to one person on Twitter who was co-parented and she was all the better for it. I had people say what a really interesting idea it would be to co-parent and lots of good luck wishes, which is always nice. I also had an email from a woman who had agreed to co-parent with a gay man and it had ended in a messy legal battle. She said she was young and naïve at the time and it sounded like a deeply unfortunate thing to happen, but I guess we just need to make sure we do it right. We know it's about protecting yourself and working on the set agreement that will also build the foundation of how we divide parental responsibilities.

Was your article intended as a form of advert to find a co-parent?

That was very much our aim! But unfortunately we've yet to have any potential co-parents come forward. It's not easy to find a match. There are a few websites that could do with some UX support that tries to match people, but it seems like loads of guys just wanted to share their sperm and weren't looking for any form of parental responsibility. We met a gay couple recently and we got talking about it as they said it had been something they had been interested in. They were very kind and that is what we are looking for ultimately: kindness. One of our plans is to be proactive and approach the LGBTQ+ centre near us to host a night, like match making, for prospective co-parents. We like the idea of building an infrastructure, even if we don't find co-parents ourselves.

Does the gender matter to you? Would you consider co-parenting with a lesbian couple?

We are very open-minded about this. We need someone to provide the sperm but gender is not important to us.

MEET . . .
Chris Powell (he/him)

Chris is a gay dad of an eight-year-old via a co-parenting relationship with two friends who live in New York.

How did the three of you end up becoming a queer co-parenting family?

I am a co-parent with two friends of mine that I've known for a very long time, Kate and Ari, who are from the US and live in New York, while I live here in the

UK. They are a lesbian and non-binary couple, and they approached me about ten years ago to get my thoughts on starting a family together. It was something I'd been approached about a few times by lesbian friends, but I'd always felt the situation wasn't right for me. None of them was looking for a father figure within the family and I'd always imagined myself being a parent, so we were not on the same page. I understand that the situation of being a donor works well for some people, but I didn't think it would work for me. So, when Kate and Ari approached me, and I did have it in the back of my mind that maybe they would at some point, they ended up saying all the right things in terms of what they were looking for. They had been thinking about alternative family structures and were interested in building a queer family on our own terms. They were open to me being as involved as I wanted to be, and to make sure it worked for me as much as for them.

How did you all start planning out the logistics of starting your family together?

From the beginning I felt it was something that would work. I felt confident in them and our relationship. We had a lot of discussion over a period of time, going over everything we could possibly think of, including how we felt about the situation, how we would want it to work, what we all wanted out of it, the practicalities, and the day-to-day, until we were all satisfied that we wanted the same thing.

One of the early questions that came up was of course how I would be known to the child. I was very clear that I would want to be identified as their father, and for them to think of me in that way. That is the role I am taking on. It reflects my identity as a parent, and my emotional commitment to this other person. Sometimes when I describe the situation to other people, they still say, 'Oh, so you are the donor?' Which is technically true, but I don't use that word because it doesn't describe our relationship.

Did you take any legal steps to cover your bases? And how did them being in New York work?
At the outset, a mutual friend, who's a family lawyer, advised me to start reading case studies of situations where a similar arrangement had ended up in court. In almost every case what had gone wrong was that one or the other party had changed their mind in terms of how much involvement they wanted the sperm donor to have. We spoke to a lawyer over in the States and had a full mediation session. Together we wrote up a document that isn't necessarily legally binding but serves as a written statement of intent and which could be referred to if there was ever any conflict or misunderstanding. It covered a lot of the practicalities like how much financial involvement I was going to have, how much time I could expect to spend with the child as a minimum and what would happen if they broke up.

Kate and Ari are based in New York so that has always been part of the setup and we knew going in there was going to be a lot of distance between us, as I am based in the UK. They said to me, 'We know the distance is a thing, but we are coming to you because we want to do this with you as a person.' It felt right. Like them, for me the people were more important than the proximity. There is a huge element of trust involved and whatever the setup or wherever we lived I wouldn't have been able to go into it if I didn't feel like I trusted them completely.

We took the whole thing one step at a time. Initially we discussed me coming to New York at least four times a year. I knew it was my responsibility to build that emotional relationship so that when I came it didn't just feel like a family friend turning up; I was there as the child's father. I try to be physically there as often as I can and usually visit for up to two weeks at a time. We also Zoom, Skype, etc. regularly. What became clear early on was that intimacy was not going to be a problem and not once have I felt any awkwardness between the child and myself. One obstacle we hadn't foreseen of course was Covid, which meant that I had to stop travelling over. It was frustrating, especially for them, as a year for a six-year-old is a long time. We figured it out and talked a lot over Zoom and started to play video games online. We've found playing games together is one of the best ways to connect, especially at this age when they don't really want to sit down and have a conversation. We play games and then chat at the same time which is really nice. I can tell they are as invested in my role in their life as I am, which feels great.

Even with the distance, have you been able to be part of decision-making?

For big decisions, such as which school they will be going to, they will usually involve me in the conversation, but I trust them to make the right choices. I don't really understand the American school system anyway! They are great about keeping me up to date on changes in the child's life, but I know we have a mutual understanding and so I'm unlikely to disagree with decisions they make.

How has it been for your extended family? Did they fully understand?

When I first told my family about our plans to co-parent, I think they were initially slightly surprised but, overall, they were just excited. They had all the questions you'd expect, especially on where they fitted into everything. Just as it was important for me to be acknowledged as 'Dad', it was equally important that our child see all these people as their extended family, their grandparents, and to have close relationships with them. My co-parents have brought the child to visit their UK family several times, and my family know they are welcome in New York at any time, although I usually try to be there too when they do go over. At the same time, my own one-on-one time with my kid is very precious, so I must protect that. It can feel like a bit of a tightrope to walk.

What does the future hold for you all?

I'm looking forward to the future. Kate, Ari and I are still great friends and get on really well, but it will be nice to have a more independent relationship with my child as they get older. Because of the distance, and their age, everything is still mediated through the other grown-ups, even small things like setting up the laptop to Zoom or setting up a time to speak. But at some point, they will be old enough to visit Dad in London on their own, and I think our relationship will evolve and really come into its own.

And what advice would you give to anyone thinking of co-parenting?

My advice to anyone exploring co-parenting is to think very, very carefully from the beginning about what you want out of the situation and the relationships involved. Remember that the child's happiness and wellbeing is the most important thing, so put everything on the table and be as clear as possible about how you might handle different situations. It sounds obvious but I know it doesn't always happen.

LEGAL EAGLE:
Co-Parenting

LGBT Lawyers, a specialist law firm for the LGBTQ+ community, highlights some of the things to consider when thinking about co-parenting:

Create a Co-Parenting Agreement

This is a document that is drafted by all relevant co-parents and sometimes other family members or partners.

The benefit of a co-parenting agreement is that the wishes and responsibilities of each parent will be in writing for future reference. So, if you must go to court for any reason further down the line, you have evidence of any initial agreements.

It's important to note that a co-parenting agreement is not a legally binding document. However, if any issues arise down the line, it can be used as evidence in court.

A co-parenting agreement can clarify each person's duties and responsibilities in areas such as: finances, living arrangements, education, healthcare and other general wellbeing responsibilities.

Parental Responsibilities

In the UK, a child can legally have only two parents. Therefore, if the chosen birth mother is married or in a civil partnership with her partner, then they will become the legal second parent, regardless of if the other co-parent has donated the sperm.

If the child is conceived in a fertility clinic, all adults will normally be able to choose who the second legal parent will be alongside the birth mother.

Any additional parents can apply for legal parental responsibility. There is no limit on how many people can have parental responsibility for a child.

The process of obtaining legal parental responsibility for non-biological parents can be complex. The application comes with a court fee (£215 as of 2022) and there might be select criteria you need to meet so it is worth checking on what the current law requires.

Change of Circumstance

In the event of a relationship ending, you will need to agree on who will continue to care for the child. You can decide if you wish to continue with your current arrangement or amend your co-parenting agreement.

If you are a non-legal parent in a co-parenting agreement, your child will not automatically inherit from you when you die. It's important to discuss inheritance wishes with your co-parenting partner(s) and have these expressed in your will.

We have a ton more non-fun legal eagle information in 'X is for Ex-Partners, Divorce, Separation and Step Parents' (see page 340).

Talking Points

▶ If you were to co-parent, what level of shared responsibility would you feel comfortable with?

▶ Could you share a child with another person that is not your romantic partner?

▶ Do you feel you are aware of the legal implications involved in co-parenting a child?

IS FOR DONORS

 One of the many surreal moments encountered while shopping for a sperm donor is the ability to compare their 'celebrity lookalikes'. The sperm bank that we used provided a photo of the potential donor as a baby (some donors share adult photos but this is less common). Instead, the clinic staff offer their perception of them ('appears jolly!', 'kind expression'), and give you the name of a famous person that a computer algorithm believes they bear a passing resemblance to. Stu and I have tested this Celebrity Lookalike tech and we're Tom Hardy and Nelly Furtado, so that's reassuring.

Your Type on Paper: Choosing a Donor

But actually, it wasn't the fact that a donor was said to look like Tom Cruise, Denzel Washington or Ben Wishaw that gave the biggest insight into the genes we were about to add-to-basket, it was the voice recording. Once we had narrowed down a shortlist based on a few essential characteristics (we wanted him to have dark features like mine because Jenny is blonde and she was carrying), we delved deeper into their profiles. Donors write a letter about why they have decided to donate, which includes anything they'd want to say to a prospective family and a child born thanks to their donation. You get to read this handwritten letter and then hear them speak what they had written.

We listened to about forty different men's voice notes and became adept at making some quick and probably very harsh decisions about them all. As Stu says in relation to adopting, you really have to trust your gut and allow yourself to go with what feels right without worrying that it might be 'unkind' to have to reject someone. This is *your* family and the rest of *your* life: if there's ever a time to be picky, it's now.

If you really interrogated how significant your choice of donor sperm could be, you'd be paralyzed by indecision. When straight people fall in love and decide to procreate, you don't expect them to be flip-flopping over whether they made the right choice, or if there might be someone better, genetically, out there if they'd just kept looking. Okay, we all have that one friend who does exactly this, but on the whole the way it works is they fall for someone, they commit and decide to start a family together. Even if it isn't a perfect match, they'll always think the child or children they have together are perfect and wouldn't have done anything differently. My point is, because queer people using donors have the luxury of choice, and can make a decision based on specific criteria, unencumbered by any of the emotions that go with a romantic partnership, it can feel overwhelming. In the end my wife and I heard our donor's voice, and there was such warmth and kindness to his cadence, we both had goose pimples. He sounded like a dear friend we'd never met. Without giving it any more thought, we bought three 'straws' [vials] of his sperm and our journey began.

I have some friends who had a complex spreadsheet and marking system for potential donors, and spent months going over and over their shortlist, but we went entirely with our hearts and made the decision within one night (and one bottle of wine). As soon as I'd clicked 'buy', I felt confident we'd found our donor – I didn't need to keep looking.

The way clinics are set up now makes it almost as easy to buy sperm online as it is to buy an outfit from Zara. Of course, you need to be registered with a licensed clinic to have the sperm delivered and stored, so it's not *exactly* like splurging on a summer capsule wardrobe, but clinics make the process of 'shopping' for a donor as seamless as possible.

MEET . . .
Helle Sejersen Myrthue (she/her), CEO of Cryos

Helle is CEO of Cryos, the world's largest sperm bank.

What do you think are some of the biggest misconceptions about sperm donation?
That sperm donors only donate because of the money – this is not true. In 2021, Cryos carried out a study[7] on the motivations of sperm donors which showed that a very large percentage of donors have altruistic reasons for donating. The financial compensation is not irrelevant but is not the main factor of motivation for donors. Another misconception is that a sperm donor can be considered a father – this is not the case. Neither legally nor socially can or will a donor ever be considered a father to the donor-conceived children that come from his genes.

How has the proliferation of DNA testing websites impacted what you do?

DNA testing sites have not yet had the biggest impact on what Cryos does as a company, however we are monitoring the technological development in this area. Looking long term at donor anonymity, DNA testing sites, social media and other technological advances in this field might pose a challenge for future donor anonymity.

Could you explain the difference between ID release and non-ID release donors?

An ID release donor is a donor whose personal information becomes available to the donor-conceived children from that donor once the children reach a certain age. [Children conceived with sperm donated before 1 January 2021 can learn non-identifying details about their ID release donor when they are sixteen and their identity once they reach the age of eighteen. Children conceived with sperm donated from 1 January 2021 and onwards can obtain this information when they turn fifteen.] The child can ask for the information on their donor if they wish to do so, but the donor cannot ask for any information on donor-conceived children. A non-ID release donor remains anonymous, and his information will never be released to anyone.

UK law prohibits UK-based sperm banks from offering non-ID release donors. This means that, in the UK, *all* donors must agree to their details being known when the child reaches eighteen, even if those donors come from abroad.

What kind of testing and evaluations do sperm donors go through?

Sperm donor candidates complete a comprehensive medical questionnaire and participate in an in-depth interview with a set of questions aimed at identifying candidates with risk behaviours, symptoms of disease and family medical history. The medical exam also includes a background check. In addition to this, we test the quality of the sperm and a thorough physical examination of the candidate is carried out by one of our healthcare professionals.

If there isn't any more sperm available from a particular donor, can you ever make a personal request that they donate more?

No, that is not possible. If you want to make sure that there is enough sperm from a certain donor, you can reserve more straws for later use. In that way, you should have enough sperm for more attempts at a pregnancy or siblings for your donor-conceived child.

What is the limit on the number of families that a donor is used for, and is there a rationale behind this limit?

This is country-specific and varies from country to country. Since Cryos delivers to more than a hundred countries, there are many different quotas and limits. It is, however, very rare that a Cryos donor is used for more than twenty-five to fifty families in total.

Since 1 August 1991, UK law has allowed up to ten families to use the same donor.

How much do donors get paid?

A Cryos donor receives a compensation of up to 500 DKK [around €70 or £60 at the time of writing] per donation.

Can donors make any requests about who gets to use their sperm – for example if someone was queerphobic, could they request that no LGBTQ+ families use it?

No, this is not possible for the donors to decide and not something we experience is a wish for our donors to do.

We also checked with London Sperm Bank and were told: 'It is possible to specify other conditions regarding the use of your sperm donation; although none of these may be discriminatory on the basis of age, disability, gender reassignment, marriage or civil partnership, race, religion or sexual orientation.'

MEET . . .
Soren (he/him)

Soren is a Danish sperm donor for Cryos.

Why do you donate?

I donate mainly to help parents to achieve their dream. Before I started to donate, I talked to lesbian-couple friends of mine and they told me about how they became parents because of a sperm donor. That inspired me to donate as well.

I also get a small payment for each donation I make. That is partly also why I donate.

How does it feel when you find out a child has been born from your sample?

I do not receive any information about how my sperm is used. That also means I do not get any information if a child is born out of my sample.

Do you often think about the children you've helped create and wonder about their lives?

I do sometimes, yes. I hope they grow up in a healthy and safe environment with a caring family.

How do you feel about them tracking you down when they reach eighteen?

Right now, I do not put a lot of thought into it, because I know that it will be many years before anyone – if any – will track me down. But I am very open-minded. I am a non-anonymous donor, because if I was a donor-child myself, I would like to have the ability to know my biological parents. And I would be glad to see how the children's lives have turned out to be.

Did you tell your friends and family you were a sperm donor? And if so, what was their reaction?

I am very open about my activity as a sperm donor. I am proud to be a sperm donor, and I have mentioned it to most of my friends and family. Most of the reaction I get is recognition or other forms of moral support. Only one friend of mine has expressed negative emotions about my activity as a sperm donor.

Did you put a lot of thought into the 'letter' that you write as part of your profile? Was it hard to do?
Yes, I thought about it for a bit of time, and I wrote several drafts before I was happy with the final result. It was a bit hard to do, because I wanted to write a short but powerful letter to 'my children'.

What was the most challenging thing about the process?
Before I could start as a donor, there were many forms to fill out, tests and questions to answer, interviews to attend and of course the letter I wrote. But that was only in the beginning. After all the formal procedures were done, it was easy to be and continue as a sperm donor.

Before logging into a sperm bank's online database for the first time, I'd advise anyone to devote a bit of time to sitting alone and making a list of the things that feel important to you. If you are planning to have a family with a partner, ask them to do the same, then compare notes. My list was as follows:

Must haves: dark hair, dark eyes, no pre-existing genetic conditions or health concerns (clinics tend to screen for these and only stock donors who are 'clear').

Nice to have: tall, athletic, university-educated, literary, worldly.

Thankfully, Jenny's list was pretty much identical so we didn't need to have any BIG conversations – we could just crack on. Crucially, though, we were both also happy to keep an open mind and accept that we might find a donor that ticked none of our boxes but felt right for a reason we hadn't considered. I think it's good to maintain an element of fluidity in the process rather than be too rigid as you could end up closing yourself off from options unnecessarily.

MEET . . .

Freya Lyon (she/her)

Freya calls herself a unicorn because she is the rare combination of a donor-conceived person who also used a donor to conceive her own child.

Freya was conceived with the help of a donor in the early 1990s. Back then her biological mum had to apply for fertility treatment as a single mum, as same-sex marriage wasn't legal, let alone same-sex parenting. Her mums separated when she was eight, but she maintained a close relationship with both her parents. Freya and her wife have used a donor to conceive their two children.

As soon as I asked, my mums gave me the details about the donor that they were given, which were really minimal – I got hair colour and eye colour and a few bits of other info. They weren't given anything in writing. The way it worked then was that my mum said what she wanted characteristic-wise and then the doctor said, 'This donor matches what you want'. So it wasn't even really a conversation. The clinic also informed my mum the donor was a student and a street performer. That became a big part of the story I built up about him. I used to go to London for day trips and look for him among the performers in Covent Garden.

When I got pregnant myself through donor insemination, I was thinking a lot about family and genes. So, I decided to do a couple of those genealogy tests. It was pure luck that I ended up finding my donor through a second cousin, who had a hunch who my donor was and sent a DNA test to the person. She emailed me the results and it was a paternal match.

It turns out he wasn't a street performer after all. My whole childhood, I had constructed this narrative, and it just goes to show how almost irrelevant those kinds of details are but how, as a child with a donor, it's nice to have something to cling onto. It's a story, which is what you need as a kid.

I sent him an email that started with the line, 'I know that you signed up to complete anonymity, so you might have absolutely no interest in speaking to me and that's fine'.

He came back really quickly with a well-worded email. That was a way of winning me over quite easily. It was really eloquently put and it turns out he is a teacher. We emailed back and forth for the rest of the day. My biggest fear at the time was that I was going to have to tell my sister, who's my full sister, and our half siblings – because at that point I had found two of them [through the sibling donor registry]. I knew I was going to have to be the messenger.

The first time I FaceTimed my donor I was absolutely terrified. My biological mum had passed away a few years prior, and it was strange that he reminded me of her. He was instantly reassuring and really easy to talk to so the nerves vanished really fast. All of our interests are very similar.

The first thing my other mum asked me was, 'Does he feel like your dad?' And I was like, no, I've got no picture of what a dad is so he can't feel like a dad. But I couldn't deny after meeting him in person and hugging him, he couldn't just stay 'donor' in my head. I suppose I've switched to referring to him as my biological father. It feels a slightly more warm term than donor, which was fine for my entire childhood because I needed that distance.

When it came to choosing the donor for me and my wife's child, I knew I wanted to find someone who was open to meeting them at eighteen. My own experience has made me think about other things I can do to make it easier for my daughter, so that she's not having these big realizations about herself later on in life. I've started looking for her siblings now so that they could potentially be part of her life from an early age. I set up a Facebook group for our clinic and found her half sister, who is only two months apart in age. It's been really nice. We plan to meet up soon and we share pictures and news about the girls.

Other Mother Insecurities

It's funny, the things I thought would matter when choosing a donor ended up being entirely irrelevant once our daughter was born. She's so brilliantly herself. I don't need that kind of physical validation in the way I thought I would. It had been so important to us to find a dark-haired donor so our child would look like me because I was worried, I suppose, that I'd find it difficult to connect with them if they didn't. But the reality of our relationship, and our closeness as mother and daughter, is so much deeper than appearance. I see myself in her intense imagination, her love of books and storytelling, her surreal sense of humour, her confidence; and the parts of her that are unfamiliar feel exciting to get to know. Here is an evolving human being who will teach me so much and expand my life in ways I can't even comprehend right now. How boring it would be if she was just a 'mini me'.

What I mean to say is that sometimes, when it comes to using a donor, as a non-biological parent we fixate on the wrong things because we feel insecure. I remember worrying that I'd think obsessively about the donor: where is he, who is he, what's he really like, what parts of my daughter are similar to him? But in the weeds of taking care of a small person every day, I have so little time for this kind of neurotic indulgence. I rarely think about him, and when I do it's with absolute gratitude. Maybe this will evolve as my daughter gets older and perhaps becomes interested in learning more about him, but for now he's a stranger who gave us the most incredible gift and that's all we have the bandwidth to care about.

STU'S VIEW ON SHARED GENES

In a world before children, before nappies, before sleepless nights, before being so tired that I want to inject coffee directly into my eyeballs, I used to have this wish: I'd wish that a big old fairy would fly down and grant John and I the opportunity to biologically have a child, together. Both our genes, a bit of both of us in a child. I used to feel sad knowing this was never going to be a reality but remained optimistic that at least we could adopt and raise a child on a neutral playing field. Fast-forward to the present. We have three amazing children, and my heart couldn't love and adore them more. Honestly there are not enough words in the world to describe what they mean to us. If that fairy turned up one day in her big pink froufrou dress and glittery wings (well, firstly my son would love it!), then I'd say, 'No thanks, love, I take back that wish.' There is no way in hell I would ever want anything other than what we have. The fact we don't share the same genes is utterly meaningless. It never registers in my day-to-day thinking. I've never once sat there and wished they had some of mine and John's genes in them. A funny thing happened when we adopted them, well more precisely when we first met them. They became our children. I see part of John in them and parts of me. Some I like, some I don't and some I find hilarious. Poor John is going to have to put up with their diva tendencies that they have totally picked up from me. I'd never, ever wish for anything else. (Well, maybe a new car.)

Involving Friends and Family

Once we had decided on our donor, I took screen grabs of his baby photos and the written letter and shared them with friends and family. I'm not saying this is a great idea – depending on your relationships you may risk getting some negative feedback that throws you off course, but Jenny and I wanted to bring our wider families along on the journey with us and to remind them that this person should never be thought of or referred to as the 'father'; he's only ever the 'donor'. We felt it would help our parents to be involved and to feel we'd made a good and a sensible choice in our donor. Looking back, these were probably quite challenging conversations for some more traditional family members, but we didn't want any shame or secrecy involved in our pregnancy endeavours, so we started as we meant to go on, by being open and honest about the process. And however 'unusual' our parents may have found these discussions, they were good enough not to share their doubts or anxieties with us. And no one, to my knowledge, has ever called the donor the father.

MEET . . .

Lotte's mum Jenny (she/her)

Lotte asked her mum what she thought at the time they were choosing a donor and what, if anything, she thinks about him now.

I remember the first IVF baby; it was all over the news, but it had as much significance to me as Dolly the Sheep. I never could have imagined that fertility treatment would directly involve my family and give me a beloved grandchild. Even though it was all new to me I never had any negative feelings about Lotte and Jen using a donor (it just feels so unfair that same-sex couples have to pay for IVF). I don't think I realized all of the thought that must have gone into choosing your donor, though, as when you told me, Jen was already pregnant, so there was all the excitement about that. You did share the photos of him as a baby and the letter he wrote and the 'celebrity' he apparently looked like. I wondered if you needed to think you could be attracted to that man. Whoever he is, he helped to make the most beautiful little girl – it could not have been better. You chose well!

If you decide to use donor sperm and have treatment in the UK, you can only choose a donor who your child will be able to track down when they are a teenager. If you want an entirely anonymous sperm donor, you will need to have fertility treatment in another country such as Denmark.

LEGAL EAGLE:
Sperm Donation

Our friends at NGA Law share here what you need to know about the legalities of sperm donation.

If you are an unmarried couple conceiving with donor sperm at a fertility clinic in the UK, then you rely on your clinic both to provide good medical care and to ensure you will both become the legal parents of your child. The Human Fertilisation and Embryology Act 2008[8] creates a process for unmarried couples which must be followed at a fertility clinic in order for a non-gestational parent through sperm donation to become their child's legal parent. The process must be completed correctly before conception takes place, so that the requirements are met for legal parenthood to be established at the point of conception.

There are different, more liberal, rules for married couples (see below).

Information About Donors

Anyone over the age of sixteen can ask the Human Fertilisation and Embryo Authority (the UK regulatory body known as HFEA – see page 150 for more about them) whether they were conceived with donated eggs or sperm at a clinic in the UK after 1991. They can also ask if the Register shows that they are genetically related to someone they intend to marry, register a civil partnership with or enter into an intimate physical relationship with (the application must be made jointly by both partners).

Donor-conceived people whose details are on the Register can also ask for any non-identifying information about their donor from the age of sixteen. This usually includes the donor's physical appearance, height, weight, hair colour, eye colour and occupation. It may also include any statement the donor has written describing themselves (or a pen sketch) or a note the donor has written for any children conceived (a good-will message). Donor-conceived people over the age of sixteen have a right to request this information, but in practice the HFEA will also provide it to their parents before they are sixteen, if requested.

From the age of eighteen, donor-conceived people whose details are on the Register can ask for identifying information about their donor, including their name, date of birth and last known address.

Information About Donor-Conceived Siblings

Donor-conceived people may have donor-conceived genetic half siblings in other families if their donor donated to more than one family.

Donor-conceived people can (from the age of sixteen or, in practice, before with their parents' support) ask how many donor-conceived siblings are also recorded on the Register, whether they are registered as male or female and the year in which they were born. From the age of eighteen a donor-conceived person who wishes to be put in touch with donor-conceived siblings can ask to join the HFEA's Donor Sibling Register. If any of their donor-conceived siblings also join the register, the HFEA will put them in touch with each other.

Information Available to Donors

Egg and sperm donors can apply to find out limited information about the results of their donation, either from the HFEA directly or from the clinic where they donated their eggs or sperm. They can ask the HFEA whether their donation resulted in a birth and, if so, the assigned sex and year of birth of any children born. They cannot find out the identity of any children born, or that of their parents.

Married Couples and Civil Partners

A woman who is married to or in a civil partnership with the birth mother at the time of conception is automatically her child's other legal parent. The rules apply to conceptions after 6 April 2009 that take place through IVF or artificial insemination, whether at home or at a clinic in the UK or overseas. Like a married father, the non-gestational mother is named on her child's UK birth certificate and automatically has parental responsibility, giving her the authority to make decisions about her child's care.

The law applies unless it can be 'shown' that the non-gestational mother did not consent to the conception, something which must be proved as a matter of fact. If the couple are separated and/or the gestational mother or parent is conceiving as a solo mother or with a new partner, it may be necessary to collect evidence to 'show' that her wife/civil partner does not consent.

Female Same-Sex Couples Who Are Not Married or in a Civil Partnership

A non-gestational mother can also be treated as the other legal parent if she and her partner conceive at a licensed clinic in the UK after 6 April 2009. Both parents must complete and sign HFEA Forms WP and PP to nominate the non-gestational mother as the other parent, before conception and after receiving counselling and proper information about the forms.

ID Release or Non-ID Release Donors

Personally, I remember how inquisitive I was as a kid. I would have wanted the option to find out who I shared half my genes with, so I felt it only fair that I give my own child that chance when they're old enough. I know lots of people who use non-UK-based sperm banks so that they can choose a totally anonymous donor (full anonymity is legal in places like Denmark) because this feels right for them and their family. To be honest, it's probably for the best that only the kid can reach out to their donor not their parent, because a midlife crisis may get the better of me and I can picture myself inviting our donor to dinner parties to show off how handsome and accomplished he is. Imagine all these fifty-something lesbian couples secretly comparing the hot men on their arms, 'Dahling, you must meet our donor . . .' It makes me think of that film *The Kids Are All Right*. Julianne Moore and Annette Bening play gay mums with teenage kids who contact their donor. He becomes a part of their lives and suffice to say it gets MESSY.

I've noticed that there's definitely an unspoken etiquette among queer parents who have used sperm donors – you don't ask for details! The fact is, I don't want to be having a casual chat with someone at a barbeque and find out that I used the same donor as them and our kids are biologically related. I wouldn't know what to do with that information – would it mean we had to see more of each other? Would we have to tell our kids and nurture a half-sibling relationship? This is all uncharted territory. There's no right or wrong, and I know some people feel very differently and actively seek out their children's 'diblings' (donor siblings), but for me, there's something very precious and private about a choice of donor; it's not a topic for small talk.

MEET . . .
Oli Benjamin (he/him)

Oli Benjamin, whose two mums conceived him with the help of a donor in the late 1990s, found out that he had more than twenty-five siblings from his donor and went on a mission to track them all down for a BBC documentary called *25 Siblings and Me*.

Had you always been inquisitive about who your donor was?

My parents couldn't lie to me about it, even if they wanted to, because they're two women. What else would they say? That I'm adopted? My experience is different from a lot of other donor-conceived people because many actually aren't told – including a number of my half siblings – until their twenties, or they find out by accident through DNA testing. The fact is that I grew up always knowing I had a donor.

Then, when I got a bit older, I knew that to have a baby you needed to take something from a man and something from a woman, then put them together. I was just a kid, I didn't really care. Then came the conversation of, 'Well that means you have someone out there who donated something so that we could have you.' It was so gradual; there was never one point where I was immediately inquisitive about it. I just got a bit more curious one year and thought I'd find out!

And how old were you then?

Around twenty. It was just a thing to get out of the way, you know. 'Oh well, I might as well find out.' It wasn't a huge moment for me, although for some people it's the biggest moment of their entire lives.

Did your parents tell you much about him when you did start asking questions?

I think they told me something funny that he wrote on his donor profile and they told me a bit about how they wanted somebody that looked like a specific celebrity, I can't remember who it was. They kept the donor records safe in a purple file, so I would have access to them when I was older. That was good.

What did you need to start looking for your donor?

All I needed really was the donor number, in order to go to the sperm bank and ask them. The problem is that in order to confirm whether you are who you say you are, you have to go to a notary, which was just too much effort. You can go on the sibling registry much more easily, so my first contact was not with my donor. I had an email from someone reaching out to me, saying that I had over twenty siblings and now they're all excited to meet me. I was like, 'Oh wow, okay!'

Did you instantly want to meet them or did you feel any trepidation?

No, I wanted to meet all of them. I was just curious. I didn't have any reservations. I think this is why it's important for people to raise their children knowing they're donor-conceived because for some people it can be quite traumatic finding out by accident or when they're much older. In a way, I'd say that makes them less likely to feel comfortable about the situation in

general. I think it's something that should happen gradually and people should be raised knowing.

**And how would you describe your relationship with
your siblings now? Do you keep in touch with them?**
Because we're in different countries and there's a
massive cultural divide between the UK and the US,
that's one factor. I don't speak to a handful of them,
there are some I occasionally speak to and there are
a few I speak to fairly regularly.

**And for readers who haven't seen the
documentary, did you find that you had things in
common with your siblings?**
What I learned from making the documentary is that
you don't have to get along with absolutely everyone;
that shouldn't be the objective. The objective should
really be having relationships that are meaningful to
you and I'm happy that I do have a few meaningful
relationships. Initially, I saw not getting along with
absolutely every one of my siblings as being a failure,
but when it comes to it, you are essentially just
strangers. I would just say that with these sorts of
things, genetics may be the door to a relationship,
but whether you actually walk through or not is
entirely up to you.

**When you did finally meet your donor, what was
that moment like for you?**
I wanted it to be a really beautiful moment with
slow-motion running towards each other, but I think
I'd just got off a train and I desperately needed to pee.

***After you found a bathroom, was the meeting
everything you'd hoped for?***

No, absolutely not. I think the most important thing
with these things is to not have an unrealistic or roman-
ticized idea of this perfect father figure. What's to say
that a complete stranger is going to have some
extra-special connection with you? It's better to go
into it seeing them as some sort of uncle or a cousin.
Then see where that relationship leads, if it does lead
anywhere. If it doesn't, that's completely fine.

***Do you feel more complete as a person knowing
your donor now? Has it shifted anything in terms
of your identity or selfhood?***

I guess it's plugged a hole in one of the many things
I'm curious about, but I wouldn't say that just knowing
him has fundamentally changed my life.

In the future, I'm open to my daughter's donor and diblings
becoming a part of our lives. And what I've learned from
speaking to people who have tracked down their donors is that
them doing so doesn't make you any less of their parent, or
mean they love you any less. It may be challenging if and when
it happens but with openness and communication from everyone
involved it can be a bonding experience for you and your child
as they move into adulthood themselves. One thing I've learned
from my own non-traditional family is that families are mutable
and wonderfully so: they expand in ways you never could have
imagined. Queer families are, by their very nature, the most
beautifully mercurial of all – offering a colourful kaleidoscope
of possibilities. Embrace the rainbow!

Talking Points

▶ What are you looking for in a donor and why?

▶ What are you willing to compromise on?

▶ How would you feel about your child meeting their donor when they are eighteen?

▶ Would you want to connect with your child's half siblings, and if not, why not?

IS FOR EDUCATION

 'Are you worried they are going to be bullied for having gay parents?' Yes! Every LGBTQ+ parent or queer parent-to-be has surely had this question run through their brain. After all, isn't the fundamental and universal truth about being a parent that you are generally worried about your children 24/7? We are a generation that has likely experienced or witnessed homophobia at school. We carry the baggage of what it means to be a young queer kid who is trying to work out who they are while the world around them is throwing metaphoric (and sometimes real) sticks and stones at them. Is it any wonder we, and those around us, might be worried about how our kids will get on at school?

Starting School

It was two years after our daughter had first moved home that we were about to send her off for her first taste of the school system: pre-school. Our intention had always been to send her and her brothers to the local primary that was housed in a cute little Victorian building down the end of our road. We were slap bang in the catchment area but, here is another little adoption fun fact for you – and one that I feel drives most traditional families wild with jealousy: an adopted child gets priority choice to any school of your choosing. Let's just call it one of the nice perks of adoption! I remember my friend having to cut the lawn of the local vicar for almost three years to just have her children considered for the local church school. Excuse me while I revel in this joyous privilege.

So, one morning off we trotted in a little uniform, book bag in hand – her, not me, as that would have really set the tongues wagging! She was so excited about school; there were never any concerns or worries. It was us that had the butterflies. It was a big moment, because not only was she starting school, but it was the first time our family was properly heading into a situation that involved outsiders. Prior to this day, our little queer family bubble had essentially been protected from the world, as we only socialized with close friends and family. Who were all these other parents we now had to meet? Lordy, they were going to be in our life for at least the next ten years!

We live in a small-ish town and to my knowledge there are not many 'gays in the wild' around us. John and I had lived there for over ten years, yet we knew no one. Working in London and commuting home, I loved the fact that I had no connections in this town. Even John, who grew up in a village not that far away, knew no one from his youth. The sense of anonymity at weekends was glorious. There was never anyone to bump into and have forced small talk with. I could stroll down to Sainsbury's looking like a horror without a care in the world. Now it's all change. I can't walk ten metres without bumping into someone I know. School life does that to a person! Before my daughter started school, we had no idea how people viewed and treated gays in our area. So how would this school community deal with two gay dads? In my day-to-day life I never give a damn about what people think about my sexuality and I proudly own my identity as a feminine, camp, gay man, so this feeling was all new to me. What if there was a homophobe lurking under the surface of these seemingly smiley, happy parents? What if that came through in comments made by their children to my daughter? I could deal with it, but I didn't want her to have to feel different.

Linda Riley, LGBTQ+ campaigner, activist and publisher of lesbian magazine *Diva*, told us on the podcast about the awful experiences she had ten years ago when her children were at school. One of these included her daughter being uninvited to a friend's birthday party when the parents realized she was a child of lesbians. I honestly don't know how I would feel in that situation and Linda recognizes that it was an incident that is unlikely to happen nowadays. But this is very, very recent history, and history has a tendency to repeat itself. Me, paranoid?

My own worries quickly faded once my daughter started school, as everyone seemed open, welcoming and kind. The headteacher even confided in me that her own dad came out as a gay a few years ago and she is determined to foster an open and inclusive environment at the school. This was her reply when I asked her why she felt it was important to encourage a diverse education:

We want all children to grow up to have a strong sense of social justice and being willing to fight for what is right. We also recognize that it is important that children see diversity and individuality recognized so that they can develop their own understanding of themselves as individuals. Essentially, we believe that by underpinning our curriculum and school life in general with an emphasis on diversity, we are better preparing children for their lives ahead. The Relationship and Sex Education (RSE) revised policy has provided us with the backing to introduce ideas and concepts to children at a younger age. This helps us to normalize life in modern Britain and, for older children, has led to them feeling able to speak about their own individual journeys.

I could take a breath. Perhaps it was all going to be okay. I'm hoping this does indeed continue. We are one down, two to go, as our youngest boys have yet to start their own schooling adventures. Will the parents in their respective years be as fabulous as those that are in my daughter's year? My son has a more flamboyant side and enjoys experimenting with what he wears. How will those in his year take to him? It's a continual worry at the back of our minds.

It helps that change has finally come to our education system. A policy, introduced in September 2021, means that primary school children will be able to access information about all types of families and relationships within school. For a country that in its very recent history had any form of queer talk in school banned by Section 28,[9] this is a big deal. Section 28, which in itself was partly inspired by a parent protest against the book *Jenny Lives with Eric and Martin* (for more on this see 'Q is for Queerification', page 254), was an act of law that prohibited local authorities (aka schools) from 'intentionally promoting homosexuality or publishing material with the intention of promoting homosexuality; [or] promot[ing] the teaching in any maintained school of the acceptability of homosexuality as a pretended family relationship.'

'Our RSE policy was created in consultation with a working party of parents, and we are proud that it includes a statement about our commitment to recognizing the diverse backgrounds of all families within our school,' our headteacher told me. 'We have also audited the book corners and play resources to ensure that what we have to offer the children is more diverse and representative.' It comes as no great surprise that some people have got their knickers in a right old royal twist about it, and the incoming Parental Rights in Education bill – aka the 'Don't Say Gay' bill that was passed into US law in 2022 – shows there is still a lot of misunderstanding about queer 'education'.

That bill bans any conversation around sexual orientation or gender identity (only queer identity, mind; heterosexuality and cisgender identity is a-okay apparently). The conservatives of the world would have you believe that we are sitting primary school children down to learn about rimming and what it means to be a true scissor sister. What do they take us for? What is being taught is love. To echo the title of our podcast, they are being taught that 'Some Families have two dads and two mums', that not everyone feels comfortable with the sex they were assigned at birth and that relationships come in all shapes and sizes.

MEET . . .
Olly Pike (he/him)

Olly is a children's author, illustrator and YouTuber who created Pop'N'Olly, a series of books and online content that is LGBTQ+-focused and acts as an educational resource for schools. His books are now available to schools thanks to the new RSE (Relationship and Sex Education) policy, and he talks to us about his mission.

I have made it my mission to make sure that every single primary school in the UK has at least one LGBTQ+ resource in their school. We know that children aren't born prejudiced and that's why we have to introduce diversity as young as possible to stop prejudice forming. There are roughly 23,000 primary schools in the UK. As of August 2022, we've now donated over 8,000 Pop'N'Olly books. On our website, www.popnolly.com, there is a whole database of every single primary school in the UK, and it shows if they've got copies of our books or not. If they haven't, then you can donate books there to really help with our mission.

I've also been into schools and met with the children. I go in first and foremost as an author who just happens to be LGBTQ+, rather than going in to talk about being gay. I've spoken to all ages, and I always say that kids are not given enough credit for how smart and woke they are. They know children have two mums or two dads or a trans or non-binary family member. They are more interested in my number of YouTube subscribers, which I find funny. The kids are awesome.

My background is in children's theatre and television. I loved the way children's stories, particularly fairy tales, help children learn about the concept of good vs evil and how good always triumphs. They are so powerful as they have this overarching moral message. I wanted to start creating my own books that have an LGBTQ+ twist on these classic fairy tales because that is what I needed when I was a kid, and they just didn't exist, which I put down in part to Section 28. I just know that if I had had books like the ones I'm creating, it would have made life a lot easier and would have helped navigate being an LGBTQ+ teen. I've received my share of homophobic abuse. Even now, just walking down the street, holding my partner's hand. I think, when that happens, where does this come from? Perhaps because that person hadn't learned that it's okay to be LGBTQ+ at school.

What did surprise me when I first started creating these videos and books is how many non-queer families wanted this type of content. Schools and teachers were wanting content to use to teach the diversity of society. Non-LGBTQ+ parents are wanting their children to grow up into accepting adults, especially as the majority of people in the UK will at least know an LGBTQ+ person, they want their children to understand it's okay. The gender-critical movement, however, really dislike what I do. They hate that we are trans-inclusive and have non-binary fairy tales that are available in schools. They've even taken our content and manipulated it into something that is really gross and transphobic. We've managed to get it taken down, but only because of copyright reasons, not because of transphobia and bullying, which is kind of shocking to me.

'Unfortunately, we have received some challenges from parents,' my daughter's headteacher told me, which hit me like a dagger in the stomach. 'We have received complaints about our portrayal of families from some. One parent actually said to me that they would be telling their child that all families start with a mummy and a daddy and that is a fact. We also had some backlash when a child came out as non-binary and wanted to share their story with the class. It is tricky, but ultimately, we refer parents to the equality act and stress that all protected characteristics have the same standing. Very few have actually withdrawn their children from lessons though!'

'Very few'? Which means some have. And this is my daughter's school! It makes me angry, but when I spoke to my husband about it, he wasn't surprised. After all, the constituency our town falls in has been voting Conservative since 1979. Should have seen that as a red flag when we moved here. On investigation, at least our MP voted for a ban on LGBTQ+ conversion therapy, although she does have a blonde cockapoo called Boris . . . Yikes! I do have faith in the school and the teachers and it's just an unfortunate fact that we can never know who the other parents might be or what their views are. I know that all the parents in my daughter's year have been incredible, and I just hope the same happens when our two others start.

I think it's wonderful that my children will get to feel included when it comes to family conversations in the classroom, regardless of outside views, and that their friends will be able to understand that our family is full of love and just like theirs. And also it brings me such joy to know that a child who is still in the process of exploring their gender identity can sit in their classroom and see different people, and families, represented. Helping this is also a 2022 policy, Keeping Children Safe in Education, which will do more to safeguard LGBTQ+ children within school. The ramifications for the next generation and debunking the shame our generation has experienced will be huge. 'A group of Year 6 pupils approached me this year to tell me that they were setting up an LGBTQ+ support group for a few of their friends,' my daughter's head also told me. 'The child who inspired the group had previously been a worry for us – they were suffering with anxiety and presenting with difficult behaviours. The openness with which the LGBTQ+ agenda was addressed in their classroom meant that he felt able to come out and this led to an outpouring of support. Ultimately, his mental health improved too, and I was beyond proud of this group of children who were fighting for their sense of social justice and felt empowered to do so here at school.'

These policies are clearly helping create change in our schools. However, as usual with government policy, there are loopholes and murky language. We had a little chat with Andrew Moffat (an MBE no less!), who runs the incredible organization No Outsiders, to help us understand more about what the policies entail and how LGBTQ+ parents can help make sure the correct policy is being implemented. No Outsiders' vision is to create inclusive education within schools that promotes cohesion to prepare young people for life as global citizens. They have an aim to teach children that we are all different, and that's wonderful.

MEET . . .
Andrew Moffat (he/him), teacher and founder of No Outsiders

Andrew found himself in the centre of a media storm in 2019 when protesters campaigned outside his school in Birmingham. It was reported that the majority of protesters were from the Muslim faith, but other religious groups such as Christians joined to voice their support against the No Outsiders programme.

What does the family and relationship policy mean for pupils (and teachers) in schools?

The 2019 RSE (Relationship and Sex Education) guidance[10] is a great start, but if we look at the guidance, we can see that it is really left to schools to decide what is taught with regard to LGBTQ+ awareness, and when it is taught.

The guidance says:

> Schools should ensure that all of their teaching is sensitive and age appropriate in approach and content. At the point at which schools consider it appropriate to teach their pupils about LGBT, they should ensure that this content is fully integrated into their programmes of study for this area of the curriculum rather than delivered as a standalone unit or lesson. Schools are free to determine how they do this, and we expect all pupils to have been taught LGBT content at a timely point as part of this area of the curriculum.

To me, 'at the point at which schools consider it appropriate . . . ' and, 'we expect all pupils to have been taught LGBT content at a timely point . . . ' enable schools, if they wish, to opt out of LGBTQ+ awareness in their teaching if they have concerns about potential challenges from parents in their community. The challenge, then, for parents who do want an inclusive curriculum (and I really believe most of them do), is to make sure our schools hear that message.

How will it affect what teachers can teach in school with regard to LGBTQ+ subjects?

The 2022 Keeping Children Safe in Education guidance[11] will have more effect. Page 49, paragraph 202 says:

> The fact that a child or a young person may be LGBT is not in itself an inherent risk factor for harm. However, children who are LGBT can be targeted by other children. In some cases, a child who is perceived by other children to be LGBT (whether they are or not) can be just as vulnerable as children who identify as LGBT. [. . .] Risks can be compounded where children who are LGBT lack a trusted adult with whom they can be open. It is therefore vital that staff endeavour to reduce the additional barriers faced, and provide a safe space for them to speak out or share their concerns with members of staff.

I believe this guidance has more impact because of the absence of words like 'when schools feel it is appropriate' or 'a timely point'. This guidance makes clear that schools have a responsibility to care for any children who might be LGBTQ+. It is a fact. It also recognizes that even when children are not LGBTQ+, they can be perceived to be, and this can make them vulnerable. This guidance uses the word 'vital' in saying schools must provide a safe space and reduce barriers. This is what schools need to hear; it acts as a suit of armour to protect us in this work. This guidance is statutory from September 2022.

What long-lasting impact do you think Section 28 has had on us as a nation?

Let's be clear: Section 28 had little impact on my school in the 1980s because it's not as though my school was doing anything about LGBTQ+ awareness anyway that was suddenly halted by the law. I never saw the book *Jenny Lives with Eric and Martin* in any of my schools, or indeed any representation of a gay person. I'm not convinced the teachers at my secondary school were sitting round a table in 1987 planning how to support their LGBTQ+ students and suddenly Section 28 came along.

I was at secondary school between 1984 and 1988 and there was only one lesson that mentioned gay people; it was a debate in English when I was sixteen, where the topic was homosexuality, and I kept very quiet because absolutely no one spoke up in support of gay people and I certainly wasn't going to be the one to do it.

The clear message from the debate was that LGBTQ+ people were a bad thing (I remember vividly a cheer going up when someone said, 'I think all gay people should be put up against a wall and shot!'). I think Section 28 had more impact outside of the classroom as it reinforced a narrative where LGBTQ+ people were undesirable, dangerous and something children needed protection from. This ethos had a lasting impact and can still be felt today.

What advice would you give to any LGBTQ+ parent whose child is about to start school?

I work with hundreds of schools who ask me to come in and train their staff on No Outsiders and I am always welcomed with open arms and enthusiasm. It is my experience that most teachers and most schools want to do this work and are just looking for strategies and resources, and reassurance from their parents that it is wanted and accepted. If you are a parent with a child about to start school, my advice is to talk to the school, ask them how they teach about different families and LGBTQ+ equality. I know when LGBTQ+ parents have visited my own school and asked us about our work, it has given us a huge boost because it reminds us that this work is needed in our community. The school will be anxious to demonstrate their inclusive practice and your support will mean everything to them.

What advice would you give to LGBTQ+ parents who may face challenges from parents who have opposing religious beliefs?

Everyone is entitled to hold religious beliefs and I will absolutely stand beside you supporting your right to hold your religious beliefs. In No Outsiders I make clear that schools do not need to 'celebrate' LGBTQ+ people in the curriculum; in the same way we don't need to celebrate people of colour or people with a disability. We embrace our diversity; we just are diverse. We talk about diversity, we understand it but we don't celebrate our individual differences . . . what is there to celebrate? We're just different, that's all. I often say to parents or teachers when I do training, 'I love being gay – it's fantastic! I'll celebrate me being gay but you don't have to celebrate me; I don't need your celebration. If you have a faith, I don't need to celebrate your faith; I will stand with you and fight for your right to celebrate it, but I don't need to celebrate it with you.'

In schools, No Outsiders is simply teaching children that there are different people in the world, and everyone is welcome. We can't deny that protected characteristics exist; they are all there in society.

OUR VIEW:
Tips for Starting a New School

So, as an LGBTQ+ parent, what can you do to help ensure your child's school is doing what they can to support your family?

Speak to Them
Open up a conversation with your school's headteacher about how they plan to actively discuss LGBTQ+ families with all the age groups. The policies that are now in place are there for this very reason, but they need encouragement from parents to ensure they're being activated. Andrew Moffat (see page 92) says 'a simple nudge of encouragement from parents can be the green light needed for schools to address certain areas'.

Form a Parental Committee

Ask your headteacher if you might be able to form a parental committee to share resources and information to support RSE (Relationship and Sex Education). Our school had one and it was great to connect with other parents from different year groups on the subject. It also introduced me to another gay dad at the school.

Use Pride as a Reminder

As LGBTQ+ folk, we know Pride is for life, not just for the summer. But what Pride can be incredibly useful for is reinforcing areas that might have been forgotten or not addressed. You could perhaps even try to encourage some form of event that creates conversation and awareness. Get booking that drag queen for a storytime session and watch the homophobes go wild!

Explore the Library

Ask the teachers to give you a list of the books that feature and celebrate LGBTQ+ families in the school library. There are more and more hitting the shelves, including Lotte's own *My Magic Family*. Make sure the shelves are diverse. And while you are at it, make sure you also check in on wider diversity, including books that feature Black, minority ethnic and disabled people.

Hello, Straight People

Allies, wake up. If you've picked up this book to find out more on how you can support LGBTQ+ families or educate yourselves on our journeys, then you too can do all the above. Having the voice of a non-queer parent could get the school to take notice and implement what we need for equality education.

MEET . . .
Richard Orchard-Rowe (he/him)

Richard is the host of the adoption podcast *Adoption Adventures*. He has a teenage son and, as Lotte and I are only at the start of school with our little ones, we wanted to know what the full school experience had been like for his son.

What were your first experiences?

For the most part, our lives were no different from any other family: we met other parents on the playground and we saw our son making friendships. There were the occasional issues with peers not quite accepting the fact that our son had two dads, but this was so rare that it didn't become an issue. If there were problems, then the school was very quick to pick up on this and ensure that it didn't happen again. I think that it is the same for anything, making sure you are an advocate for your child and insisting that the school fulfils its role.

How did you prepare your child for secondary school?

The first thing that panicked us was the commute. He had to walk, then get a train and then do another mile's walk, all without knowing anyone. This was a major worry for us, so we did the trip several times, and got him comfortable with the route and the routine.

As for preparing for secondary school, we did all that we could to ensure that he knew where he was going, who to speak with if there were issues and that we would be there to support him. We made a point of engaging with the pastoral office and building a working relationship with them to ensure that they were prepared to make adjustments where needed to support him with his learning.

Did he have any challenges?

Due to some of our son's early-years experiences, being in a busy classroom can cause a lot of worries. As a result, our son would work hard to make himself known to the crowd and more importantly to the teacher. He could be quite disruptive in the wrong environment and the teachers had a whole class to focus on. So, it was a challenge to help them to understand his behaviour and then for him to relax in the classroom, but in time this settled down and he coped better.

What advice would you give to an LGBTQ+ parent whose child is just about to start schooling?

Connect with the teachers and find out how they are trauma-informed and what they do to support the pastoral care of a child. Talk with them honestly about being part of the LGBTQ+ community and ask them how this would be supported in the school. We had an 'off the record' chat with the headteacher and explained that if there were any concerns about us as parents we would want to know before our son attended. We explained that if we knew beforehand then we wouldn't have an issue, but if we were told it was fine and then we saw issues, we would take it further.

But in general, life has changed, things have progressed and allies are everywhere you turn; embrace that and trust that your child will be fine. Get them to celebrate that you are part of the community, use it as a strength and they will too.

Looking back, would you have done anything differently?

The first school that we sent our son to had never had a child who had been adopted, which meant that they were poorly informed in how to support a looked-after child. With hindsight, we would select a school that had a strong working knowledge of trauma and adoption.

Talking Points

▶ Can you do more to help support your local schools' LGBTQ+ education?

▶ Discuss your own experience of schooling. How does this affect your expectations for your children?

▶ What would be your biggest worries about your child starting school?

F

IS FOR FOSTERING

In June 2018 my husband and I walked up the garden path to a house. It was an ordinary path, to an ordinary house, in the middle of an ordinary street, yet inside this house our daughter and son sat waiting for their Dad and Daddy, who they had never met, to ring the doorbell. I'll never forget the feeling as we got out of the car and made our way up the path. I felt physically sick. I was so nervous. I felt that at any moment I might pass out. The emotions were so intense that they consumed every part of me. By the time the door opened I was, for all intents and purposes, a mess. My children's foster carer stood before us. We had never met him, although we had met his wife a few weeks previously at a 'child appreciation meeting'. This is a meeting during the adoption process where once you've been matched to your child/children, you get a chance to meet their foster carer. We met her in a council office in the town where our children then lived. Her husband was at home looking after them. It was surreal to know they were only a couple of miles away from us. I remember that feeling of nerves as we met, especially as the adoption process was all suddenly starting to feel very real. What I hadn't even thought about was how nervous she would be. Her hand trembled as she reached into a box of items she had brought with her to help us understand more about our future children. This was the lady who had supported my daughter for a year and had sat in the hospital caring for my son as a new-born. They loved them, rocked them to sleep, sat with them through the night, gave them medication and dried their tears. Of course she was nervous; she loved these children and wanted them to go to the best home and I can't imagine how hard it was for her knowing they would no longer be living with her. Each item she brought with her gave us an additional piece of the puzzle. Wrappers from the food they enjoyed, a name tag from when our son was in hospital, a cuddly toy that our daughter got for her second birthday, an item of clothing she was wearing when they first came to them. I remember the smell of the cuddly toy and I could picture our daughter cuddling it. I held it close before putting it back in the box to be returned to its owner, who sat oblivious at home with her *Peppa Pig* tea set. As a sidenote: as much as I love our children's foster carers, I hold them personally responsible for the *Peppa Pig* obsession our children had. I say 'had', as I soon moved them on to bigger and more wonderful things like *Paw Patrol* (insert eyeroll!). God, I hate *Peppa Pig*.

Back to the doorstep on the day of the first meeting. While we knew his wife, the man in front of us at the front door was a stranger. He smiled and made us feel welcome, and then suddenly our daughter popped up behind him with the world's best smile. That smile will forever be etched in my memory. She laughed and I melted. My daughter has the best laugh. It's deep, cheeky and, dare I say it, it's a dirty laugh that I'm sure will be echoing around pubs in years to come. It's the type of laugh

that when she gets the giggles it becomes infectious, and you have to laugh alongside. Whenever I hear it, I'm always transported back to that day. We have a video of her laughing during that first meeting which I could watch on repeat forever. She pulled us into the front room where our son lay on the floor; he was seven months old. He looked at us with his beautiful almond-shaped eyes and I fell deeply in love with this little boy. During our adoption training we were told not to worry about having to fall in love with children straight away. Our social worker explained that you have never met this child, so how can you love them straight away? It's perfectly normal to take time to get to know them and start the falling-in-love process. I was prepped for this but, honestly, hand on heart, I can say I fell down the biggest rabbit hole of love that I will ever experience. I remember feeling exactly the same when the four of us walked in and met our youngest son a couple of years later at his foster carers' home.

The Introductions Period

We had begun what they call the introductions period. This is where you spend approximately ten to fourteen days slowly getting to know your children and for them to get to know you, trust you and allow you to become their primary caregivers. You might find yourself going through the introductions process in a totally alien area with no one around for support. In our case, we had travelled approximately 150 miles and were staying in a local Premier Inn in an industrial town. Some advice, dear reader . . . Premier Inns are never meant for more than one or two nights; fourteen nights ended up pushing the limits of our sanity, as introductions are incredibly draining, both emotionally and physically (i.e., you've gone from sipping cocktails in your local bar to suddenly running around after small children!), so if possible don't just accept what the local government childcare services offer accommodation-wise and try to find something that gives you some form of home comfort. Each day we would come back to the inn exhausted, with no way of cooking or preparing food, limited only to the Harvester downstairs or the KFC drive-thru opposite. I dreamed of a bit of home cooking and a sofa from which to watch some trash TV to just zone out from the intensity of the week.

Our introductions started with just an hour to meet our children. We left their house and sat for the rest of the day in our Premier Inn trying to make sense of what had just happened. The next day we spent a few hours with them. The one after that we spent the whole morning. The next we went out to the park with the children and the foster carers. And then the next, we took them out alone. It was so surreal to be leaving them each day when all you want to do is scoop them up and take them home, but it's designed this way for a reason. It allows them, and you, to get to know each other. By the end of the two weeks you will be arriving at the foster carers' before the kids wake and then putting them to bed at night. For both us and the foster carers there was no denying it was a strange experience. You are essentially taking over their house. It was definitely uncomfortable for the foster carers, and we felt resistance. We understood though, as they were protective and in love with these children that were soon not going to be part of their daily lives anymore. It wasn't a natural situation for any of us.

Could You Be a Foster Carer?

I've often said I don't think I could be a foster carer. My husband has always been keen but I wanted to be a parent first before I could give a child a temporary home. Selfishly, I also don't think I could say goodbye to them, and now, having watched my children's foster carers say goodbye, I'm sure my heart couldn't take it. When that time came, she held our son so tightly in her arms and you could feel the heartbreak vibrating through her. Both foster carers had come to drop the children off at our house to complete the introductions. My husband got the lucky end of the stick as he stayed downstairs with our son, who as a baby was not aware of what was happening, so he could have a good cry. After a brief 'see you soon'-style goodbye, I had taken my daughter upstairs to play in her room. We tried to keep it as light as possible for her, as we didn't want to turn it into another traumatic experience and highlight another loss for her in her young life. Sitting with her and listening to them leave while trying to hold on to my emotions was one of the most difficult things I've ever done. I eventually had to take myself to the bathroom to break down and I think I sobbed for a good thirty minutes.

You have to have a certain strength to be a foster carer. It isn't for everyone but perhaps it's the perfect way for you, dear reader, to become a parent? Bear with me as I become a foster care salesperson. The care system is close to breaking point in the UK and they need more foster carers than ever to help them look after the many children who need it. Once our children are grown, I hope to be able to work with AKT, a charity that supports LGBTQ+ young people aged sixteen to twenty-five who are facing homelessness. You see, it's not just babies and toddlers that need a home. I'd love to open up our house to a queer teen who needs some support, love and respite from the situation they have found themselves in. Perhaps this is a light-bulb moment for you? Forget surrogacy or IUI. Stuff trying to be a co-parent. Adoption too much of a headache? Foster!

Okay, sales pitch over. Back to my experience. We stay in contact with all the foster carers that looked after our children. They are important to their life story and their identity. There are no hard-and-fast rules that state you have to remain in contact, but we very much believe that it's essential for our children to have that connection. Hopefully it made saying goodbye (for now) that little bit easier.

INSIGHTS:
Setting the Fostering Myths (Anything But) Straight

Just like adoption, you may have a lot of questions about fostering. The fostering agency, Capstone, have helped demystify some fostering myths:

Well, it would be a short chapter if in fact you couldn't be gay and foster, but, to clarify, can queer people foster?
Of all the components that go into a foster carer, your sexuality is not on the list.

I'm single. Does that count me out?
Foster carers are not required to be married. They need to have a desire to look after children and young people and help them work towards a brighter future. As a

foster carer, you are part of a larger team so there is no need to have a spouse to share the responsibilities of caring for a child. You never foster alone; there is a strong team working with you.

If I rent and don't own my home, will that affect me fostering?

You do not need to own your home – it's acceptable for it to be a rented property. However, you do have to check with your landlord before applying and have them provide approval for foster children in their property. You will also need to provide not only financial security, but stability too if you are living in rented accommodation: it would not be recommended to keep moving around if you are taking care of a foster child.

I want to foster but don't want to give up work. Can I still foster?

The reality is that when you become a foster carer, your first obligation is to the child in care and this is a 24/7 job. However, fostering may turn out to be a sporadic job and you might not always have a placement and, without a placement, there is no payment. When you apply to be a foster carer, you discuss your job and your desire to keep it. Arrangements can often be made to accommodate it along with fostering – for instance, if you have a spouse or partner, one of you can always be available for the child.

I am retired, so am I too old to foster?

There is no upper age limit. There are, however, health requirements. If you are in good health, mentally and physically, and have a high energy level, being a senior citizen is not an impediment to being a foster parent.

I don't have my own children. Will that disqualify me?

Experience is not required to be a foster parent. This does not mean that you don't have all the necessary mental, physical and emotional equipment necessary to foster a child.

As for the experience, you will receive ongoing training and support. If you have never had a child and therefore think that you will not know what to expect from a child placed with you, do not be concerned. A supervising social worker will be available for you from the beginning of your assessment and throughout your journey as a carer.

Talking Points

▶ Do you have the emotional resilience needed to foster?

▶ If you already have children, might you consider fostering?

▶ Would fostering be a good way for you and your partner, or you alone, to start your parenting journey?

▶ If you have adopted, have your opinions of foster carers changed since you adopted?

▶ Would you keep in contact with your child's foster carer?

G

IS FOR GENDER

 She/Her, He/Him, They/Them, Ze/Zir. As the very subtitle of this book alludes (you didn't think we meant the letter 'Ze', did you?), there are many different gender pronouns we can now celebrate and use to identify ourselves. Hurrah! We can finally break free of our gendered constraints and explore identities that we feel relate to our lived experience. Yay! Rejoice for liberation.

If only. As anyone who has struggled with gender identity will tell you, the road is still long. And in terms of parenting? Forget it. We seem to be a long way off breaking free of the 'mother' and 'father' shackles. Nor has the commercial world woken up to the fact that, shock horror, little boys might want to wear Disney Princess night-time pullups rather than Pixar *Cars*. Becoming a parent is like being continually hit round the face with a massive gender stick as you find yourself challenged by day-to-day 'mummy' and 'daddy' stereotypes. Cue us trying to awkwardly sing 'We are living in a heteronormative world and I'm a non-heteronormative girl/boy/person' to the tune of 'Material Girl' (it doesn't work but bear with us as you get the point!).

We decided to have a look at the *Cambridge Dictionary*[12] definition of 'mother' and 'father'.

Mother (noun) – a female parent

Father (noun) – a male parent

Fairly self-explanatory, but then again where are the options for non-binary parents? (Let's stick a pin in that, and come back to it; see page 126.) It was when we looked at the examples of how the noun can be used that we hit the gender-stereotyped nail on the head.

'The supermarket was full of harassed-looking mothers with young children.'

'My father took me to watch the football every Saturday.'

These are actual *Cambridge Dictionary* examples. To spell it out, mothers are viewed as the caregivers; they are maternal and loving but are also harassed and need a nice bunch of flowers on Mother's Day to make everything alright. Dads are the fun ones who pop in and take the kids out to give Mum a bit of a break and don't really have any emotional connection. How boring and frustrating it must be to be a straight parent and to have these gendered rules of parenthood hanging over you, dictating how you go about your daily parenting duties. One thing Lotte and I have embraced is the idea that as queer parents all these rules go out the window. We make our own rules and there is no weight of expectation on either of us to perform a certain 'role' in our parenting. A common theme throughout our adoption process was that we had to constantly demonstrate how we would address the fact that our children wouldn't have a female figure around the house. While we could easily address the shared parental responsibilities, there is no denying that, quite simply, neither John nor I has a vagina. What does that mean for our daughter? What would we do when she was older and needed to relate to someone about her period? And what would it mean for her to grow up in a house surrounded by four men? During our panels we made the point very clear that although we are two men, we are surrounded by a large group of women who would have a very real and close relationship, not only with our daughter, but with our sons too. And we've kept that promise. Whenever we stay with my mum or sisters, we encourage them to let our daughter be in their room when they get changed, maybe even shower together. It's important to us that she sees bodies that reflect her own and to start building that intimate relationship with the female members of her close family, and while we hope she will always be able to come to us to discuss anything, she will know that she can always chat to her aunties.

So if it was down to just our little family unit, we would be fine, but we have the rest of the world to contend with when out and about. Many struggle to get their head around the modern-day definition of what a mother or father can be or that queer parents do indeed exist. Case in point was when my husband and I walked into a grand National Trust house in the middle of Cornwall. Our three children buzzed around us while we brimmed with the frantic energy any parents visiting a stately home with toddlers will have experienced. 'Don't touch!' 'Get down!' 'Come here!' 'Don't touch!' 'Get off that!' 'Don't touch!' 'I told you not to touch!' So when a kindly-looking older gentleman from the Trust, probably a volunteer, approached us, our minds were already a little scrambled. He took one look at us, two men together, and said, 'Mums' day off, is it?' BAM! Walloped with that gender stick again. We stood with a blank look on our faces as he continued. 'Your mummies gone off shopping for the day, have they?' BAM! Walloped again. He was addressing the children this time. It was their turn to give a blank look before refocusing their attention on destroying every priceless artifact in sight. Our response was one that many queer parents will be familiar with. We did nothing. We stared blankly for about two seconds, smiled politely, and walked away. In that precise moment we were shocked but also had more pressing matters at hand (i.e., a missing two-year-old who no doubt had climbed into a seventeenth-century sideboard for fun). I regret not taking the moment to address it. I'm sure he was a friendly old man, different generation, blah blah, but honestly if we are going to make change, we can't allow for these type of excuses any longer. Not only was he completely oblivious to the fact that we are two gay men who are, GASP, parents, but the sexist undertones were very much real. I wish I had taken the moment to say, 'We are a two-dad family; this is my husband. As much as I love shopping, I'm enjoying this day out with my family. Thank you, sir, goodbye.' Then, especially as I'm sure his intentions were good, perhaps he would be a bit more open in his thinking in the future. (We explore how to deal with this kind of obtuse comment more in 'W is for Who's the Real Mum?', see page 334.) He may have even had a conversation with his mates down the Dog and Duck that night and told them this story. They too may take a moment to think it over as they take a sip of their pints and re-evaluate what they say, do and think. Although, I'm 75 per cent sure one of them is likely to have said, 'Bloody faggots are breeding now. Can't they just keep it out of our faces.' Groan.

And mum is indeed the word. Before becoming a dad, I never quite realized just how much it's used and how alienated it's made me feel in the context it's used. 'Mother and Baby' classes, 'Local Mums' Facebook forums, 'Mother and Baby' magazines, the 'Mums WhatsApp' groups and even my own beloved Spice Girl Emma Bunton released a book called *Mama You Got This*,[13] although to be fair to Baby Spice, it's obviously riffing on their tune 'Mama', so I might be biased but I'll throw her a bone.

Early on, when searching for a non-'Mum and Baby' parent group in our local area, we finally gave in and decided to take our littlest to a session called 'Mummies and Little Ones'. Perhaps us being there would even incite some sort of change? Let's just say the experience was not pleasurable. The instructor/group leader/dictator (whatever you want to call her) decided to completely ignore the fact we were two gay dads, a point we made very clear at the start when we gave her a friendly hello. It almost felt she was doing it on purpose when she continually addressed the 'mums' in the group and hit her peak when she announced that the 'Mother and Baby Yoga Class' would be taking place on Thursday this week, not Tuesday, 'but perhaps not one for you two' while looking daggers our way. Safe to say we ripped up the leaflet given to us on how to sign up for regular classes. The thing I don't understand about the whole fixation on 'Mum and Baby' is also how damaging this constant use of mother/mum/ mummy in relation to anything parenting is to women who are trying to fight for equality in life and the workplace. It continually fuels the notion that women must stay at home with the kids and doesn't help liberate dads (queer or straight) who may want to be the ones to take a career break or become a primary carer. Groups, communities and the media should be welcoming dads into the mix. How about this for a revolutionary idea? Why don't we just use the word 'parent'?

My friend let me borrow a cookbook she had loved and recom- mended it because it allowed you to make recipes for you and baby . . . genius. The book is called *Young Gums* by Beth Bentley (she/her).[14] As I pulled it out of my bag, I then happened to notice the subtitle: 'A Modern Mama's Guide to Happy, Healthy Weaning'. Urgh! Why? I decided to email Beth to ask her about this choice and her thoughts on the fact that the continued use of 'mama' and 'mum' in parenting helps no one. She quickly came back to me. I think it helped that I was trying to be constructive and explore the debate rather than criticize her. 'The modern mama of the title is me, it's my guide to happy, healthy weaning. Which is why it's "A modern mama's guide" vs "The modern mama's guide",' she explained. Makes more sense now and why I didn't think of that bloody use of syntax! She continued: 'I understand that's unclear though and it's really crap to have made you feel alienated and marginalized when what you're doing [adoption] is so powerfully positive. I agree with you on the narrowness we see re perceived ideals, standards, norms etc. of parenthood. It's bullshit and it's (even as a white cis woman) so boring, unreflective and alienating to see the same old tropes of parenthood everywhere always.' Couldn't agree more, Beth! This isn't solely a queer issue and I hope that together with our trad-parents we can find a way to start breaking it down. Lotte has a cishet female friend whose husband looks after the children so she can continue her career. 'Every time I walk past a sign advertising a "mum and baby group" on my way to the office, it makes me feel like I'm somehow less of a mum because I'm working,' she says. 'It's as if I've had to choose between being a mum and being a "person". In my life and career, I've always felt equal to men. It's only since having a child that the stark realities of the different expectations society burdens mothers with have become apparent.'

MEET . . .
Anna Whitehouse (she/her), aka Mother Pukka, journalist, author and broadcaster

We talk about allies to the queer community – straight people who stand up and support the queer community. But allyship works both ways. Without getting J. K. Rowling all riled up again, a lot of the discrimination and inequality that women have faced for thousands of years mirrors the queer experience. In fact, the true definition of allyship are groups that are associated by a common cause, so we had a chat to Anna, a parent who is trying to make a difference in the world of parental equality.

Anna, can you talk to us about parental inequality?
I've been campaigning for flexible working for everyone, not just mothers, since 2015. In all that time, every talk that I've ever given within companies and businesses has been to the women's network, which is ultimately an echo chamber of agreement. Gender inequality isn't an issue just for women to fix. One of my biggest issues is a sort of bricks-and-mortar physical issue with the world at large, which is that mothers are just assumed to be the ones wiping the baby's ass, essentially. I think we all sort of applauded Marks and Spencer's for including a dad changing area, but that was in 2020. That we're all clapping for such a basic shift is extraordinary. I went on a press trip with a *New York Times* journalist to Sweden and she was looking around at all these men with their babies and she said, 'Why are there so many male nannies out here?' And I was like, 'They are dads. Parenting. This is what equality looks like.'

Do you agree that some parenting language is too gendered and work needs to be done to help support the mission for parental and workplace equality?
When I launched Mother Pukka it was a direct response to the fact that I felt so targeted by publications such as *Mother and Baby Magazine* etc., when actually no one was talking about the bit in between. You have *Vogue*, *Stylist* and magazines saying 'this is the wedding dress you should wear' and 'this is how you go from day to night', but no one was talking about the middle bit, which I found myself in, which was being pushed out of the workforce for simply pushing out a baby. A lot needs to be done to break up those

networks which are solely for women telling other women about issues. I ask why are they not parent networks? Why are they only women or mother networks? I specifically launched Mother Pukka with the strapline: 'For People Who Happen to Be Parents'.

Why do you think there is a reluctance from some to adopt 'parents' as a simple use of language, especially when it's so inclusive?

I think probably the reason is that mothers are deemed to be more vulnerable commercially. That's good for business because they want to prey on women's insecurities, whether that's how they look or how they feel. Ultimately, there's no denying that women go through more biologically to have a child. There is a biological inequality that happens when a baby lands, but the job, the role of parent, is divided in two. I find it astonishing that, for quite clear commercial reasons, we're still being targeted because they know the mother's going to be so exhausted and broken that she'll be the one that goes, 'Right, well, I need this product to fix that numbness that I'm experiencing'. I initially got applauded for using the word parents in all my communications, and I just thought, 'But it's so basic?' It covers both sides of the coin or one side of the coin if we are talking about inclusivity. 'Parent' covers single parents, two parents parenting, three parents parenting. It's strange that we are then coming back to those networks.

To be clear, in case it's not obvious through our chat with Anna above, one thing we are not suggesting is the erasure of motherhood. What most people who get uptight about new vocabulary being used seem to not grasp is that we only want to *add* to language, not take anything from it. It's time to stop, think and question if a different terminology can help someone feel included. I recently went to a garden centre where there was a calendar called 'A Mum's Organisational Calendar'; that piece of tat is what we want erased, not motherhood. 'We've really struggled with general patriarchal assumptions,' say bisexual couple Lucy and Paul, whom we spoke to about this. Lucy explains that her workplace didn't even have a shared parental leave policy in place, despite it being required by law for more than five years. 'I basically had to write one while pregnant. They had wrongly assumed that I would be the one looking after the baby. People just can't seem to accept Paul as an equal parent. I am always the first person that organizations phone, even though we've specifically requested Paul to be the primary contact. On one occasion the nursery even decided to phone my mother-in-law, who was listed as an emergency contact before Paul.'

I should also add that John and I often get a dose of positive discrimination when we seem to be congratulated when out and about for doing absolutely nothing but day-to-day parenting. 'Awww, what a good dad,' I was told while pushing my daughter on the swing one day in the park. Excuse me? 'Well done!' I was told by someone while taking my two kids on a dog walk through a field. Are you serious? Why do men get congratulated for doing simple mundane parenting tasks? The fact that someone goes out of their way to praise parenting when a male is involved just highlights the issues we have as a society due to painting women as the expected caregivers. As a side note, now we have three children under the age of five, and if I'm out with them alone, sometimes with our two dogs, then actually I'll take all the praise I can, as let me tell you, it's fucking hard! Praise away!

LOTTE'S VIEW

When my daughter was first born, a health worker weighed her then passed her back to me with the unforgettable words: 'Go to Daddy.' It was only as we walked home from the children's centre, pushing the pram in that hyper-careful way you do when it holds precious newborn cargo, that we looked at each other and burst out laughing. 'Did that actually just happen?!' I don't mind being misgendered. There have been times, when I've been leaning into my more masc gender identity, when I've actively wanted to be read as a queer boi. But 'Daddy', in this context (!), did not work for me. I like being 'Mama' as it differentiates my role from my wife, who our daughter calls 'Mummy'. But I don't feel that there's a hierarchy of motherhood between us, like one is *a* mum and the other is *the* mum. I totally agree with Stu that this commoditized and hyper-feminized version of mum stuff is banal and unhelpful and excludes anyone who doesn't fit an outdated hetero stereotype, but I've found my own queer way into motherhood and I'm happy with where I am.

We spoke to Alexandra Heminsley (she/her), the author of *Somebody to Love: A Family Story* and a coparent to a five-year-old with her ex, D, a trans woman. She says:

I became a mother in the absolute peak of the Insta-mum trend. I went from having social media feeds that were talking about the Mueller report,[15] to seeing a really small group of white, straight women talking about their kids. I felt genuinely tormented by my experience coinciding with that. I think it was such a pernicious point in social media and branding history, the way that people were kind of branding motherhood and shipping it out for sale. I didn't have any queerness in my feed. There was nobody that I could relate to. Kris Jenner (who had been married to Caitlyn Jenner, a trans woman) was pretty much it at that point.

I had to break out of it. And I'm pleased being part of a queer family helped free me from a type of motherhood that I think could have got me otherwise.

Mother's and Father's Day

Parents' days are perfect examples of how gender notions are so far back in the dark ages. The explosion of stereotypes is like something from a 1980s Woolworths shop front. Mums get flowers, pink cards, a lie-in or breakfast in bed – it's all very cutsie and twee. Dads on the other hand get cards with pints, cricket and football – it's all jokey blokey claptrap. Trying to find a Father's Day card for my husband is near impossible, as I can spend hours searching through the gendered bullshit to find something that aligns to his interests, and guess what? I often will find the 'perfect' Mother's Day card for him. It doesn't help that, in our family, I'm 'Daddy' and my husband is 'Dad', so that wipes out 50 per cent of the cards on offer, especially the younger cute cards, which all seem to lean towards 'Daddy', aka me! I had a chat to trans parent Freddy McConnell (he/him), a solo 'seahorse' father, about how he deals with Mother's Day and Father's Day. 'I find Mother's Day and Father's Day all pretty silly,' he said. 'I'm pretty cynical and feel they're all just marketing gimmicks. But the only thing that makes me nervous around these days is the idea that someone might try to celebrate me on Mother's Day. My kids are too young to really care about any of it anyway so luckily no one has ever tried that. I just do my best to ignore it. I celebrate my own mum [meet Freddy's mum Esme Chilton on page 191] and sometimes the nursery are very sweet and get my eldest to do a card for Nana on Mother's Day. They also checked with me that I wanted that to happen, and I did. She's a mother figure for our whole family.'

I have felt the pressure of Mother's Day and Father's Day more and more since my children have started school. We decided to hit the subject head on and I had a chat to my daughter's teacher about how on Mother's Day we make a fuss about John's mum and my mum and it's an opportunity to spoil the nannies. It means that when everyone else in school is making Mother's Day cards they can join in and do some special cards for our mums (saves us buying a separate card as well, bonus!) Being two gay dads, you would think Father's Day would be like Christmas in the Oakley household. Anyone who knows me, and knows what I get like around my birthday, would imagine me screaming at the top of my lungs, 'It's our day, OUR day! Worship us, children!!', but honestly, it's more of a logistical minefield. Who spoils whom? Who gets the lie-in? Who gets taken out for dinner? We cancel each other out! Therefore, I'm hoping all this changes by the time the kids are old enough to make us a nice breakfast in bed and go and buy us flowers. In the future I can only dream that they might take their ageing dads out on the town for a slap-up meal.

LOTTE'S VIEW

Father's Day unsurprisingly barely registers in our house. I do try to send my dad a card but as he doesn't drink beer or like sports or scatological humour, I struggle to find anything appropriate in the shops. Last year I sent him flowers as I realized I'd never done so before, whereas my mum gets a bouquet from me at the first sniff of an occasion. I think he really appreciated it. As I was growing up in the 1980s and 90s, my father was the opposite of a basic blokey dad trope. He did all the cooking and housework and was as involved in my life as my mum was. Because this was my role model of fatherhood, it blows my mind when I see things on social media about useless men and lazy dads. Who actually are these people? And why are their wives making inane TikTok videos about them and not filing for divorce? Straight people, honestly! Maybe when my daughter gets older Father's Day will make her aware of not having something that others do, but we can celebrate any number of the wonderful men in our lives instead – and it sounds like Stu might enjoy the extra attention!

Don't be afraid to speak to your child's school about how your family likes to celebrate Mother's Day and Father's Day, if at all. Remember that while teachers may have had experience of dealing with sensitivities around these days, including single or deceased parents, they might not have had to address your situation. They may also try to second-guess something, so be clear on how you'd like your little one to be part of the activities.

All of this begs the question: should we scrap the idea of dedicated Mother and Father Days? In a world where we are striving for gender equality, wouldn't the idea of 'Parents' Day' be a simpler, less gendered approach that also serves anyone who has lost a parent or is a single parent? In fact, there is now a Non-Binary Parents' Day on 18 April each year. My parents never really celebrated either Mother's or Father's Day, as both felt you should respect and love your parents every single day, and I do think there is something in that.

Pink is for Girls, Blue is for Boys
(and Other Nonsense)

It's not all about us either (although the megalomaniac in me would argue against that!). The other frequent slap-round-the-face-with-the-gender-stick we get comes from our children themselves and the boxes the world tries to put them in. From before they're even born, with the dreaded gender-reveal parties, this pink/blue silliness begins. I never quite realized just how gendered society was until I had children. We still live in a world where girls can only like unicorns, rainbows, fairies and Disney princesses. Boys can only like cars, monsters, football and diggers. Everything from clothing, party accessories, toys, bedding, home décor and beyond perpetuates these stereotypes. In our house I was adamant that we were going to break down these gender tropes and not place any particular emphasis on any of our children, but honestly, it's really, really hard. The world is against you. The moment my daughter went to school she started becoming more and more 'girly'. It doesn't matter what you do at home, it spreads like a disease through their social circle. I remember my heart sinking when my son wanted to have a princess cake for his birthday and my daughter declared, 'Princess cakes are for girls. He can't have one.' 'Who told you that?' I snapped back; I was fuming. 'He can have whatever cake he wants, as can you.' I was so upset and, in that moment, I realized that no matter how hard you try to break down these stereotypes, society will also beat it into them. I will talk more about my son's gender identity in a future chapter (see page 244), but he loves everything that you stereotypically associate with girls. We let him live his truth but it's not easy, or always logistically possible. Underwear is a perfect example of this. He wants pink pants, he wants princess pants, he wants unicorn pants, but can you get these anywhere? No. We could get him knickers, but they are not designed to house little boy bits; it would fall out the side and I think he might be too young for tucking. The same with night-time pants. Huggies do

Disney Princesses for girls and Pixar's *Cars* for boys. They are specifically designed for boys and girls based on where the urine will come from in the night, so it's not just a case of giving him the princess ones. It's time for parents – queer AND cishet – to be able to let their children live their lives without these ridiculous gender constraints. It's a vicious cycle that repeats, repeats, repeats.

Non-Binary Parenting

We spoke to Kai (they/them), the parent of a three-year old (Kai's wife carried), about their experience of not conforming to the mother/father binary. They said they were lucky as all the doctors and midwives they met during the pregnancy and labour were very respectful of their pronouns. 'I asked that they made a note on our records so I didn't have to keep explaining at every new meeting. There were times when I would have just let the misgendering go over my head, but my wife is a stickler for these things and she would correct everyone all the time! We found that once we'd told someone my pronouns they made a real effort to get it right.' Kai says the harder part has been since the birth, when everything from the NCT WhatsApp Groups to the Baby Sensory classes present 'Mum' and 'Dad' as the only options. 'I always introduce myself as our daughter's "parent" and I can tell that just blows some people's mind. They don't know how to be with me.'

Assumptions about what makes a 'mother' and a 'father' are so loaded. While for many trans people being acknowledged within these binaries is important and validating, non-binary parents are challenging all of us to interrogate our unconscious biases. A more fluid approach to our child-rearing roles can benefit all of us, particularly our straight friends!

Names for Non-Binary Parents

We asked some non-binary parents to tell us what their kids call them. Here are some responses:

Mapa
Zaddy
Bubba
Maddy
Par
Zaza
Nini

Talking Points

▶ Has your opinion on gender shifted since having children?

▶ How do you feel your own gender identity might influence your parenting?

▶ What steps do you feel you can take in your life to help support gender equality?

H

IS FOR HARD TIMES

We have a theory that queer people learn to assert a degree of control over their reality from a very young age. This stays with us into adulthood (as manifested in everything from the relationship we have with our bodies to our career ambitions . . . and, of course, parenthood!). Its root might be in the fact that as kids we were constantly having to manage feeling different from our peers – controlling when it was safe to let our true selves shine and when it was better to hide. Or perhaps it stems from the necessity of having to 'come out' – making a grand and definitive statement about our identity and desires, then having to make it again and again for the rest of our lives, in a way that cis heterosexual people never have to. Being very good at putting feelings in boxes and developing efficient strategies for dealing with difficult things – bullying for example – can be a direct result of an LGBTQ+ person's formative years. And while Stu and I were lucky enough to be from loving and supportive families, and to never have directly suffered from homophobic abuse – still we find ourselves to be Type-A adults who like to assert order on chaos and hold ourselves to impossibly high standards (something we'll explore more in 'P is for Perfectionism', see page 237). What this means is when things don't go to plan, we have in the past really struggled to accept that it isn't our fault. But there's nothing like being a parent – and the road to getting there – for helping us embrace the glorious chaos that is life and connect with the raw reality of our feelings more than we ever have.

I remember when Jenny first told me she was pregnant. It was a cool October evening and I'd been out for a drink with a friend. She'd texted to ask when I'd be home, which was rare in our laidback marriage – it's normally at least midnight before one of us starts wondering where the other is. We weren't due to do the pregnancy test for another couple of days, so when I walked through the door later that night, it took me a while to understand what the wand she was waving at me, featuring two parallel blue lines peeking out from a little rectangular window, actually meant.

Fast-forward four years and I longed to see those lines for myself – their absence was a regular marker of my 'failure' to conceive. But back then, after we'd embraced and shouted, 'THIS IS MAD' and 'I CAN'T BELIEVE IT' back and forth a few times, I absolutely did believe it: we had decided to do a thing, we had planned for a thing, the thing had worked – it was all exactly as it should have been. In retrospect, I don't think I appreciated the miracle this pregnancy was. It worked the first time we tried! Using natural IUI! I should have been wildly, wildly happy but instead we both just powered head-first into the reality of pregnancy and never really stopped to marvel at this growing embryo's very existence. I wonder if you can only ever truly experience a high if you have known its equivalent low.

Because our children weren't conceived during a night of passion but as a result of an orgy of administration and organization, we thought we were 'prepared'. Ha!

Nobody arrives at parenting without any baggage, but many of us queer people are lugging an extra Louis Vuitton trunk along for the ride, and perhaps that made adjusting to parenthood harder too.

If you'd asked me how I was shortly after I made the decision to stop trying IVF, having undergone three years of fertility treatment, I would have said 'fine' (turn to 'I is for IVF', page 145, for more on this). I quickly reframed this 'failure' into something empowering – I chose the time to stop. I took back that control and once I had made the decision, I didn't want to dwell on it. I didn't want to interrogate the disappointment that lay heavy on my chest, the shame that twisted deep in my gut or the envy that hit like a wave whenever I heard someone else's good news. Nope, I was fine. But the truth is, it's really hard to let go of the dream of carrying a child. Especially when it was going to connect me to my non-biological daughter in a really beautiful way, as the children would have had the same donor. So, there was a lot to let go of.

I count myself lucky not to have ever experienced a miscarriage, but I wonder if in some ways actually seeing the blood, feeling the pain, might have helped give me the closure I needed. Instead, the whole experience felt extremely abstract, and I got so used to the disappointment of finding out I wasn't pregnant every few months, it became banal and everyday. I went through so much in terms of injections, appointments, procedures, but there had been no baby at the start of it, and no baby at the end of it. When else do you spend so much money and devote so much time on something you don't ever see the result of – and don't say damp-proofing your house. Nothing had changed, and yet so much had.

MEET . . .

Kate (she/her)

**We'll talk more to Kate and her wife in 'I is for IVF'
(see page 145) but here she shares with us her
experience of miscarriage.**

I miscarried at eight weeks and we found out at the
twelve-week scan. After the initial shock and grief,
honestly, I felt incredibly powerful. This sounds strange,
but I felt the most female I've ever felt in my life. Weirdly
empowered and really strong. Just like, if I can do that,
I can do anything. It sounds really out there, but I had
this weird moment where I was about to go in for my
D&C procedure [to have the embryo removed] and
they put me on a bed and I was lying, looking out of
the window. I'd never been in hospital before for a
procedure, so I was quite nervous and I just felt this
incredible, powerful feeling. Like, I had so many women
behind me. All my ancestors were saying, 'It's alright,
you know, we've all been here. We all do this.'

So how did I eventually lean into my real feelings about ending
my IVF journey and move on without quashing them down into
a deep, dark place within myself in a profoundly unhealthy way?
Exercise. It sounds so simple, but honestly, getting out into the
local park twice a week with a trainer made me experience being
in my body in a way I hadn't since starting IVF. As a queer person
who feels closer to non-binary than female, embarking on fertility
treatment and hoping to get pregnant meant loosening my grip
on the way I like to show up in the world. I enjoy having a flat
chest and not looking feminine, but inhabiting a space between

gendered ideas of body shape and fashion style became harder as the hormones I was injecting over so long put weight on my hips and stomach and quite dramatically – to my eyes anyway – changed my shape. I had reasoned that it would be worth it.

After my first exercise session, as I gasped to catch my breath and realized my heart was no longer used to beating so fast, I burst into tears. It felt so good to move, to get sweaty and to get out of my head and into my body. As I jogged around the park, I felt something physically shift inside of me. Alongside talking to my friends and family and writing about my fertility journey, which helped me mentally work out my emotions, exercising regularly freed me from the weight of what I'd been carrying: hope, loss, anger and a resignation to my body becoming unfamiliar. As well as workouts, I also found just having to be in the moment when looking after my three-year-old daughter a great panacea.

I might not ever get pregnant, but I can get strong again and feel good, feel myself. I'm at peace with not ever being able to carry a child. I don't regret trying and I don't beat myself up for 'failing'.

INSIGHT:
Ask a Fertility Counsellor

Jamie Forster (she/her), an MBPsS, MBACP Specialist Fertility Counsellor, on waiting, wanting and what to do when things don't go to plan.

What advice do you have for people going through the two-week wait (2WW) to find out if they are pregnant?

By this point in treatment, individuals and couples have already been through a huge ordeal, and it can be the first time patients reach out for counselling support. This is partly because clinic communication slows down, there are no more appointments, and there is nothing left to do but reflect and wait: the perfect storm for high anxiety. People I see at this time are often stressed, tired, worried and obsessing over every choice they've made the past few months, and agonizing over every tingle, ache or pain.

There are six things that I encourage people to do to smash the dreaded 2WW.

1. Step away from Google.
2. Plan ahead and have something to look forward to (a break away, short course online, a good long book, a series to binge-watch).
3. Practice self-care – I know this seems silly because people in treatment are generally the most health-focused people on the planet. However, continuing to focus on basic nutrition, hydration and exercise during the 2WW is very important. Not just because you are trying to support a growing embryo, but

because it helps you feel more in control and will support your overall emotional wellbeing.

4. Journaling and counselling can help you keep on top of the emotions you are feeling and keep you grounded. It is important to know that the thoughts you are feeling are normal and have an important part to play.

5. Relaxation techniques such as meditation, gentle yoga and mindful walking are fantastic ways to focus on your mental health and keep your anxiety in check.

6. Practise loving kindness – I go back to this time and time again because it is so incredibly important. Life is tough, but fertility treatment takes the cake on self-induced stress. You must remember that you are doing everything you can to take care of yourself and to fulfil your dreams of becoming a parent. The process is going to be filled with highs and lows, but no matter the outcome of the treatment, you are doing what you must do to support your future.

Why can feelings of guilt and shame come up if we experience pregnancy loss or infertility? What kind of questions should we be asking ourselves when wondering if it's the right time to stop trying?

We are essentially groomed from birth to believe that being a successful adult somehow includes parenthood and having children. So when it doesn't work, we can often feel deep sadness, shame or guilt and assume that something must be inherently wrong with our bodies, like we are broken in some way, less than human. The truth is, we aren't taught properly about fertility or reproductive medicine, rather we are led to believe that fertility treatment such as IVF automatically equals baby, but sadly, for many, this is simply not true.

In my experience when people are coming to the end of their fertility journey, they are naturally starting to consider what life might look like on the other side. They are starting to wonder about what a life without children might feel like; can they be happy, can they be fulfilled, will they always feel somehow left out of society? Often they are exhausted by the continuous decision-making, endless appointments, the poking and prodding of their bodies, the giant pause button that looms over their existence.

Sadly, there is no series of questions you can answer to determine if you should stop trying. I only encourage people to pause, breathe deep, find some grounding and think ahead to ten years from now, imagine yourself after the pain has left, the stress is gone, the emotions processed. Can you picture yourself at peace? Feeling the tug of those difficult emotions at your heart, are you able to console yourself with the knowledge that you did everything you could at the time? Fertility treatment is more than just trying to have a baby; it is about utilizing all the resources available to you, so that on the other side of treatment, regardless of the outcome, you can find peace knowing that you did everything you could do.

If we have experienced loss or infertility, is it okay to feel resentful of other people's pregnancies and births?

To be honest, I don't see how you could be struggling on a fertility journey and NOT feel this way! Of course, it's okay to have thoughts of jealousy and resentment; having these feelings is a natural and normal response to seeing someone experience the one thing you want the most in the world, but can't seem to achieve. Repeated cycle failure and pregnancy loss is so painful and difficult, and watching people achieve these things so easily can make you feel like someone you're not. The best way to manage these feelings is to show yourself some kindness; what you are doing is hard, so give yourself a break.

Learning how to check in with yourself and then respond appropriately to those needs is one of the best ways to work through negative thoughts. This means pausing to assess how you are feeling. If you are feeling a bit anxious or stressed, then perhaps giving yourself permission to say no can be the kindest thing to do for yourself. If you are having a good day and feel strong and grounded, then go ahead and get stuck into your day! It is important to remember that these emotions are not permanent: you will feel different tomorrow and different again the day after, so go slow, breathe and be as kind to yourself as you are to the person you love the most in the world.

In what ways does being LGBTQ+ make TTC (trying to conceive) or loss even more challenging?

One of the most obvious challenges for LGBTQ+ people is the discriminatory policies that keep you from being able to access fertility treatment in the UK. While this is finally being challenged, there is still a long way to go to making treatment accessible and fair for everyone.

The emotional aspect of treatment is highly complex, so for anyone who experiences loss after fertility treatment, the experience of grief is often aggravated by the intense planning and emotional investment it took to achieve pregnancy in the first place. However, for LGBTQ+ people, their grief can be minimalized or overlooked due to many assumptions that are made. Assumptions such as the pain is worse for the gestational carrier, or for transgender parents who can experience significant dysphoria in regard to their bodies or specific body parts as a result of pregnancy loss. Lesbian couples might have to deal with the assumption that if one partner fails to carry, they always have a backup. For many it diminishes their entire fertility journey and does not respect the experience for that person or couple. These discriminatory biases can interfere with your ability to process the loss and continue with a fertility journey, and there is often a lack of representation for the LGBTQ+ community in the support resources set up for baby loss.

Do you think it is beneficial to talk more openly about experiences of miscarriage?

Talking can absolutely help process the loss and grief of baby loss, but it's about finding safe and inclusive spaces where you can speak openly without fear. Talking to a counsellor who will allow you to explore your feelings of sadness without judgement can be so helpful in processing the grief.

How can therapy help when going through these things?

The British Infertility Counselling Association (BICA) says that 'Infertility is known to be one of the most distressing experiences for anyone who expected to plan a family. It is often a shock, threatening hopes and dreams of how they imagined the future. If this is happening to you, you may be surprised at how hard it is to cope with your emotions and with being surrounded by other people's babies and families. Relatives, friends and colleagues may not be very understanding or realize how much grief you are feeling. Not everyone will appreciate that a miscarriage is a bereavement or that undergoing fertility treatments is stressful, offering hope and anxiety in equal measure.'

Finding a counsellor that can hold a space for you while you explore all of these complex emotions can be an invaluable resource for fertility patients. It can help you learn to communicate your feelings to your partner, or if you are on your own, can give you that place to get it all out, and it helps to learn how to articulate the complicated emotions and normalize confusing feelings. We wear so many masks: one version of ourselves at work, a different version at home or with friends. Finding a counsellor you connect with gives you a space to just be yourself, just as you are, no expectations or judgements; someone to sit with you and hold a space for you to just be. There is something very special in that.

There's a growing awareness of post-natal depression, and rightly so. What of the mental health challenges many new parents feel, regardless of how their children came into their world?

MEET . . .
Didi (she/her) and Priscilla (she/her)

We hear a lot about post-natal depression, but how about post-adoption depression? Does it exist, how is it manifested and what can we do to feel better or to support someone in feeling better? This is Didi and Priscilla's story. They adopted their daughter Ava eight years ago, when she was one year old.

Priscilla

Post-adoption depression definitely exists – we both experienced it, although it manifested in different ways. It seemed to come out of nowhere. Days generally felt dark and long.

Didi

I felt like a fraud in a way, I felt uncomfortable calling myself a 'mummy' or even saying 'my daughter'. In a practical sense I knew she was and I was a mum, but emotionally I couldn't relate . . . it felt foreign. I was, though, very aware that I wanted our child to be okay, so I acted my way through activities and daily routines. But, when she was napping or down for the night, I fell into dark moods and became fearful. Our relationship took a back seat, although when our mental capacity allowed, we tried to be there for each other. Then one day the darkness began to lift, some of the important things in our relationship like laughter and conversations came back and we started bonding emotionally with Ava and as a family. Being called 'Mummy' and saying 'my daughter' then felt right and true.

Priscilla

I had heard it said many times – nothing can prepare you for a child, but in my experience, this was very true. I hadn't foreseen the impact of a child on my sense of autonomy. Didi and I had been together for nine years before adopting and had lived quite a spontaneous lifestyle! We enjoyed socializing, travelling and really enjoyed each other's company. I hadn't considered how much a child would consume so many of my thoughts, leaving little room for the life that I once recognized. Knowing that our child needed us was my driving force in the early days. I threw myself into 'doing' and busying myself to cater for her and although she was adorable, the monotony of parenting and the cycle of activities seemed endless. I missed 'our time' desperately and tried my best to support Didi as I knew that she was also struggling. Then, around four months later, the cloud seemed to lift. We got to know our child and developed a bond; we started to build little traditions and started socializing again. I can't pinpoint a specific point where it changed – all I knew was that over the next few months, the name 'Mama' became a title that I was able to proudly own and I realized that I loved her.

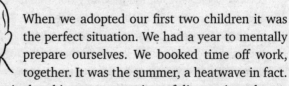

When we adopted our first two children it was the perfect situation. We had a year to mentally prepare ourselves. We booked time off work, together. It was the summer, a heatwave in fact. We were excited and it was a crazy time of discovering who we were as a family, and we had fun working out the how of it all. If I had read about Didi and Priscilla's story of post-adoption depression back then, it would have seemed incredibly alien to me. However, I first spoke to Didi and Priscilla after the arrival of our third child. As detailed in 'A is for Adoption' (see page 26), he was a surprise addition to the family when we discovered our children's birth mother had had another baby. Rather than a year to get our heads round the idea, or even the nine months that some parents get, we had five weeks. I now know how Sonia felt when that baby popped out on the Jacksons' sofa in *Eastenders*, to Dot and Sonia's surprise!

Not only did he arrive in our lives incredibly quickly, it was a completely different time of life for me. About three weeks before we got the news that he existed, I had made a huge life decision: I was taking redundancy from the job I had adored. My career was more than a job to me; it was part of my identity. Without a new, surprise, child in the mix it was already going to be a difficult time for me. Those few months were a bit of a whirlwind. Who was I? I was stressed, angry, irritable and became, I can call it now, depressed. I was depressed. I loved my new son. He was incredible, there was no question of that, but there was part of me that just felt incredibly unhappy. I don't think this was pure post-adoption depression, and the two life changes were completely linked. Fast-forward a couple of months and I started to find a groove. I'd taken some time off to focus on me before throwing myself into freelance work.

And then, before I knew it, it was March 2020. The world went into lockdown and everything changed. My mental state tumbled. I loved lockdown to begin with as it released me from the pressures of trying to work out what I wanted to do next in my career and gave John and I the joint parental leave we were not able to have the second time round. Plus, of course, it was a beautiful summer. I know I'm not alone when I say the second lockdown during the early months of 2021 was the worst. That's when things really went downhill. Being a depressed parent was hard, really hard. Being inside with the kids, in the winter months, while trying to forge some form of career, sent me further and deeper into my anxiety. I remember once just lying on the kitchen floor crying in the middle of cooking dinner, while the kids climbed over me like feral animals.

John and I really struggled; I was putting it all on him. All my anger, all my frustration, and it was too much. It almost broke us, but right at the final snapping point, he pleaded with me to go and get help. Something I'd resisted for so long. My company offered me counselling when I first left but I did not enjoy my first session: it was done in the psychiatrist's home, which reminded me of my grandad's house, and I didn't gel with him. I felt hugely uncomfortable, and it just put me off doing it again. I also had been hesitant about ever reaching out for help because of the adoption system. I felt by admitting I had a mental health disorder I would be opening myself up to questions from social workers and be judged. Could it potentially affect another adoption should another sibling come along? It felt better to just try and manage it myself, except I wasn't. However, after a particularly fraught twenty-four hours I phoned my doctor and sobbed on the phone. We chatted and she felt I should try an anti-depressant. A cloud lifted. It felt talking about it, to a professional, was a step in the right direction. I was prescribed sertraline and underwent some cognitive behavioural therapy to help my brain work its way out of its anxiety and depressive thoughts. I'm proud of myself for making this step. My treatment has made me a better parent. I needed to look after me to be the better parent to them. I love them, and John, so much and I encourage any parent who is feeling low, anxious, depressed, suicidal or experiencing any form of mental health issue to not feel too proud, not feel worried and just get help. It could save you and your family.

Why Do We Do It?

Parenting demands resilience and that you dig deep into your emotional reserves every day. It's the most demanding job we've ever had. So why do we do it?!

Here's why: nothing beats the pure joy that is looking into your child's eyes and seeing the wild depths of potential. Kids are hilarious and fun and so bonkers you're forced to access your inner child to get on board with every mad moment they throw at you. They bring you out of yourself and teach you to be in the moment and embrace the chaos. The first time they tell you they love you, the way they reach for you and only you when they need a hug, the things they whisper as they fall off to sleep at night and how they make you see the world anew through their eyes – it's so worth it.

Talking Points

▶ Do you have a good support network around you that you can lean on when things get tough?

▶ Could it be worth booking some sessions with a therapist before and during your parenting journey?

▶ How do you deal with difficult things – are you vocal and emotional or do you withdraw?

▶ What do you need from your friends or your partner in these times?

IS FOR IVF

'I definitely don't want to do IVF!' . . . Six cycles of fertility treatment later and I look back at my blissful naivety with fondness. How little I understood about the process and how I underestimated my own emotions – I thought it would be easy to stop trying to get pregnant if IUI (intrauterine insemination) didn't work for me. But, suffice to say, it wasn't. IUI is where sperm is inserted via a catheter into the uterus on the day of ovulation, and is the closest thing to 'natural' conception. Some people call this the 'turkey-baster' method, but as a vegetarian household this was not a kitchen utensil we had lying around, and it strikes me as a rather glib and potentially offensive term anyway.

What Exactly Is IVF and How Much Does It Cost

Before we get into the eye-watering costs of IVF treatment and the inequality same-sex couples face in accessing it on the NHS in the UK, as well as more about my own experience of trying, let's get back to basics.

INSIGHT:
IVF (In Vitro Fertilization)

Gavin Kemball (he/him) is Consultant Gynaecologist and Fertility Specialist at Lister Fertility Clinic, part of HCA Healthcare UK.

What exactly is IVF?
IVF stands for In Vitro Fertilization, and essentially means fertilization outside of the body, as opposed to fertilization through intercourse/insemination, which occurs inside the body.

What do all the IVF injections do?
As many of us know, IVF involves lots of injections. Broadly speaking, there are two types of drugs. These are mainly injections, although a few can be administered as a nasal spray. One type of drug is designed to 'super stimulate' the ovary, so that instead of only one egg growing at a time, more eggs are able to grow. The number is dictated partly by the egg reserve, or supply, of the ovary. The second drug is designed to prevent the body's natural instinct of ovulation occurring. This allows collection of the eggs at a suitable time,

when they are at their optimum maturity, which is difficult if the natural workings of the body are unchecked.

What happens at an egg collection?

Even though an egg is microscopic, they grow in a cyst-like structure called a follicle, which is around 15–25 mm in size. At the egg collection, a patient is given an anaesthetic or sedation, and then, using ultrasound guidance, a needle is inserted through the vagina and into each follicle. The fluid is drained, and hopefully the egg is floating in this fluid, which is passed into a tube, to be taken to the laboratory. Here the egg is inspected, and either fertilized with sperm, or frozen, depending on the type of cycle. It is a quick and generally very safe procedure, and most patients are able to go home later the same day.

What's a blastocyst?

A blastocyst is the name for an embryo that has grown to such a size that it is ready to implant into a uterus. Generally, this takes five days from when an egg and sperm are introduced to each other, and fertilization occurs. However it may sometimes take six or even seven days to occur. A blastocyst consists of over a hundred cells, and is beginning to show signs of differentiation into cells destined to form the placenta, and those destined to form the baby. The embryologist grades the embryo based on how much differentiation has occurred, and how well each group of cells are tightly packed together. This enables them to choose which embryos are more likely to implant into the womb, and which might be suitable for freezing.

What's the difference between a fresh and a frozen cycle?

A fresh cycle is used when an embryo is placed into the womb without having been frozen first. Typically it occurs during an IVF cycle, where eggs have been collected and fertilized, and a suitable embryo is placed into the womb a few days later (i.e., five days for a typical blastocyst). The womb has been 'prepared' by the hormones that are circulating due to the IVF cycle, although often the hormone progesterone is added, either as a suppository, or as an injection.

A frozen cycle is when an embryo has been frozen previously, and so is then removed from the freezer, thawed and placed into the womb at the appropriate time of a menstrual cycle. This invariably involves much fewer medications.

As mentioned in the previous chapter (see page 129), my wife Jenny was pregnant after one single round of natural IUI. So when two years later I decided that I would give pregnancy a go myself, after much soul searching of the *but as a queer person do I want my body to change in such an overtly gendered way?* variety, I had assumed it would be just as easy and straightforward. Ha ha. It was neither.

After three unsuccessful rounds of IUI, I wasn't as ready to stop as I had thought I would be. During each agonizing two-week wait to pee on a stick and celebrate the presence of a pair of faint blue lines (or commiserate over the solitary one line, as was my case), I fell deeper and deeper into *wanting*.

Emotionally, during that time I couldn't help but think about how amazing it would be to have a baby that shared my genes, using my daughter's donor – connecting me to my wife and our children like a constellation of stars. I couldn't help but 'go there', and while I was holding the very real possibility that it wouldn't work in my head, I was also allowing space for the possibility that it would.

Mentally flipping between these two life-altering scenarios during the time I was trying to conceive (or TTC if you want the much-used online acronym) was quite exhausting, but each passing day tied me tighter into the process of IUI. No way was it something I'd be able to walk away from as easily as I'd hoped. 'Stay positive' is what everyone always tells you, which is nice at first but, after two years, hearing this made me want to bury my head in a 'Live, Love, Laugh' cushion and cry.

Trying IVF

Getting pregnant became a test I simply had to pass. And the annoyingly high-achieving swot in me couldn't settle for failure. I'd never *failed* at anything in my life before, so I was driven to keep trying; particularly because when I asked doctors *why* it hadn't worked, I'd be met with shrugs and a patient smile. Sometimes it doesn't, they'd say.

As same-sex couples, we often go into fertility treatment assuming the only thing standing in the way of starting a family is the lack of sperm or eggs between us, so it can be doubly hard to deal with difficulties you, your partner, co-parent or surrogate may have trying to get pregnant on top of this.

Having found out more about the process of IVF through talking to doctors at the fertility clinic, it no longer seemed like a scary science experiment and was more like a manageable route to a desired outcome. It made me wonder if I should have gone straight to IVF rather than spend approximately £7,000 on IUI first. This is certainly something to consider if you are thinking about embarking on donor conception. On reflection, personally, I needed to go on the IUI journey in order to feel ready for IVF.

I approached the Human Fertilisation and Embryology Authority (HFEA) with some questions. The HFEA is the UK's independent regulator of fertility treatment and research using human embryos. Set up in 1990 by the Human Fertilisation and Embryology Act, the HFEA is responsible for licensing, monitoring and inspecting fertility clinics to ensure patients and everyone born through fertility treatment receives high-quality care. The association answered most of my questions, but there was one that they didn't seem able to answer: what are the IVF success rates for LGBTQ+ people specifically? It seems, like in so many areas of healthcare, research that benefits our community just isn't a priority. And it would be interesting to know the answer to this question, because while cishet couples on the whole seek IVF because they have fertility issues, many queer women, trans men and non-binary people do so because it's the only way, and they don't necessarily have any fertility issues. So where is the research and data into success rates for this community? I wasn't given an answer, though I was told that in 2019, 2,435 IVF cycles (4 per cent of all cycles) involved a lesbian couple, a four-fold increase compared to 489 cycles in 2009 (1 per cent). How many of those cycles resulted in a live birth, compared to the 64,774 cishet cycles, remains to be seen.

Many people are put off trying to conceive with IVF due to the horror stories around it. When you start googling and reading forum posts (PSA: just don't!) you'll no doubt hear about the bruises from injections, or the pain of an egg-collection procedure or some other ghastly account, but I'm here to tell you that for me, and the majority of people, it can be emotionally complex but is totally manageable. Remember, people are most likely to post on a forum if they've had some kind of exceptional experience. In the end, I quite enjoyed doing the daily injections as during a process that felt wildly out of my control and in the hands of the gods (or doctors), having the routine of filling a syringe and pressing it into my stomach twice a day gave me a sense of agency. And as for the egg collection – as a parent to a toddler, any opportunity to spend a day lying down was welcomed. I had the procedure under sedation which was also one of my favourite bits of the whole experience, as it offered the kind of deep sleep I hadn't enjoyed in three years!

Reciprocal IVF (aka Egg-Sharing)

Another route to consider if both people in the couple have bodies that could carry a baby, is reciprocal IVF. This means one person's egg is used to create an embryo which is then transferred into the other person's womb. We spoke to Kate and Claire, who did exactly this.

MEET . . .

Kate (she/her) and Claire (she/her)

How did you decide reciprocal IVF was right for you?
Claire: I wasn't so keen to carry a baby at first and Kate really did want to. Once we realized we could do it this way around, we just thought, it's perfect.

With the naivety of going into it for the first time, we thought, *We'll do it this way round first. And then we'll do it the other way round next time.* We both wanted to be involved. We wanted it to feel like the closest we could get to having our child. And we do everything together, why not this?

Where and how did you find out more about process?
Kate: This was 2015 when we first started looking into it. We live in rural Cornwall so there wasn't exactly a huge LGBTQ+ network locally we could ask. There wasn't a huge amount online either, but we found out

that the London Women's Clinic offered it. And if you donate your eggs for someone else to use then you get a significant amount of money off.

Did you involve friends and family?
Claire: We told a few friends but we didn't tell our family. Not because we didn't think that they would take it well. It was just . . . I think we just wanted to go into it privately. It was a long drawn-out process and actually, by the end of it, everyone pretty much knew what we were doing. It took five years in total. We tried three fresh cycles and two frozen cycles and our son was born from our third fresh cycle.

Was the process more challenging than you were expecting?
Kate: That is an understatement. [See page 131 for Kate's experience of miscarriage.]

What was it like trying again after the miscarriage?
Claire/Kate: We tried again with a frozen embryo and it was weird; I just knew it wouldn't take. Then we regrouped, bought different sperm and got pregnant. And that was our son.

And what about the plan to swap and for Claire to carry Kate's eggs?
Claire: Eighteen months ago, we switched to trying it that way round. Kate said she wanted her body back. And her work back. And I thought, well, that's only fair. I get that. Plus, going through labour and stuff with Kate took some of the mysticism away and actually, I thought maybe I could do this. It's quite good to do

it both ways round because we each know what the other one has gone through now.

So how has that journey been going?
Claire: It didn't work. It was hard for us to adjust to Kate stimming (injecting the IVF drugs). It didn't feel as right. It just felt a bit awkward. And actually we realized we're so much better doing this the other way around. Kate can be more emotionally sensitive and so stimming affected her more.

So Kate's been trying again with my eggs, and experienced another miscarriage. And that was a real kick in the teeth. It's been a lot harder for us to get over, for many reasons, but it was our last vial of sperm from our son's donor and the donor has now gone into retirement.

You mentioned that you donated some of your eggs. Do you ever think about any children that may have been born thanks to your donation?
Claire: I do every now and then but actually I assumed no one got pregnant from them because we didn't – I don't know how rational that is or not. I donated seven eggs and obviously they don't tell you what happens to them beyond that point. You just do it, and you walk away. But if the child wants to get in contact when they're eighteen, they can do.

How do you feel about the possibility of somebody getting in touch in the future?
Claire: Oh, it's quite exciting. Had we never come away from fertility treatment with a child ourselves, I might think about it more. It comes up when we talk to people who've got siblings from the same donor as us.

So you've been in touch with people who have children with the same donor?

Kate: We know of eighteen siblings currently, all over the world. Mostly America and Australia. It's been super useful because we reached out when I miscarried and said, has anyone got any sperm left? And a lady has some that we are looking to buy. So actually it was a massive lifesaver, and an incredible feeling actually that there is this group of strangers who potentially can help us.

What advice would you give a couple that are going into reciprocal IVF?

Kate: Talk about it. Be open with your feelings and be really mindful of each other. Because the pressure on each person at different points is really full on, and the other person needs to be the cheerleader. Like, when one of you is getting ready to have eggs collected, you really feel that weight of responsibility, but as soon as that's over, you're like, here's the bat, over to you! Being mindful of each other's position is something I think I've learned in the last couple of months. Especially if you become the pregnant person, it becomes all about you for nine months. And then once the baby's born, it's still a bit about you. I've recently just been very aware that Claire has been through a lot. It's still her egg. So with the miscarriage, I'm the one physically going through it, but it's her egg and it's been our journey.

Claire: I think it's quite easy to get into your own head space and deal with your own emotions. But it's a journey for both of you that you both have to talk about.

My other advice is just really look at your health. It can be quite a strain on the process having all those restricted diets, but it is easier when there's two of you doing it.

Sometimes as queer people we can be reluctant to do anything too 'medical' as we may have had negative experiences with doctors in the past and dread having to 'come out' to numerous people in positions of authority. But please know that most people embarking on IVF in a private clinic or via the NHS will feel well cared for by a staff of amazingly kind people who are by now, thank God, experienced in helping queer, trans and non-binary couples. It's certainly the kind of service one expects when paying for private treatment that costs up to £10,000 for every cycle of IVF. Given the amount I'd spent at the clinic, frankly I'd have expected a red carpet to be rolled out for me at every appointment.

MEET . . .

Laura Rose (she/her), founder of LGBT Mummies organization and Proud Foundations

Laura campaigns for equity and equality in the world of maternity, fertility and general healthcare for LGBT+ people and their families.

What is so unfair about access to IVF for queer prospective parents?

That it's so disparate across the UK. And in addition, until recently, depending on your local Integrated Care Board's (ICB's) criteria, it was costing LGBT+ couples up to £24,000 to have private treatment before ICBs will provide funded access. And by that point many people have either run out of money, become pregnant anyway, or it's not financially viable for them. This means that many are unable to start a family by their first chosen route, and are forced down alternative paths to parent-hood, or don't have children at all. However, with the new Women's Health Strategy[16] changes, the discrimination regarding the costs we incur compared to heterosexuals has been removed, but the 'postcode lottery' still remains. Also, many in our community have been left out of the strategy – single people, gay dads. Non-binary people were left out of the language in the strategy, but, in meeting with the Department for Health and Social care, we have been told they are included. Also in our meetings, we were advised it is a 'Ten-Year Strategy' and that ICBs would review their fertility funding at a localized level, meaning some could decide to not offer fertility funding at all and once again our community misses out on the opportunity to create their family. We at our organization LGBT Mummies feel it's a human right to have a family by your first chosen route if medically possible and that equal access should be provided to us, equal to that of our heterosexual counterparts, so there is still more work to do to ensure true equality for all our community.

What advice do you have for couples considering IVF but worried about funding it?

Look into alternative options and research all routes to parenthood to ensure you are fully versed in the costs, legalities and parenthood of any future children. Even if you know or feel that you may be 'fertile', fertility can diminish, access can be removed, and you may need to consider alternative paths to parenthood and need to be prepared for this. We also always strenuously advise you to seek legal counsel before any journey to ensure you understand how your family will be protected and can plan ahead, because for LGBT+ families, the law isn't always on our side and you need to protect yourselves, future children and any donors too.

Do you think clinics have a duty to be clearer about all the associated costs of IVF and have this information more easily accessible?

Definitely. The HFEA regulates all clinics but there are clearly areas whereby the clinics need to provide more clarity in regards to additional costs that may be incurred – a full list of possible medication and costs as well as possible add-ons – as a fertility cycle may change and additional tests, medication or treatments may be needed. People should also be directed to the HFEA website traffic-light system to see if there is any benefit before paying out for add-ons. Providing guidance around the cost implications means people are more prepared and the additional barrier of financial burden is lessened if people are aware of what they need to save 'in case' of further costs, and they can have a more positive fertility journey. It is a special life-changing experience and one that should be enjoyed where possible!

What needs to happen to achieve equality?

Legislation is so discriminatory for those who cannot afford private treatment and who do not want to go down the cis heteronormative route of marriage or civil partnership – and if they don't, they're not legally able to be on their child's birth certificate and then have to go through second-parent adoption. There's not enough regulation around home insemination to protect people and future children. Also, trans and non-binary parents have issues around how they are listed on birth certificates and we feel a whole review is needed. The legal and health systems are so gendered and not fit for purpose when it comes to our LGBTQ+ families – there's so much to do.

What was the most challenging thing about your IVF journey?

There were so many challenges. The move to IVF from IUI was a huge jump. For baby three, after three failed IUI cycles (following a natural IUI cycle pregnancy on the second attempt for baby two) and finding out my ovarian reserve had diminished by half at the age of thirty-three, within three years of our son's birth, just floored me. No one prepares you for your fertility diminishing, and then the move to IVF during a pandemic was an experience in itself. Having to go through IVF alone, with my wife being so far removed from the process, was daunting, but we had to press forward, not knowing how long my fertility would sustain. Secondary infertility is rarely discussed, especially in our community, and when it hits you personally it can have a great impact. I also wasn't prepared for the hormone changes and the multitude of different medications I was on (neither was my wife!) and how it impacted my emotions. There definitely needs to be more education around the side effects and what changes your body undergoes – something, through our global community and our educational arm Proud Foundations, we are working on with the health system and its organizations, so that they can better support our community in the care that they provide and in the workplace. We have so many barriers and implications to overcome as it is as a community. There needs

> to be more understanding of our paths and how the
> process can impact us physically and psychologically,
> and how people can support us through that – from
> family and friends, to employers in the workplace, and
> society as a whole.

I tried three cycles of IVF. There were a few lows: running to
the local ASDA at 10 p.m. to beg the pharmacy to give me a
needle because it wasn't in the pack with the syringe and I had
to do my final injection that night; cutting my finger while
opening a glass ampule of the drug Menopur and desperately
trying to call the emergency clinic line to ask if I could still inject
the liquid given that it now had shards of glass and blood in it.
There weren't exactly highs but there were some nice moments,
like after having the embryo transfer and walking through
central London on a bright winter morning feeling as if I was
carrying a secret stash of gold. And the one and only time I got
those longed-for two blue lines on a pregnancy test and promptly
called my friends and family with the news that it had worked
and received an outpouring of love and joy. Sadly, the next day
I had a blood test to 'confirm' the pregnancy and it revealed
that my levels of HCG – the hormone that's produced in early
pregnancy – had dropped and I was no longer pregnant. It was
what's known as a chemical pregnancy and it marked the end
of my IVF journey. I shared more about how this made me feel
and why it felt like the right time for me to stop in the previous
chapter (see page 130). But for now, I'd like to reassure anyone
reading this considering IVF that the experience taught me so
much about myself and what motherhood really means to me.
I'm a better person and a better parent for it. A poorer person,
yes, but I don't resent the amount of money I spent because I
had to see the process through. I believe it's always better to

try and fail than fail to try. Here are the nine things I learned from IVF:

1. You can do hard things
I had always thought I was squeamish and scared of hospitals. Actually, I was a lot stronger than I knew. You are too.

2. Letting go of control is important
Once you're on the IVF rollercoaster there's nothing you can really do to change the outcome.

3. Being kind to yourself feels good
I quit my punishing exercise regimes and allowed myself to eat what I wanted when I wanted and to nap any time I could. IVF takes up too much mental energy to continue to restrict and control other things in life at the same time.

4. Talking makes it better
Rather than trying to hide what I was going through I chose to be radically honest about it with friends and co-workers.

5. It's okay to feel a bit jealous when friends get pregnant
I'd become very good at being happy for other people and tried so hard to deny any niggles of envy or resentment. My therapist taught me to allow these feelings in, face them and move on.

6. Don't try to do it all yourself
I'm very independent and it was tempting to shoulder the IVF process myself, particularly as many of my appointments were during the pandemic and my wife wasn't allowed to join. It took a while, but I learned to involve her in the experience even if it was just checking the doses of drugs before I took them.

7. Accept your changing body

Injecting hormones into your abdomen is going to affect the way you look and feel about yourself. It's important to change your expectations about how you might want to look during this period; it's only temporary.

8. Acupuncture, supplements, yoga, fertility books can help you feel better . . .

But don't invest too much in them working because if you don't get pregnant you'll have even more to feel resentful about.

9. When straight people tell you that they got pregnant when they were super relaxed on holiday and advise you to relax a bit more, don't just smile and nod

Be an educator and call people out on the things they say without thinking.

Talking Points

▶ What are the benefits of trying IVF without doing IUI first?

▶ How many times would you try and how might you anticipate feeling if it didn't work?

▶ Would you and your partner both be open to IVF? What would be your biggest challenges emotionally?

IS FOR JUST GO FOR IT

 Not that we are at all jealous of heterosexuals, but another thing they have up on some queers in the parenting game, whether they see it as a positive or not, is the element of surprise. I'm talking about the scene you witness in multiple films and TV programmes where a lady starts to feel a bit queasy, her boobs get a bit sore, she's a bit bloaty. She runs to the pharmacy to purchase a pregnancy test. She sits by the toilet waiting to see if two little blue lines appear . . . 'Oh my word, I'm pregnant. How did that happen?' she squeals, and then works out how to tell her unsuspecting partner. It doesn't quite work like that for everyone in the land of queer parenting. I didn't wake up one morning with a raging hangover, a man in bed, then two weeks later had a letter arrive saying, 'Congrats! Your one-night stand has meant you are now able to adopt. Your child will arrive in six months.' Obviously, many straight folk spend a lot of time planning the when and where of it all, but that element of planning is fairly mandatory for LGBTQ+ parents-to-be. The process of starting to plan is incredibly daunting. Is it the right time? Are we going via the right path? Should we consider an alternative way to become a parent? These are all questions where there is no right answer, and they will keep on coming right through the process. Choices can be a blessing for us but it's also a bloody big burden. Lotte's and my motto? Just do it (although we think that might already be trademarked . . .).

However, it's easier said than done, especially when dealing with some of the literally life-changing decisions. The biggest choice John and I faced when adopting was not the actual decision to jump headfirst into the world of adoption and the subsequent training courses about trauma-coping mechanisms and probing social workers. No; it was when we had to choose our children. Mind-blowing stuff. Although adoption and donor conception are two very different routes to parenthood, there are many points where mine and Lotte's stories suddenly merge and feel relatable to one another, and this is one of those. John and I had to choose which children to adopt, and Lotte and Jenny had to choose a donor. Both of us have compared this point in the process to being on Tinder. Both are a bonkers, yet essential, part of both the adoption and donor-selection process.

As debunked in our opening chapter, 'A is for Adoption', one myth around adoption is that you don't get a choice in which children will be placed with you and will ultimately become yours (see page 20). It's very much the opposite. If our adoption panel was not surreal enough, it became even more bonkers when we were whisked straight into a room after our approval to meet Gwyneth Paltrow. WTF, I hear you cry? Yes, our family finder was in fact named after a major A-list actress, but for her privacy we will call her Gwyneth to give you some sense of the surrealness of having her name pop up in my emails. At our approval panel a group of ten independent 'judges' (let's not sugarcoat it!) sat around a table and reviewed our report with our social worker. We were invited to join for part of it to answer some on-the-spot questions about our history, desire to be parents and techniques we would use when dealing with challenging parenting situations. We then were asked to leave while they sat around and had a good old kiki about us. Ears burning, we were then invited back once again to learn our fate. Honestly, *Popstars: The Rivals* has nothing on this lot. As you know by now, we were approved and that's when we were taken straight from the approval room to meet Ms Paltrow. No time like the present to start choosing your kids!

Gwyneth Paltrow explained that she would give us a couple of days to take everything in – thanks, Gwyneth – but that she wanted to take this moment to check we were still happy with the top-line choices we had already made. The stuff such as gender, number of children, ages, disabilities, HIV status – you know, the simple things (!!). I'm sure we nodded, as by this stage we were in quite a heightened state of emotion. Gwyneth Paltrow said she would send us over a few profiles of children she thought might match our choices and would give us access to a special website that we could log into, allowing us to view the profiles of any child that was then under an adoption order in the UK. Once home, John and I decided we would be really structured with how and when we reviewed profiles. It was one of the best decisions we made and, honestly, I would recommend this to anyone else going through this process. We agreed we would only look together and would set aside a time to properly focus and go through the options. It was a mix of wanting to see how the other reacted to a profile and to also give the process the importance that it deserved. We didn't want to be sitting on the sofa alone flicking through profiles like one would review a dating app, swiping left or right. Gwyneth sent us over some profiles to look over.

We sat down and took a deep breath as we clicked on the first one. It was very surreal. There was generally a picture of the child/ children and some very basic info about them. How were we supposed to feel? In essence if that child was not the right one for us then if felt like we were rejecting them. It took some getting used to! Logging into the online profile site was incredibly over-whelming. There were hundreds of profiles and as we slowly started looking through them, seeing each little face staring at us from the screen, it felt harder and harder. We also had to create our own profile, which we were encouraged to sell ourselves with . . . Match. com eat your heart out! Within the first few days of our matching process, we had seen almost a hundred profiles. However, there were two siblings whose profiles had been in the first batch sent by Gwyneth Paltrow that had caught our hearts, and we asked to have more information on them. They were a sister and brother. She was two years old and her profile had a link to a video. In it she was playing with a little dolly, she then gets up and starts running round in circles laughing as she goes. Her laugh was infectious. She then fell onto the carpet with a thud but got right back up and, giggling once more, started running around. In the corner of the room was a baby's crib and the faint murmurs of her little brother, who was only three months old, could be heard. There was no photo of him, nor any real details. As he was only three months old, his case was still being processed by the family courts and as such they were limited on what could be shared. There was something about these two. Still to this day I can't fully explain it. They stood out and we were more than intrigued. Once we had more information about her, still nothing much on him – not even a name – we went back to Gwyneth Paltrow. I saved the email I sent:

> Lastly, we really like the sound of N and Baby L and curious to know what you would envision the timeline to be if we did happen to get in a meeting with their social worker and things were to progress? I guess we are a little apprehensive that it's been less than a week since our panel and we could already be on the path of matching . . . while exciting it's quite daunting for things to move so quickly so just wanted to go over timelines in our head.

Things progressed pretty quickly after this, and their social workers came down to meet us the following week. It had been less than fourteen days since we had been approved to adopt and here we were having a meeting about our potential children. Note my mention of being apprehensive in the email. I went into a bit of a tailspin; it felt too quick. After that meeting with the social worker, Gwyneth removed our profile from the online site. I panicked. It felt like by deciding too quickly we were not giving the others a chance. What if the perfect child was still out there and we had missed them. Having this amount of decisive fate in your hands is an incredibly overwhelming feeling.

LOTTE'S VIEW

As you'll remember from the chapter 'D is for Donors', my wife and I had a similar attitude to choosing sperm and getting the process rolling (see page 61). Maybe it's why me and Stu are such good friends: we are people who like to make a decision and stick to it. Dilly-dally around us at your peril!

Ultimately those two children that we first saw and enquired about became our children. That one decision led to the family we now have. Honestly, it's quite mind-blowing when you really think about it. I cannot imagine a world that would be any different. These are our children; it's incomprehensible to think of them being with anyone else or for us to have different children. But is that because we made the 'right choice' or did we feel something in our hearts and go with it? We then fell in love with our children, and they fell in love with us. We learned things about each other and got to spend time figuring one another out.

Would that have happened if we had made a slightly different choice? Potentially. It's why we say, 'Just do it', because you can agonize and go over and over things, or second-guess your choice, or worry, but as Will Young says, 'Sometimes you walk past the good ones cause you are trying too hard to see them.' It's bloody hard not to, but try not to overthink things. What will be will be and whichever decision you make, it will ultimately be the right one and you won't look back.

Talking Points

▶ Is there such a thing as a good time to become a parent?

▶ Do you struggle trying to be decisive? If so, how do you think that might affect you during the process?

▶ Are you aware of the many active decisions queer parents need to make?

K

IS FOR KIDS

They fuck you up, your mum and dad.
They may not mean to, but they do.
They fill you with the faults they had
And add some extra, just for you.

 A little spot of Philip Larkin's doom and gloom parenting poem 'This Be The Verse' for you to enjoy, and something Lotte and I used to recite to test our mics in the early days of recording *Some Families*. Not really the best parenting affirmation, so perhaps we should put our own queer spin on it . . .

They make you fabulous, your Dad and Daddy
They may not mean to, but you pick up their sparkle.
They fill you with all the hope they never had
And add some extra magic, just for you.

Perfect, because let's face it, we do add our sparkle, magic and fabulousness to our children's lives. Not all LGBTQ+ parents are taking their kids to Drag Brunches or dancing round the living room to Gaga, but the very nature of being queer and identifying as LGBTQ+ surely projects some essence of our wonderful selves onto them. Or is it the opposite? What if Larkin is right about the gays as well – that our children may inherit our own gay shame, or the lack of different-gendered parents fucks them up royally?

We spoke to Professor Susan Golombok (she/her), who has studied queer families since the 1970s, and she says, OFFICIALLY:

Yes, in some of our studies we found LGBTQ+ people do make better parents. The next question of course is why? Children are not born, generally, by accident to gay parents. That an awful lot of thought and planning has gone into this means they are raised by parents who really want to have them. So therefore it's not surprising that the parents are very involved, committed, warm, loving and interact a lot with their kids. Going through the adoption process, or years of fertility treatment, means that if couples are not quite so committed to having children, they may fall off along the way. And they may think, actually we want to do different things with our lives, and they don't keep going. But those who actually make it to the end of the adoption process or assisted reproduction, which is arduous and difficult, and actually do end up having children after all of that, they seem to be people who just really, really want to be parents.

Gold stars all round for us, then!

But what is it really like to be the product of a queer family? To live in a house with two dads or two mums or an LGBTQ+ solo parent? Or to live through a parent coming out as trans? It's not something Lotte and I have experienced. And our children are still so young it's hard to know if our being queer has had any real impact on them. My son would just laugh and call me a 'big fathead baldy' if I asked him about my parenting style. To really help us understand and perhaps to give some reassurance to those wondering what a child might feel, we spoke to some people who have queer parents.

MEET . . .
The Kids

Ella (twelve) – Daughter from a three-mum family

My name's Ella. I am twelve and I have three mums. My mummy is called Emma and my step mum is Cheryl. They are a gay couple. I also have a mum that lives in London, her name is Beth and she used to be married to Mummy. My sister is called Molly, she is fourteen and is autistic. We also have a dog called Barney, he's basically my fluffy brother. People never really ask me questions about my family, but if anyone were to do so I would answer that I have three mums, because it is normal. The best thing about being in my family is that I have many people to love me, I mean the more the merrier! Any challenges that my family has? Nothing major to be honest. I have nothing to do for Father's Day, but we've set up a thing where we do Father's Day for Cheryl.

Zoe McCready (she/her; now-adult) – Daughter of a trans parent

My family includes me, my older sister Immy and my younger brother Nat. My parents are my biological father and Sam, who was my mum for the first eight years of my life. I call him Sam. I don't see him as my dad, and I definitely don't see him as my mum. To me he is just my parent; gender does not come into it. I know there are gender-neutral terms for parent, but none of them suit me or my family. I don't remember there being a big discussion about how I would refer to Sam or his pronouns. I gradually stopped referring to him as 'Mum' over a few months. It wasn't forced or emotional; it just felt natural. As he became more and more masculine-presenting, it felt odd for me to call him 'Mum', especially in public. My biological dad played a big part in my younger years, however my parents split when I was eight, and we moved to Brighton, while my dad stayed in Essex. I would say that Sam has had the biggest part in raising me.

I was around ten when Sam transitioned. Most people think that his transition must have been a major and emotional life adjustment for me, but I don't see it that way. There wasn't a defining or pivotal moment; his transition seemed much more a gradual process. It did not feel much had changed, as even before he was out, he presented as masculine. Visibly, there wasn't a lot to adjust to. Emotionally, it felt like nothing had changed much either. I always saw him as the exact same person. If anything, it was a better time for all of us after his transition, especially as his mental health improved. We were happier as a family. For us his transition was a positive change rather than being upsetting or difficult to deal with.

Although I wouldn't have been able to express this at the time, overall, Sam's coming out felt like a natural progression of events, after his split from my dad, and after we had moved from our Essex hometown to Brighton. His transition did coincide with me leaving primary school and entering secondary. However, for the first two years of secondary school, I was home-educated. During this time, my friends were mostly family friends whose parents were friends with Sam, therefore it didn't feel like I had to explain anything to them. When I joined mainstream secondary school in Year 9, I did struggle to adjust. It was difficult for me to make friends and fit into established friendship groups. I felt like having to explain my home situation was an extra layer in difficulty while I was trying so hard to fit in. There was a lot of homophobic bullying at school, and I would often hear transphobic 'jokes' being thrown around. To my knowledge there wasn't anyone openly out, so it was a completely foreign topic for most of my year group. I kept my home situation private. If anybody asked, I simply had a mum and dad like everyone else. Once I did settle in and find better friends, I felt like I was too deep into a lie to explain properly, therefore I simply introduced Sam as my dad.

Once I got to university, I found everyone to be so much more open-minded and progressive, and finally felt comfortable to be open about Sam. My first day of halls, I straightaway explained to my flatmates about Sam, as I wanted to be rid of the complicated situation I had created for myself at school. Now I find that when I do tell friends about Sam, I usually don't go into a heavy explanation. I prefer to mention it in passing, rather than having a deep conversation with everyone. People are welcome to ask questions, but I feel like most people don't for fear of offending me.

To other children in similar situations, I would tell them that they are so lucky to have such a unique perspective that will give them a better understanding of gender issues so early on in life. It will make them a more accepting and open person.

Read Sam's personal story in 'T is for Trans' (see page 297).

Rhys (thirteen) – Son to two dads, James and Owen
The best thing about having two dads is that I have two amazing parents that I can go to for different things. To me they are Daddy and Dad'Ow. My dads always told me to be honest and proud of who I was and our family. To be honest I don't really get asked much about them at school. When I was younger kids wanted to know why I didn't have a mum. I just was honest and said I was adopted because my birth mum was unable to look after me. I've had a few random questions like, 'How does it feel to have two dads?' I just say no different to how it feels having a mum and dad.

But again, it's not spoken about really. People just know I guess, and it's not brought up. Occasionally people have said random things about mums and then apologised to me as I don't have one, but it doesn't bother me. I do go to my dads for different things. Daddy is stricter with schoolwork and going out, plus he has different interests to me. He likes the theatre stuff and crap music! Daddy is more for cuddles and love. Dad'Ow is more fun and we do more sports together and he's not always taking photos; Dad'Ow is more like my friend. My dads talk to me about my adoption and sometimes they are too honest about it all when I'm not bothered. I don't think about it so much but I know my dads always want to make sure I'm okay. I've always known my story since I came home. Having gay parents does make me feel part of the LGBTQ+ community, but I haven't thought about it too much. I did find it hard a year or so ago because some kids in school were not kind about gay people. Sometimes people use the word gay as a bad word but my dads explained it's best to ignore it. We've always celebrated Pride though and it's fun.

Annie (they/she; nineteen) – Child of a lesbian mum who came out later in life

I speak about my family openly because I don't feel it's odd or weird; my family is just a little different to a 'traditional' family. I think people need to become more open to hearing about it as it isn't a strange or weird topic; it's normal. My school life was pretty rough because I never really fit into an educational system. The negativity I had at school was probably because not everyone does find it as normal as I do. It never really affected me because I just chose to not associate with people who were rude or negative towards me or my family. I do have a different relationship with both Mum and my mum's partner, Lucy. They do not live near me, so I play online video games with Lucy and have life updates with Mum. I do go to both for advice and help, though. I came out as pansexual at the age of fourteen, and then as non-binary at eighteen, so I was already part of the LGBTQ+ community when my mum came out, however with my parents also being LGBTQ+ it makes me feel even more included as we all go to things like Pride and celebrate events together. I would love to have a family in the future, I'm not sure how yet, but I'd love to experience having a family of my own.

***Freya Lyon (she/her; twenty-eight) – We met
Freya in 'D is for Donor', who herself was raised by
two mums***

My family is made up of my mum, my non-biological
mum, who I called my Gaggy (and still do!), and my
younger sister. We also had the occasional cat and
grandparent! There was no huge realization for me that
my family was special, or different from other families.
I had to make my non-biological mum her own card for
'Gaggy's day', for example. We went to a lot of 'rainbow
family' events with other gay families and I started to
recognize those families were different from those of
my school friends. My mums gave me the confidence
to own my story. I was never hesitant about telling
people about my family, and I was casual enough about
it to shrug off any funny remarks with: 'Yeah, and?'

I was raised during Section 28, so gay families couldn't
be talked about in school, and I did notice moments of
it playing a part in my family being isolated. My non-
biological mum was mistaken as my grandma at the
gates, and she decided that was probably safer while
I was at primary school. I came out at fourteen, so being
a teenager at school then was much more about me
being gay than my parents being gay! Teachers were
generally a bit rubbish at remembering I had two mums.
I had a couple of arguments in Religious Education
classes on the 'debate' over IVF, but I had friends who
would back me up and I felt overall like it was just
ignorance rather than outright discrimination.

One of the best things about growing up with two
mums was having two lots of strong female energies
raising two young girls – me and my sister were, and
still are, a force to be reckoned with. We marched at

Pride as toddlers, we were raised by badass feminist lesbians who may have had their own issues but never ever let an injustice pass them by. I credit them for my constant drive for equality and pointing out discrimination loudly and without fear.

When I came out to my biological mum (my parents had split up by this point), she told me I had chosen a hard life. It was a tough point – she had a lot of internalized homophobia and she didn't consider herself gay anymore. I see now she had a big battle going on inside her. She sadly never got to experience the gay joy of my wedding as she passed away months before it, but I wish she could have seen that times have changed. My non-biological mum was fantastic. She called me after I went on dates, even ironed my shirt and drove me to the date with my now-wife.

I heard repeatedly that I was probably gay because of my parents. I think I maybe believed it in part too, but I also didn't see it as a negative thing as I didn't see being gay as negative. My mum certainly did, and it drove a wedge between us, but I was determined to show her that the world isn't as cruel anymore. Sometimes I'd just agree when people said it was 'inevitable' that I was gay, especially after my sister came out as gay too! I do wonder if it'll happen with my daughter. People were shocked enough that we didn't find out the gender before she was born (or with my current pregnancy), but I'm hoping I can raise a kick-ass confident kid who responds like I did: 'Yeah, and?'

My advice to any LGBTQ+ prospective parents is that it IS scary, but having a kid full stop is bloomin' terrifying. The confidence you have in yourself, and your sexuality or identity, is key to giving your child the confidence to know their family is just as valid and important as anyone else's. No part should be hidden for fear of what the world may think, and when they see you embracing life and taking it by the horns, then they will want to do the same.

See more about Freya's story of being a 'unicorn' in 'D is for Donors', page 68.

Theo Toksvig-Stewart (he/him; twenty-eight) – Son of two gay women, one of whom is the TV presenter and author Sandi Toksvig

Our family is eclectic. I've got gay mums, one of my mums remarried later in life, but there's also my dad – he has been married twice so I have six half brothers and sisters in addition to my two immediate sisters. One of my mums adopted my younger sister when we were adults, and my mother's partner has a daughter from a previous marriage. I still have to count on my fingers when someone asks me how many siblings I have.

I'm the youngest of my immediate siblings, and my mums divorced when I was one, so the dynamic is something I've grown up with. It is totally normal to me. My biological father was a family friend who my mums asked if he would be their donor. This was a very conscious decision for them. They were potentially worried about the idea of a 'mystic father figure' that can come with an unknown donor. I don't know any other kids my age, or my sister's age, that have queer parents or are part of a queer family. It was very new for them at the time, and they were entering the unknown, so I think they wanted someone they knew, could point to and say, 'This guy is technically your dad.' We've never called him 'dad', but he was essentially an uncle- or family-friend-figure presence. He and his family lived nearby, and we'd see them and our half brothers and sisters all the time for Sunday lunches and different events.

When I was at school my family setup still felt very normal to me, but then I don't know how it could feel otherwise because it's all I've ever known. I couldn't tell you what it's like to have a mum and a dad. I know we were lucky; we grew up in quite an accepting area, although we were definitely an anomaly. Although it was a Christian school, the head and our teachers were inclusive and accepting of the whole 'gay' thing. There were definitely times when I felt like we stuck out; I have a visceral memory of a class where we had to draw our family tree. The teacher was describing how to do it and I looked at my blank page thinking, 'I haven't got a clue how to draw this thing'. I asked questions about 'Where do I put this mum? Well, they're not together anymore, but where do I put my dad, because he's been married twice, but he was never actually married to my mum', etc. I could tell by the look on her face my teacher didn't have any better idea of how to draw the tree than I did.

I didn't *not* tell people I had gay mums, I just didn't go around saying it in the same way you wouldn't tell someone you just met you have a mum and a dad. If someone asked, then I would explain it to them. I do remember kids having quite a hard time processing the fact my mums were gay, so conversations would be quite long. A lot just couldn't get their heads around it, or would tell me I was lying, or that it didn't make sense. There was nothing I could say to that apart from

'I'm here, aren't I?' As we got older, I realized a lot of the questions were quite intrusive that you would never ask someone from a heteronormative background. I know it was just curiosity, but there was an unawareness and an entitlement behind the questions; they wanted to know how it 'worked' rather than what it was like. 'So, which one is your *real* mum?' was definitely on the greatest hits.

Once someone in the playground told me that me and my mums were going to jail because they were gay. He told me his mum had said that. I remember that being really upsetting as I was very young and gullible. I went home crying and telling my mums what had happened. They reassured me they weren't going to jail. When I asked why they would say that, my mum said, 'Because they're ignorant and you should help them with that.' But when people did try to hurt us, it always kind of backfired. We have a story about my sister, who when a kid tried to tease her in the playground saying, 'Your mums are gay!', she just said, 'Yes, that's right. Did you need more information?'

One of my mums is well known. I don't know whether her being in the public eye helped people be more accepting or put our family more intensely under the microscope. Maybe both. It's strange as a lot of homophobic people love my mum. There is some weird celebrity double standard when it comes to homophobia. If someone in their own family was gay, they'd be unable to talk about it or disown them, but they are more than happy to meet Mum, shake her hand, and take pictures with her to show their friends. It didn't stop intrusive questions at the school gate, though, especially from those that have that middle-class entitlement. My other mum recalls a very curious woman who wanted to know about 'lesbian sex'.

I always loved our family situation. I never had a feeling where I wished anything was different (maybe sometimes I wished they'd chosen a taller sperm donor), even when I realized we were the only ones like us. I liked that it made our family special, and ultimately everyone wants to be special. Who wouldn't want two mums? My mum said that when I was little I used to say 'having two mums is great because when one is ill, you still have the other one to look after you'. Everyone in our family is really kind and generous to each other. I can't say if that has anything to do with the fact that we were 'different'. Ultimately, love is the most important thing. If a child feels loved it doesn't matter where that love comes from. I had two incredible female role models in my life, not counting my amazing grand- mothers, sisters and aunties. We never had different names for each of my parents. If both were in the room and we said 'Mum', I think the intonation of how we said it let them know which one we were talking about. Now my sister has had kids it's opened a conversation about what we call the grandmothers, especially as we have three of them. It helps that one is Danish, so she can be 'Mor Mor'. It's funny as 'mor' is 'mother' in Danish and I literally have 'mor mums' – it's all about the mums.

The fact our family is not all biologically connected has never been an issue or even a thought that I've had. I can speak for my sisters on this in that it just hasn't factored in our family life. It helped that we were so aware of who we all were as a family from such a young age. I don't know if this is the same for other people who have something about them that is considered 'different', but I don't believe anyone ever 'feels' different; it's our surroundings, environment, society that tells and treats you as such. I think if society sees you as 'different', for good or ill, you have no choice but to be aware of it. You have to accept not everyone's going to get it. For example, I say I'm half-Danish although there is no genetic link on that side. But my mum is Danish, and I've been going to Denmark pretty much every year since I was born. I know the food, the culture, we sing Danish songs at Christmas, I can name and order my favourite pastries (that's about it language-wise). It's so much more than genetics.

Sometimes LGBTQ+ families get painted with broad happy brush strokes, as if we want to prove that we are better and untouchable. Of course we're not perfect, we're a family. We fight, we annoy each other, we're all different, imperfect people. Part of being a family is learning to love everyone for who they are. My mums did a lot of work after they split. I didn't see everything they did to get to a position to co-parent. They put us first and managed to salvage a friendship that allowed us to share loads of family events and holidays, which not all divorced parents are able to do.

If I was to give any advice to a queer parent starting their journey, the only thing I could suggest is that you don't keep anything secret. Anything that's hidden or held back becomes a source of shame. If a child is given all the information, they feel secure. Demystify it early on. My youngest sister is adopted, and she is very aware she is adopted. We celebrate her birthday but also her adoption day. If you wear your differences as armour, then they can't be used to hurt you.

Talking Points

▶ Did you have older queer people in your life when you were younger and if so, what did they teach you?

▶ What do you think are the positives of having LGBTQ+ parents?

▶ Are you worried that queer shame could impact your own parenting?

IS FOR LABOUR
(EMOTIONAL AND LITERAL)

 Queer parents create loving homes for children because we have to really, *really* want them. We plan for them, we analyze ourselves, our motives, our challenges and desires in order to make our family happen. And then when our children do arrive, another cause for self-congratulation is that LGBTQ+ families are not necessarily burdened with the heteronormative traditions dictating who does what in a relationship that so trouble our straight friends. You can read more on this in 'G is for Gender', where we cover this in depth (see page 111).

Who Does What and Why?

Yep, we're talking about emotional labour (we will segue seamlessly into actual childbirth labour at some point in this chapter too – Stu has his hands over his eyes in preparation). Now almost four years into parenting, Stu and I both have the 'who does what' bit figured out. But in our marriages, it continues to be a constant conversation and negotiation. And it certainly took both of us a while to find our rhythm in this respect.

For example, two months before the birth of my daughter, I found myself fighting back tears having spent the afternoon putting together a chest of drawers, only to discover that I'd built it upside down. I had wanted to surprise my pregnant wife by assembling the nursery furniture. But as I heard her key in the door, I was sitting on the floor surrounded by unused screws, a wobbly chest of drawers and various pieces of a cot.

I'm no good at DIY. Jen isn't either really. 'We need a husband!', we sometimes joke when the tap won't stop dripping. And it is a joke, because I know lots of men who are as challenged by manual labour as we are, and lots of women who are better at it. Where non-binary people fall in the IKEA flatpack continuum is an area as yet undocumented by science.

MEET . . .

Lucy (she/her) and Paul (he/him)

Lucy and Paul are a bisexual couple from Oxford. They have a three-year-old.

Do you think the division of emotional labour and the things you both do as parents is less weighed down by hetero expectations as you are both bi?
Paul: I think this is true. I as a bisexual cis man feel much less concerned about traditional ideas of masculinity and my traditional role in the family than I otherwise might. I have always tried for us to be as equal as possible in raising our child, being sure to

take on sole childcare responsibilities. I can't claim that this is uniquely because I am bisexual as I know many straight men who are also doing this but I can't help but think it has helped to free me from internalized gendered assumptions.

Lucy: I don't know if it's because we're bi but I wouldn't rule it out as a factor. We've been extremely deliberate about dividing childcare equally, and Paul did 50 per cent of the parental leave in the first year. Even though his work's policy is extremely generous, he was the first man in his department to ever take it up. This laid the foundations for a truly equal parenting relationship, and meant that I have never been the default parent. He currently works compressed hours to do one day a week's solo childcare (I do two). A big part of why we felt more free to arrange our lives like this was that we don't put any store in gendered assumptions about labour distribution.

Somehow, though, my pre-baby DIY disaster felt different to my usual flatpack failures. It left me contemplating what my role would be when our daughter was born. For the first time, I worried that what Jen and I contributed to family life would be weighted differently. As she recovered from childbirth, I'd do the heavy lifting; and Jen would have an intensity of feeling for our baby from giving birth to her that I'd never experience. Suddenly it mattered that I couldn't build a cot. I had a new role and I was already failing.

Women in straight and het-assumed relationships have long taken on the lion's share of household chores and emotional labour (the unpaid work of caring). In Britain women do about 60 per cent more unpaid work than men, according to the Office for National Statistics.[17] But, as a same-sex couple, we assumed (smugly) that we'd avoided that imbalance.

Before having a kid, Jen and I never argued about chores and were equally good at the emotional labour, too. 'We need a birthday card for your brother,' I'd text Jen. 'Got one already,' she'd reply. We'd both notice when the water in a vase of flowers needed changing, and offer to cook or run a bath if the other had a tough day. It was a happy, instinctive flow.

STU'S VIEW

John and I had also always been equally involved in domestic life and played to each other's strengths. As a perfect example, John is a great cleaner but a notorious clutter bug. I zoom round the house decluttering in a way that Marie Kondo would be proud of, but I avoid the bathroom and bleach at all costs. When we first got the children home, we were both on adoption leave. The attachment period within adoption is such an important thing to get right that we both decided we wanted to be at home for as long as possible. It meant that there was no expectation on the other from the start to be the primary caregiver. We shared the load. It was clear from the outset that my husband's dream would be to be a stay-at-home dad, while I was always honest about my ferocious career ambitions. My identity is my work. I love it and get immense pleasure from the films and projects I work on. For me, being a full-time caregiver was never an option. However, that didn't mean I turned and ran and left John to pick up the nappies. We worked on a system that allowed us to both be around for the children when needed and to support each other. We tried a shared Google Calendar to manage our week, but it didn't quite work out! We prefer an old-fashioned bit of paper on the fridge that we review each week to see who is available to pick up or drop off the kids. It's worked out on who has meetings when or who needs to be in a physical space at any point in the week. We also make sure it's as balanced as possible so there is an equal share of looking after the kids.

Becoming parents made the distribution of emotional labour an issue in a way it never had been. When my wife was breastfeeding, I felt guilty, and a bit jealous, that I wasn't involved. Eventually, we settled on 'combination feeding' – I'd give the baby four or five bottles of formula a day and Jen would breastfeed the rest of the time, which allowed her to rest more and me to experience our baby falling asleep in my arms – albeit often at 3 a.m.

When I returned to work as creative director at an advertising agency – after negotiating a month of parental leave, while most of my male colleagues took the statutory minimum of two weeks – it was Jen's turn to feel resentful. She is as ambitious as me, so why should I be the one who got to disappear into an adult world?

Returning to work was a wrench for me, too. The whole experience brought feelings of inequality into sharp focus. But I could empathize with Jen and acknowledge it in a way a lot of straight men apparently can't (I actually reckon they can but it's easier not to). So I decided to leave my job and freelance, allowing Jen, a freelance journalist, to take on more work.

Childcare brought further challenges for me. I was writing a book to a hard deadline, and as I slipped out in the mornings to quieter environs, I could tell Jen felt envious. But once the

book was finished, it was my turn to feel conflicted as I took our daughter to 'rhyme time' in a church hall while Jen was busy launching an online magazine.

Our work–family balance needs constant negotiation and flexibility. And we only have the one child! On Sunday nights we compare diaries and evenly distribute school drop-offs and pick-ups. Communication is key and we do it well – something I recognize in all my female-couple friends. Perhaps women talk and listen in a similar way, whereas men and women often have different approaches.

Right, that's the easy kind of 'labour' sorted. Now to the actual having a baby bit.

Labour, As in Birth!

Okay, so being the person not actually giving birth at a birth, whether you're with a surrogate, co-parent or partner is a role like no other. Your job is cheerleader, fetcher of things and most importantly advocate for how the person in the throes of labour, who may not be at their most articulate due to, er, trying to bring a baby into the world, wants to be treated and what they need at any given moment. For me, that meant lobbying for a C-section after three days of labour and making sure everyone who came in and out of our room knew we were both mothers-to-be and didn't say anything stupid or ignorant during such an intense time. I also, and Stu loves this, brought a pink globe lamp into the hospital with us so that we could turn off those ghastly overhead lights, along with a fan and some aromatherapy oil to waft a calming scent throughout the hospital room.

Extra? Moi?

MEET . . .

Esme Chilton (she/her)

Esme is the mother of Freddy McConnell, a trans man who gave birth (twice). He made a fantastic film about his first experience of pregnancy and labour called *Seahorse*. Esme was Freddy's birth partner and here she shares her top tips for anyone else supporting a friend, partner or family member through the experience.

What do you think Freddy wanted and needed from you in the role of birthing partner?

Obviously, he's a single parent with no partner. He and I are quite close and I've been there with him all the way through his whole journey of transition. I suppose he wanted company and somebody who had some experience and knowledge of giving birth (I've been a birthing partner for friends and other family before). I think I'm quite a practical, steady person who is good at not panicking and being calm. Also, for Freddy, it was important to be supported by somebody who really understands the issues for trans and non-binary people in healthcare settings (or any settings, really) and to be able to hold the space for them, and, if necessary, remind people of language and that kind of thing. Because in the heat of the moment, especially because we had lots of medical professionals coming in on shift, I would just gently and quietly say, 'You know, he's the dad.' Or, 'That's perhaps not a great word to use in relation to my trans son who's in labour at the moment.'

How else did you ensure that people in the hospital were treating Freddy with respect?

There was quite a lot of work done in advance, making sure that when we went to appointments and things people were made aware of issues that may arise. So there was a bit of pre-empting. And I suppose I saw myself as a bit of a barrier for Freddy, not that he needs protecting; he's quite tough. But particularly with other hospital staff like cleaners or the people who bring lunch – I would just keep my antenna up and maybe have a word in a quiet way, just to explain, so no one would say anything inappropriate.

What was the hardest thing about being a birthing partner?

You go in with this great excitement, and then it doesn't happen for ages and ages, but you have to keep really positive for the person without being like, oh my God, I'm going to have to be here another night and I'm not going to get any sleep! You've got to be that positive and consistent force in the room because people come and go on shifts and it can be challenging having to explain things over and over again to different people. It can be difficult to keep your own energy up.

Did the experience bond you and your son in new ways?
It's just that sort of primeval, basic, profound thing that you're doing for somebody else. There's nothing like it, when you're there in person and they are relying on you so much. You're bound to feel even closer than you probably feel.

What advice would you give a birthing-partner-to-be?
1. Take snacks, tins of gin and tonics, olives, houmous, dips, crisps. You know, all sorts of things you'd fancy when you're just hanging about really.
2. You are the communications manager, so keep everyone updated and reassured so the person in labour isn't worrying about responding to messages.
3. You can never take enough photographs, even if it seems annoying and silly, like Freddy would be like, 'Oh for God's sake, Mum!' But afterwards, it's so great to have all those photographs.
4. Have two playlists: one for when you need calm and one for when things are getting intense and you need motivation. The Bach Cello Suites are the best pieces of music for actually giving birth to. When Freddy was having the caesarean, the second time, he desperately wanted to listen to that because it made him feel so much in the moment, so I had to quickly rummage around in my bag and play it on my phone.

STU'S VIEW

The final episode of *Friends*, one of the most-watched moments in TV history, has Monica and Chandler present at the birth of their adoptive twins. In true *Friends* style, the scene is a saccharine moment that was the cherry on the cake of a very unbelievable take on the adoption process. The birth mother, Erica, agrees to have the couple adopt her babies while pregnant. This view of adoption, aka 'The One Where She Gives Up Her Baby', is not reflective of the UK adoption process in any way. The vast majority of children who are up for adoption are up for adoption because the authorities have had real, and just, cause to show the children are experiencing neglect, trauma, abuse and more. We were not present for our children's births. Neither do we have many, if any, details. But that doesn't change the fact that it was, and always will be, a massive part of their life story. It's literally the start of their life story. They may have questions when older that we just can't answer. How long was the labour? Was my birth mother okay during it? Did she have anyone to support her? Did she hold us when we were born? Did we cry? Were we okay? Did we have any breast milk? I think the one thing I can do to try to reassure them is that I don't even know the answers to the above questions about my own birth and it's not something I've ever asked my mum. Perhaps it's only when you know you can't have the information that it becomes more important? After all, it's not something any of us remember, and most of our parents try to forget!

Giving birth is a hugely intimate experience and not only is the way it happens different for everyone, but the planning and intention-setting varies from person to person too.

INSIGHT:
Ask a Queer Birth Specialist

AJ Silver (they/them) is the author of *Supporting Queer Birth* and the founder of the organization The Queer Birth Club, a fantastic resource for our community.

What can be some of the challenges for pregnant LGBTQ+ people?
A lot of the difficulty around pregnancy and labour comes from the assumptions made by healthcare professionals or birth workers. It might, for example, be, 'Well, you are not going to want to carry because that's going to cause you dysphoria'. It's a massive assumption that for non-binary and trans folks pregnancy would cause this. It might do for some people, but not for others. It's the sweeping assumption that may restrict people's self-efficacy of wanting to say, 'Actually I'd quite like to carry my baby.'

What can we do as queer people in medical spaces to feel confident asserting ourselves and asking for what we need so that we are comfortable and safe?
I think, firstly, before you go into those conversations, remember everybody feels that way. So whether you're LGBTQ+ or not, there's a great portion of the popula-

tion that feel as if they can't say things like, 'Oh actually, no, I wanted to give birth in water' or 'I don't think induction is right for us and our family'.

A lot of people say things like, 'I'm not *allowed* to go past forty-one weeks' or 'I'm not *allowed* to have a vaginal delivery or a pelvis delivery'.

From obstetricians, surgeons and healthcare professionals to hypnobirthing instructors, and people who run baby yoga sessions – whoever it is – their mission statement is to support you in what you do.

So, if you're finding that you're in a position with a healthcare professional or a birth worker who you don't think is hearing you or is perhaps not understanding why certain elements of your birth plan need to be upheld, then there are options.

For example, if you are inducing lactation within a same-sex relationship, or within an LGBTQ+ family, and they're not understanding why that's important, it's not your job to explain or justify. You don't have to prove to them that you are worthy of receiving that support, because the starting point is that all people deserve humanizing and individualized care that is tailored to them. So as an LGBTQ+ service user, you don't have to say, 'I need to teach you about why this is important for queer folks.' You are allowed to change healthcare professionals. You are allowed to change birth worker. It's difficult for people that are in more rural communities, but you are allowed to say, 'There's clearly a personality mismatch here.' You are allowed to change hospitals as well. You don't even have to go to your nearest hospital. You don't have to feel bad that you're taking up services or causing a fuss.

There's so much fear and anxiety associated with birth and labour. In your experience as a doula, can you tell us anything about how amazing and beautiful it is?

When you're a new baby doula, you have a mentor who you can go to and have a debrief about your births, which is really important, so you're not dragging those births to other births, and your own experience of birth into other people's births. One of the things I said during my very first debrief was that I wasn't prepared for how beautiful it would be. I couldn't stop staring because there is so much power and beauty and connection and love in the room. It's wild. And I've seen beautiful births like that with trans mums and trans dads and non-binary folks and same-sex families. And I've seen that with cisgender and heterosexual people, you know, it is universal and it is beautiful.

Once we stop panicking about birth and viewing it as an emergency situation – which, don't get me wrong, sometimes it is, but in a lot of cases, it's not – we're able to just view it as the incredible thing it is.

Everyone thinks that doulas are cis, het, skinny white women with long hair, toe rings and floaty skirts. But there's a different kind of doula for every different person. Empowerment can be found in so many different kinds of birth. Just because your birth isn't in a picturesque river creek, it doesn't mean that it can't be beautiful – as long as people are believed, supported, held and cherished in that powerful yet vulnerable state – that's what a beautiful birth is.

Because of the overt medicalization of trans and non-binary and intersex folks going through those journeys already, we can bring fear with us into these medical spaces. And that doesn't mean that you're silly or that you should be tougher, but it also doesn't mean that you have to let that fear take the right to be excited and happy about the prospect of giving birth from you. Although there are risks and there are complications that come from pregnancy and conception and birth, the vast majority of people will have safe and wonderful births. We are allowed to be excited about it!

Talking Points

▶ How do you balance emotional labour in your
relationship?

▶ What would be important to you or your
co-parent/surrogate when giving birth?

▶ What are your preconceived ideas of birth?

IS FOR MY FAMILY
(AND HOW WE TALK ABOUT IT)

Let's get ready for some BIG conversations. First up, as queer parents-to-be, we might find ourselves regularly having to talk to our own parents or friends about our intentions to start a family, and people expect a level of detail from us that heterosexual couples trying for a baby aren't subjected to. You don't get Aunty Carol asking her straight niece when she's ovulating, but asking a lesbian going through IVF for the dates of her next treatment? Perfectly acceptable.

For many of us, when we came out as gay or trans, our parents assumed this meant we'd never have children, so it might take certain people in your life a while to get their heads around your intentions. Even if they're happy about it, their first reaction could come from a place of unfamiliarity, fear and confusion, so try not to hold this against them but instead be willing to bring them on the journey with you and open their minds.

It can be helpful to start sowing the seeds early so that by the time you do have children, everyone can just enjoy these tiny humans without feeling that they have unanswered questions or 'don't understand how it all works'. Giving your parents or family members a copy of this book is a great way to begin the conversation and help them understand the challenges you might face along the way.

At this stage, allow people to make mistakes and say 'the wrong thing' at first. There will come a time when it's not acceptable, but these early chats are when it's best to get all the issues and potential faux pas out of the way, because once the child is in your world, you don't want any negativity or ill-placed 'concern' from your nearest and dearest.

Setting Boundaries

Before talking to your parents or siblings for the first time about wanting to have kids, have a chat with your partner or be clear in your own mind about your boundaries when it comes to answering questions. You don't owe anyone anything and are perfectly within your rights to say your version of 'no comment' at any stage of these early chats. But in our personal experience, being really honest and sharing almost everything with our families at every stage of the process, of adoption and donor conception respectively, ended up being a really positive approach.

When you do eventually become parents, you'll want to check in on those boundaries again so that you are clear on where you draw the line when talking about your family. It's often deeply dependent on context – you're not going to open up to a nosey stranger about something you might have no problem sharing with a close friend, but it's good to be prepared. Maybe you don't want to give specifics about the donor or the birth family; maybe you don't want people to know whether it was yours or your partner's sperm you used for surrogacy, or why you decided to co-parent with this friend and not *this* one. All totally fine! This is your family's story to tell, how and when you want to.

OUR VIEW:
Responses to Common Questions

How to avoid the inevitable 'But have you thought about X?' response to saying you are doing 'Y'

'We've thought long and hard about this and explored all the different options. We have decided that adoption/fostering/donor conception/egg-sharing/surrogacy, etc. is right for us. There are lots of reasons why this is the case, but maybe right now we could just tell you more about the route we've chosen rather than go over the ones we haven't.'

How to avoid well-meaning constant check-ins about how things are going

'We're just starting out, but we'll let you know when there are any significant developments.'

How to respond if someone says, 'But aren't you worried they'll be bullied or face prejudice because their parent(s) are queer?'

'We're confident we'll raise a strong, brave and independent person who grows up feeling so loved by all their wonderful friends and family that they can face whatever the world throws at them.'

What to say if someone says, 'I just think all children need a mum and a dad'

Permission to roll eyes, flick hair, walk away. But if you can be bothered to confront this, try saying, 'Children need to feel loved and secure. Our kids will be surrounded by role models of all genders and won't feel the lack of anything in their lives'. If you want some data to back up your instinct that children don't specifically need a male and a female parent to thrive, see the chapter 'K is for Kids', where Professor Susan Golombok shares the findings of her thirty-plus years of research into the subject (see page 171).

How to handle catastrophizing questions
'Well, there are lots of what ifs in this process but we're going into it with positivity and we'd love it if you could support us in that.'

Owning Our Narrative

As LGBTQ+ people, we are used to coming out. We have to do it on a daily basis at the supermarket checkout, the GP's, to delivery people and taxi drivers. It's a pain – but what it has done is steeled us for unnecessarily intimate conversations with strangers. And once you have kids, you'll find yourself having a lot of them.

We like to pre-empt questions about our families by loudly and proudly asserting ourselves before anyone has to ask. There's a sense of power in owning the narrative in this way and it protects us from being caught off guard. This might mean at the newborn baby drop-in, when all the other mums have obviously postpartum bodies, you say, 'Hi, I'm Lotte – it was actually my wife who gave birth.' Stu tries to slip into conversation as quickly as he can that he and John adopted the children. 'We know that the moment they meet us and see we are two gay dads they will start wondering the how of it all. I'd rather just be straight (first time for everything!) and answer the inevitable question. We are proud to have adopted and we teach the kids to be proud of being adoptees; there is no shame in it. That doesn't mean we want to immediately share intimate details of our children's life story (that's our kids' choice to do if they wish when older; it's their story), but at least we have addressed the pink and sparkly elephant in the room.'

We've also found it useful to be really clear with new people about what our children call us. To the uninitiated there's little to differentiate Dad from Daddy or Mummy from Mama, but for our kids, their two parents' names are as different as 'Mum' and 'Dad'.

Something we've both been really aware of is providing consistency for our children in the language used about their family from all of their caregivers. A conversation with a child-minder, schoolteachers or grandparents so that they know Lotte would never refer to her daughter's 'father' but rather her 'donor' goes a long way. Likewise, in Stu's case, explaining why we don't use the phrase 'taken from' in terms of adoption is hugely impor-tant. Once we've passed on this kind of information, ideally in a face-to-face conversation, followed up with an email or text message, we're not afraid to pull people up on it when they don't get it right. It can be easy to shrug off mistakes in that very English way of not wanting to make a fuss. But it matters.

Teaching Pride

Something that's a lot harder to control is what happens when our children encounter other children who ask them about their family. And perhaps they do so in a way that feels confronta-tional. There's going to be a time in their lives, and hopefully we can put it off as long as possible, when they are made to feel different. All we can hope is that we've given them enough confidence and equipped them with enough tools to be able to talk about their families with pride.

Do
- Be honest with your children.
- Talk to them about their family and how it was made even before they can talk back.

- Say the words 'gay' or 'trans' – we have been conditioned to see these words as 'inappropriate' for children to know about or say. This is the sad legacy of Section 28 and living in a world that centres on heterosexuality.
- Tell them that every family is different – some have two dads, one mum . . . some even have a mum and a dad.
- Be ready to answer deep questions at awkward times.
- Smile, laugh, be playful and affectionate as you have these discussions.
- Let your child know they can ask you anything, at any time. Nothing is awkward or difficult to discuss so nothing is off limits.

Don't
- Pretend you're just like everyone else.
- Tell a child they are extra special because of the way they came into your world.
- Put things off until they're old enough to understand.
- Whisper or avoid words like 'adoption' or 'donor' – these are not dirty words.
- Say anything that isn't true.
- Expect these conversations to happen in a linear fashion.

We've talked to our children about their origin stories from before they could talk back to us. This means there's no big reveal moment where they find something out about themselves. They grow up always knowing. When she was two, Lotte's daughter was fond of telling people that she had 'Two mummies and a donut'. She meant donor. Having a healthy sense of humour, as with so much of parenting, is key!

Of course, at three a child can't understand the nuances of her conception, but she can grasp the basics, like whose tummy she was in. As queer parents we are constantly having to come out throughout our child's life – every new school or club or holiday, it never stops being something we have to at the very least acknowledge and most often explain to others. But the way we discuss it within the family gets inevitably to a deeper level. As parents of older children you may have spoken to them about their origin story throughout their life, but that's not to say new questions or desires might arise. It's a conversation that will go on long into your child's adult life and it will shift and change as they do and your relationship with them evolves too.

INSIGHT:
Our Queer Family Friends

We asked some of our queer family friends how they talk to their young children about their birth. Turn to the chapter 'K is for Kids' for an insight into conversations with older children and teens (see page 172).

Adoption

We adopted my son when he was just fourteen months young and he has been aware of his setup since day one, even when he was too young to even know what the 'traditional' family setup looks like. Now, at eight years old, we talk all the time about how he has two dads, some people have two mums or neither and families come in all different shapes and sizes. Our friendship and family group is diverse and I love it because he gets to see all different kinds of family setups and it's amazing. Kai knows he was adopted, and we've never hidden that from him. We don't want a big surprise reveal when he's eighteen; we want him to always have known from as early as he can remember that this is how his family came to be. We're so proud of our journey and so proud of him.

Tom Cox (he/him) (aka Unlikely Dad)

Donor Conception

'Some bodies have sperm and some bodies have eggs. You need sperm and eggs to make a baby and as Mummy and Mama both have eggs, a kind man gave us the sperm we needed to help make you. He's called your donor.'

Lotte Jeffs

Fostering

I get mistaken for their dad all the time and after the first few weeks where S would declare emphatically 'He's not my dad!' before I could get a word out, I would say 'I'm not your dad, am I, but I love you like a dad.' Now we often just let it slide. K recently said to me as we looked at his secondary school contract, 'You don't like it when they call me your son.' I explained that I didn't mind at all, but that I know his sister used to mind, and that I felt it was better when schools used language that covered all the different kinds of families. I don't think we ever said, 'You're part of the family', because it was three years before we knew for sure they weren't going to be moved on, but we did say 'This is your home'. The emphasis is on making them feel safe and secure after a trauma or series of traumas. But I didn't want to make false promises to them. I did promise them that I would do everything in my power to allow them to stay here.

Josh, foster carer

Surrogacy

'Papa and Daddy can't have babies growing in our bellies. So we looked for a woman who could grow our babies in her belly for us. We looked and looked and looked and finally, we found her.

Annie said she would love to carry and give birth to Daddy and Papa's babies. And so she did: for almost nine months (that's how long it takes!) she had two little baby girls growing in her belly. And when it was almost time, she went to the hospital. Just a few minutes later two little girls were born. As soon as Daddy and Papa laid eyes on these girls, they fell in love with them. They knew they would love them for ever and ever. How could they be so sure? That's easy: they knew it in their hearts.'

Ferd Van Gameren, dad via surrogacy

Co-Parenting

'Mummy and Mumma and Christian were the best friends in the world. We had so much love for each other, we thought if we mixed all our love together, we'd make an amazing baby. And we did! Now Mummy and Mama are your parents, but Christian helped make you and that's why he's such an important person in your life and always wants to come to your birthday party!'

Ellen, lesbian mum via known donor

Bisexual Parents

I plan to always be open with my daughter about my bisexuality, in any age-appropriate conversations about crushes and romance. I hope to tell her that some people like those of their gender, or another gender, or any gender, and how the latter is what applies to me.

Paul, dad via natural conception

Do Say Gay

At this early stage of our children's lives, we've prioritized normalizing the words associated with the way they came into our lives and we've worked hard to remove the residue of any internalized shame that we may carry ourselves as adults. As we explored in 'E is for Education', so much of this is a result of our own upbringing at a time when it was illegal to even acknowledge the existence of gay people, let alone celebrate LGBTQ+ families, in a school context (see page 87). This is why we believe it is so important to speak openly and confidently with our children and all the people in their lives about our gender, sexuality and the way we became parents.

We have to fight the sense that talking to children about being gay is somehow not appropriate. Heterosexuality is so prominent; it's everywhere but we don't notice it. People will happily joke about a boy baby flirting with a waitress or a little girl having a 'boyfriend' at school. But imagine if we joked about a girl having a girlfriend or a boy baby flirting with boys? Not that we ever would – because in our opinion placing any kind of sexuality on a child, even as a harmless joke, is not okay. But we use this example to demonstrate the difference in the way heterosexuality and homosexuality are perceived. Our children need to know that their parents are gay and for that to be as uninteresting and unexceptional as it is to know someone is straight.

Making these conversations we have with our kids about conception, family and what it means to be queer light and happy when they do happen is so important. It's not always easy, though, as sometimes they come when you least expect it and you've got to be prepared! Like the time Stu's daughter asked why she didn't have a mummy while putting her shoes on for school one morning, or the time Lotte's daughter asked her why she couldn't make her a baby sister in her tummy in the middle of a kids' birthday party. While both of these innocent questions got to the heart of our deepest insecurities and challenges as parents, we couldn't let our children know that. Here's what we both said in these instances:

> *Stu:* It was the perfect scenario to remind her that she grew in her birth mother's tummy and go over her life story. As well as focusing on the facts and where she came from, we focus on what she does have, which is two loving dads, rather than what she doesn't, to reinforce a positive.

> *Lotte:* I said something like, 'I really wish I could give you a brother or sister but I tried to make a baby in my tummy and it didn't work. That was disappointing. But you're my baby and I love you so much! We really want you to have a sibling too and maybe one day we still will.'

And how did our kids react? Did they look us lovingly in the eye and say, 'Thank you so much for sharing, Mama/Daddy, you've really given me a great age-appropriate perspective on that issue'? No, of course they didn't. They looked us lovingly in the eye and said, 'Can I have a snack?' or simply ran off without any acknowledgement at all. But rest assured all these moments, all these micro interactions and answers to their out-of-the-blue questions, are all logged in our children's minds for future reference. They matter, so keep leaning into the difficult conversations.

Oh, and for anyone reading this wondering what not to say to LGBTQ+ parents, turn to 'W is for Who's the Real Mum? (and Other Awful Questions)', where we'll be sharing the worst of the worst and how we respond (see page 334).

Talking Points

▶ What are your lines in the sand in terms of what you're happy to share and not share about your family?

▶ What do you find difficult talking to your children about and why?

▶ How did your parents talk to you about important or challenging subjects when you were young?

▶ Do you remember any big reveal moments from your upbringing, and if so, what effect has that had on you as an adult?

IS FOR NURTURE

I'll tell you the moment I recognized the true impact that I have had on my daughter's character, despite not being genetically related to her. She had just finished a rendition of 'These Are a Few of My Favourite Things' sung originally by Julie Andrews in *The Sound of Music* and later by Lotte Jeffs in The Kitchen. E, who was three at the time, had insisted on making the sofa a stage for her performance, while her mums were to sit on the floor in absolute silence. When finished (after holding the final note of 'so baaaaad' as I'd taught her), E took three bows and then insisted we do the thing where I pretend the whole of the street is cheering for her, and then the whole of the country and then the whole of the world. *That's my girl*, I thought.

The nature vs nurture debate is nothing new. In Ancient Greece, Plato believed that we are born with our thoughts, ideas and characteristics regardless of environmental influences. In

the 1600s, John Locke argued that the mind begins as a blank slate so our personality, interests and flaws are all determined by our experience.

Today people continue to have strong beliefs on both sides of the conversation, but more and more research is being done into the interaction between nature and nurture. I'm no scientist, but surely it's common sense to assume people are a complicated melange of both inherited and learned attributes? Have I just solved one of psychology's greatest conundrums? You're welcome.

Talking about nature and nurture can be a particularly triggering subject for LGBTQ+ people because the idea that you can choose to be gay (nurture), rather than, in the words of Lady Gaga, being born that way (nature), is at the root of much homophobia and behind the argument for conversion therapy *shudders*. It's also a debate that rears its head during discussions around gender identity and transitioning and as such can have very negative connotations for trans and non-binary people who have their existence constantly undermined by people obsessed with the 'biology'/'nature' of their bodies.

But I hope we can discuss what nature and nurture can mean to the queer parenting community in a useful way.

INSIGHT:
Heteronormative Parenting

Dr Daragh McDermott (he/him), Professor of Social & LGBTQ Psychology at Nottingham Trent University, talks to us about the impact of heteronormative parenting.

How do you think the way that we were parented affects us as parents?

I think that there's a huge amount of learned behaviour that comes from having watched and grown up with your parents. Often that can be replicated, but many people actively try to behave differently.

As queer parents who most likely grew up with straight parents, how much are we battling against a heteronormative template of parenting?

Yes, people are looking to put their own mark on it. But equally I think that there is an underlying anxiety that people experience as a queer family, which is *what are the potential impacts that this might have on our children?* In some instances, you do see a number of LGBT+ families present in quite a heteronormative way, so as to try to minimize the risk of their children experiencing the things that they may have experienced, as an LGBT+ person, be that homophobia, transphobia and even sexism as well.

How might gay shame or internalized homophobia affect us as parents?

It impacts people differently. Some people carry quite a lot of internalized homophobia or negativity; other people have gone completely past that point in their own life experience or they were raised in a family – and this is becoming more and more common – where homosexuality was very openly talked about from a very young age. Many people brought up in these kinds of liberal, open-minded environments are becoming parents now. Many of the stigmatizing effects that we might have seen historically, or that maybe you or I might have experienced, are dissipating. Or at least they were. If you had talked to me three years ago, I would've had a much more positive outlook. But I'm starting to be a little bit more sceptical or cynical about the direction of travel with some of the rhetoric that we're experiencing, particularly in the UK at the moment about trans kids and trans families around nature vs nurture and how we risk 'training' our kids to be trans. Which are the same arguments that people would've had about homosexuality in the 1970s and 80s. There's also the risk of a leaking effect; that the arguments that have been put out against trans people – I've seen one or two murmurs of them opening up some of the questions about same-sex families or same-sex relationships and bringing back some of that really negative rhetoric that I'd thought we'd dismissed.

What are your views on the nature vs nurture debate and why it is significant for LGBTQ+ families?

Critically, we just don't know enough. And it's very unlikely that we will ever know enough to be able to really understand the root fundamental 'nature' causes for someone's sexuality. There is increasing evidence to suggest that there is some kind of genetic aspect to it. But how, or why, that takes place – we just don't know. The risk is that the desire to try to understand those questions then opens up the possibility that they can be used in very malevolent or malignant ways, such as, *If we know what the cause is, then we can fix it.* That is an incredibly triggering sentiment for many queer people. But all we have to do is look at the kind of ex-gay movement and conversion therapy to know, from the people who have gone through those programmes – the evidence is just not there. They don't work. You cannot pray the gay away; you cannot change somebody's root of identity. People can repress it and try to live some kind of alternative life that isn't living as their true and authentic selves. But that doesn't mean that there has been a fundamental change or shift. And the only reason that people feel the need to engage in those kinds of behaviours is because of the environment that they live in and the *nurture* that they face.

It's more important to provide that positive, inclusive space for people to grow and to develop in adulthood as well. Sexuality in and of itself is not a binary. It's not a fixed entity. It's something that can adapt and change. People can have a very strong, emotional attraction to people of the same sex, but maybe not have the sexual attraction, and vice versa. And so, again, all of the assumptions around nature and nurture are based on this premise of sexuality and gender being binary terms and that you can either be one or the other.

Despite not sharing genes, as E has gotten older I've loved observing the little mannerisms and quirks she may have picked up from me. Okay, she looks more like my wife and her side of the family, but actually as I said in the chapter 'D is for Donors', really she looks entirely herself. Likewise, her personality is completely unique. It'll be interesting to maybe meet her donor or half 'diblings' (donor siblings) one day and see what characteristics they may share. But as I've gone deeper into the parenting journey, and she becomes a fully formed person, what she has inherited becomes less and less important to me. Instead, what really means something is seeing how the way we communicate, the books we read to her, the silly jokes we share have helped shape her character. All the hard work we have put in shines through in this formidable four-year-old and it fills my heart with so much joy, there's no space for any of those niggly anxieties about the fact that she shares 50 per cent of her DNA with a stranger.

INSIGHT:
Therapeutic Parenting

You'll remember Didi and Priscilla adopted their daughter eight years ago, when she was one. Here we'll ask them about how 'nurture' plays an important part of therapeutic parenting, which is something all adopters are trained in.

What does nurturing mean?
From our perspective, nurture involves empowering our child, fostering an environment of openness, sharing unconditional love and instilling boundaries and structure in a considered way. Each child is different

and therapeutic parenting involves structuring your style to meet the needs of your child.

We believe in having boundaries and teaching our child to self-regulate, however our focus is on reasoning and helping her to understand her behaviours as opposed to reacting to wrongdoings with instant punishments.

If a child has experienced trauma in their life before you become their parent or carer, can you eradicate the damage done through nurturing?

No trauma can be eradicated irrespective of how young that child was at the time. However, we do teach our daughter coping strategies to help her manage her behaviour. This has included us seeking external therapeutic support, joining adoption groups (for children and adopters) and educating ourselves on what it means to be an adoptive parent. We've received support through post-adoption services, fellow adopters and the National Association of Therapeutic Parents.

How do you talk to your adopted children about what they may have inherited health-wise from their birth parents?

It's a story that needs to be deconstructed and built up over time. So the information is relayed to the child in an age-appropriate way.

We have given our child the information on her birth family over the years. However, although we say 'age appropriate', this has to correspond to where she is emotionally and the amount of detail she can receive at that time.

We are transparent and always answer any questions she has, no matter how spontaneous they may be!

Chosen families have always been at the heart of queer culture, and nowhere exemplifies this more than the drag houses which, especially during the 1980s and 90s, provided a home and surrogate parental figures for many young queer and trans people disowned by their families.

INSIGHT:
Family and Drag Houses

Simon Doonan (he/him) is a writer, bon-vivant, window dresser and fashion commentator. He has worked in fashion for over thirty-five years, and is the author of *Drag: The Complete Story*.[18]

If you look at the documentary *Paris is Burning*, it's the linchpin of everything to do with Black drag, and the idea of family is explored repeatedly in it. It's an unconventional milieu, but the ideas are very conventional. Pepper LaBeija says, 'I need to school my children, they don't listen to me, they buck my authority.' LaBeija, as a drag mother, maintained quite a traditional idea of family. She would take in these young kids, but she wouldn't take any crap from them, they had to do what she said. You see that through all of *Paris Is Burning*, this sense that the way you care about these kids is to give them structure. People like Pepper LaBeija had very specific ideas about family. She herself had two children; she was both a mother and a father. If you read her *New York Times* obituary, it reveals that she died at fifty-three and left behind two children, a son and a daughter.

What was the hierarchy of family in drag?

In drag houses there's the Mother, the Father, their Legendary Children and the Legendary Children upcoming. The word 'children' is used very broadly, encompassing people who are in their twenties and even in their thirties. It just means you're new to drag. In *RuPaul's Drag Race* today, they still say 'Drag Mother' and 'Drag Sister' to show solidarity with your group.

Who would be the Drag Father?

I think the Father role is probably a little less clear and may also be about some handsome guy that was needed to escort. It was more like, the Drag Mother is the picture, and the Drag Father is the frame, if you will.

What did 'chosen family' mean to young queer people on the drag scene and particularly young queer people of colour at that time?

If you look at *Paris is Burning*, which is the best document of that era, something that always strikes me about it is how happy people seem. You don't hear the family complaining, you don't hear them disgruntled, they're just sort of hilarious and happy and they love being at the Balls. I think the family brings them happiness and there's no real reason for them to be happy – they don't have much. I would say the vast majority of them went on to die of AIDS; there's very few survivors of that generation. Their lives were so challenging and fraught with conflict and complications, but all you see is this shimmering ability to rise above it, which I find immensely touching. My generation were gay when it was still illegal to be gay. We had to find that place and you find it with each other, where you're just happy.

You mentioned structure and discipline in terms of what these houses could provide to kids who had been rejected by their parents. Is there anything else that you think the house structure gave to these children?

I think the need to create some financial stability or any kind of financial opportunity. It's easy to underestimate that if you're not a poor person, if you're not from the wrong side of the tracks. That need to know where your next meal is coming from.

I met the Xtravaganzas and hired them regularly for events and when I worked at Barney's, we booked them multiple times, just as Madonna was employing them around the same time.

We would pay them obviously and they were immensely professional; they showed up on time, they were really good in rehearsals, they were incredibly co-operative because drag has a very complex relationship with the whole idea of earning a living. To put food on the table, to pay your bills, to make your contribution to the family's finances if you can. I think that the drag family helps with that because so many queens back then ended up falling through the cracks.

Creating this family structure was also a radical thing to do, as it queered this incredibly heteronormative ideal of family with a mother, father, children, dinner on the table, eating together and so on . . . .

Yes, they wanted the heteronormative version of it: they wanted dinner on the table, they wanted new clothes, they wanted stability. For them, they didn't have to pretend to be marginal; they were. What they wanted was a bit more of that bourgeois stability because they could take their pick from the marginal, tough experience from gritty street life; they had that any time they wanted.

Could you talk a little to the devastating impact that AIDS had on these queer families?

I remember in the early 1980s, hearing about 'gay cancer' as it were, reading the first articles about it and thinking, 'Well these are the gays that go out to the Mineshaft every night and have multiple partners'. Then all of a sudden my roommate had this big, purple mark on his neck and I took him to the doctor and asked for a referral to take him for treatment and was told there were no treatments, there was no referrals. It's very hard for people to understand that there were incredible people, just hitting their stride in their twenties, dropping like flies. In the voguing community, I'd say teenagers, not just guys in their twenties. I lost three former boyfriends and multiple friends. It just went on.

Probably the family nature of it helped enormously when AIDS hit; people looked after their ailing family members, but then there just weren't enough family members left.

Nurturing of course means taking care of our own children and providing them with everything they need to thrive in today's world. But whether we're parents or not, as queer people I think we deeply understand the need to take care of ourselves, each other and nourish our community as well. We are role models and cheerleaders, shoulders to cry on, allies and activists for each other. Many of us will have opened our hearts and our homes to other LGBTQ+ people and provided support and guidance along the way.

So sing it with me: 'We are fam-i-ly!...'

Talking Points

▶ What does the word nurture mean to you and when in life have you most felt it and by whom?

▶ How important is it to you that your child shares your genes and why?

▶ What do you have in common with your own parents?

IS FOR ON YOUR OWN

 Part of celebrating LGBTQ+ families is about being able to break down the rigid traditions that seem to surround family life. As we've explored, a family can be made up of multiple dynamics, regardless of gender. So where does the idea that a child 'needs' two parents come from? Rhetorical question, as I think we all know the answer – thanks, heteronormative patriarchal traditions! The one universal truth we can all agree on is that a child needs love. They need care, nurture and trust. So, do we really think that cannot come from just one person? Some may argue that a child 'needs' two parents because two is better than one, that a child can be so much more enriched with two parents. But if that is the case, why stop at two? I bet my ass that those who think two parents is the only, and best, option are also anti-co-parenting. Surely, based on their logic, three, four or even five parents would be better? I did look into some research about single-parent families but to be honest it was so overly heteronormative-focused that I gave up. 'The mothers wanted the fathers to be involved and the fathers contributed a lot during pregnancy . . . ' said one BBC report. Oh bore off. What we want to focus on are single queer parents. However, one thing I'd like to address right off the bat: why 'single'? Again, it's a perfect use of improper language, as all it indicates is your relationship status. The term 'solo parent' feels much more accurate.

Many solo parents have found themselves in this position due to separation, but many have purposefully gone down the path of solo parenting as an empowered choice. With all the tools we have at our disposal, is there really any reason why we can't use adoption, donor conception, and more, to start a family when we want to, rather than waiting around for the right partner? And, of course, some people don't even want a life partner – does that mean they shouldn't want children? Lotte and I met with some LGBTQ+ solo parents to get a sense of what one might need to consider if going it alone. And for those facing a separation, what might the future hold? We hope these stories give you the hope, courage and determination to own your own parenting destiny.

MEET . . .

Cathy Reay (she/her), a relationship anarchist

Cathy is a single mum of two. She identifies as a queer, disabled, polyamorous woman and her children are aged eight and four.

I was in a straight-presenting monogamous marriage for almost ten years with the father of my kids. For most of my life I have been very fixated on curating my own version of the nuclear family. I believed that's what success and happiness is. When my second daughter was just a few weeks old my marriage ended, and I then became a solo parent.

Being a solo parent can be exhausting because you are the only person responsible for physically and emotionally caring for them. You're making sure that they're nurtured and nourished and then, beyond that, you are also trying to live up to societal expectations. Society deems single-parent households as 'broken homes' and that is something that I've had to wrestle with internally.

I created the nuclear family I thought I always wanted, then that nuclear family imploded, so now it's me and the kids. While we are incredibly social and have many friends and people who care for us, we are isolated at the same time, because ultimately when anything goes awry, it's on me.

I realized I was queer quite late, only in the last couple of years, and it's meant my friendship circles and networks have dramatically shifted in that time. I'm still kind of really finding my way within queer spaces, but the queer connections I have made so far have been incredibly nourishing. People really hold space for us as a family and care and check in on us. There is no judgement, which has been incredibly refreshing, as I've found it hard hanging out with 'straight' mums. My queer friends have been a lifeline.

As a single parent, you can internalize the thought process that you are just half of a whole. I try not to think this way. When I look at us, I know we are in the best place we could possibly be as a family. I love being a single parent because I can obviously parent to my own preference. We are defiant against the odds, being a queer family, a disabled family, and a single-parent family. I want to show my kids that being a single parent is possible, and it's not miserable. We have an amazing time together.

I identify as polyamorous, and I only started practising polyamory as a relationship style a couple of years ago. I don't think I am ready – and may never be ready – to integrate my romantic relationships fully into my home life, but I enjoy having the two exist and occasionally cross over. I think the kids seeing me in healthy relationships is positive and empowering for them.

Navigating school life and other people's questions has been interesting. I don't walk up to parents and go, 'Hey, I'm polyamorous', but I get asked if I am dating anyone. Before telling them, I try to scope out the type of person they are and what their vibe is. Ultimately if someone is not going to understand this basic fact about me then they are never going to be people that are important to my life. The one thing I don't want is for the kids to have to navigate negative conversations about me. Realistically a lot of monogamous people do not typically understand polyamory. They might be scared of it or think it's cheating.

My kids love meeting new people, whether they're people I'm dating romantically or not. They just love interacting with new adults and I think it's important for them to meet people in the queer community who will really embrace who they are. It's not all about sex either, at all. I question why sex is always at the absolute top of the definition of being in a relationship. I work backwards and think about how important friends are to my life. Why am I putting the people I have sex with at the absolute top? I'm leaning towards relationship anarchy but I also realize that I've been conditioned by the relationship ladder for so long and it's going to take a lot of work deconstructing that.

MEET . . .
David K. Smith (he/him)

David is a widower and single dad. He's the author of *tw-eat together: big feelings and short recipes for those who cook and eat with love*.[19]

Tell us about your family.
My immediate family is me and my son, who is now nine. My husband Sam and I adopted our son when he was about two. However, my husband passed away when our son was six, so now I am a single parent.

When did you and Sam decide you wanted to have a child?
Honestly, I'd always known I wanted to be a father, ever since I was small. Coming out as gay was challenging for me in several ways, not least because I thought that would stop me from ever having the family I wanted. In those days, gay parenting was not an accepted part of everyday life. Maybe it still isn't, but it's a lot closer. I then met my husband Sam in 2005. He had cystic fibrosis, and so we obviously thought that parenting was not for us because of his

health challenges. In fact we never even discussed it. However, in 2011, shortly after our civil partnership in 2010, Sam had a double lung transplant, which transformed his health and potentially opened up a whole new phase in his life. We therefore explored becoming parents.

Adoption was definitely the route we wanted to follow. We were both 'socially minded' people. We were aware that very many children suffering from neglect and abuse were taken into care, sometimes never finding a permanent family, and we felt we could offer a great home to kids like that. The need is so great for those kids, and although they can have many challenges as a result of their history, the potential to be a genuine force for good as a parent appealed to both of us. As such, we went through the adoption approval process with a local authority and adopted our son in late 2014.

Could you tell us about what happened next and what you faced as a family?

Sam developed a rare and unexpected type of rejection of his lung transplant and suffered from significantly declining health from 2018. He passed away in early 2019, when our son was just six years old. Throughout the process, as well as navigating my own emotions, I was always conscious that I was guiding our son through the process too. For a child who has already lost their birth family, then 'lost' their foster family, to 'lose' his Pop was extremely challenging. To some extent, I'm not sure I ever really mourned myself, as I was too busy supporting my son. Overall, he has coped well. However, it has obviously not been easy for him. He has some additional needs, and these can make it hard for him to manage his emotional response to things, so for me, working with helping him regulate and understand his emotions has been an important job.

What have been the biggest challenges since becoming a solo parent?

Honestly, it's very hard. I was working full-time, in a demanding job as a university academic running a research team and collaborating with scientists across the world. It had involved lots of travel away from home. I have had to rationalize my work very significantly, cutting out most of the travel. Covid and the rise of virtual meetings has somewhat helped there. I am also now working part-time to try to balance the needs of my son with the needs of paying the mortgage. It does sometimes feel like all I do is either parent my son or work. I feel that as an individual myself, I have somewhat disappeared. I think all parents feel like this a bit, but single parenting is particularly intense in that regard.

Do you have a good support network around you?

My son's additional needs (and demands of work) can make it quite difficult for me to connect regularly with others. With the Covid-19 pandemic coming along relatively soon after my husband died, the sense of social isolation has been somewhat compounded by that. In my experience, therefore, single parenting has been quite an isolating experience that others do not understand very well. You can't just pop to the pub on the spur of the moment in the evening if you want a chat, as there is no one to look after your child. Meet-ups at weekends inevitably involve your child having to be there with you, which limits the ability to really discuss things. Furthermore, finding effective childcare for children with additional needs is difficult. Sam's parents have been supportive, which has been lovely, and they have a very strong ongoing relationship with me and their grandson.

Does being a gay widower come with its own challenges?

As a gay widower, who is also a parent, you definitely feel that any sense of gay identity begins to slip away. You are just the 'single dad'. There is no obvious marker that you are gay, and to some extent you feel forgotten and overlooked as a person. Many gay men are not interested because you are a parent. Hook-ups or dates are just a non-starter, also for all the reasons described above about the difficulties of finding time for myself. Furthermore, many other parents don't really see you as gay, or recognize that part of your identity may be important to you. Events like Pride are important for connecting with other gay parents, and York Pride is really inclusive, with an outdoor festival event that has lots of activities for kids, so that has been helpful.

You didn't plan to be a solo parent, but have you found positives in being one?

You can make all the decisions; this can also be a negative. But I can decide to do what is right for me, and especially my son, at all times. What does my son need to get out of a holiday? I can just deliver that for him with no compromises. What activities do we want to do on a weekend? I get to choose. What's for dinner? The answer is whatever he and I want. My relationship with my son is extremely strong, much stronger than before I became a single parent. He relies on me totally, and I think I rely on him more than I would often acknowledge.

I love that you have cookery books and share your journey of coping via food on your social channels.

Sam and I always both loved cooking. We used to argue over who was going to do it, and both looked forward to spending time in the kitchen. Cooking became therapy for me after Sam died. It was one of the rare times that my son would be happy in his own company, if he knew something delicious was being prepared in the kitchen. It gave me some precious thinking and relaxation time. My son also likes to join in sometimes and is a very adventurous eater who likes to play an active role in deciding what we have for dinner. Capturing that in my books and on social media was important for me, as was wrapping up the simple recipes in the stories of things Sam and I had done. I would say writing my cookbook/memoirs was the best therapy I had and was the only bereavement therapy I have had. I know my son also values them deeply, and often looks through the books to decide what he wants for dinner, or to remember stories about his Pop. I wrote the book for the three of us: myself, my son, and also for Sam.

What advice would you give to someone who, for reasons beyond their control, suddenly finds themselves in a solo parent situation?

I wish there were some easy words I could offer, but there aren't. I'd say if someone offers to help, grasp that help with both hands; it's rare, and hugely valuable. Do try to find other parents in similar situations who understand.

INSIGHT:
Solo Parenting

Advice for those thinking about going it alone or facing the prospect of being a solo parent from solo-parent veterans.

Cathy Reay

Ask yourself: what is your definition of a 'partner'? What is your definition of a family? Because you can make it up however you want. Your friends can be considered family. What society puts on us is that we need a partner to help us because it's hard being a parent. But why does that have to be a partner? We just need help. I'm sure people in two-parent families will tell you that even they are not enough sometimes. It's so invaluable having a network and community of people that surround you physically or emotionally when you are raising your children. If you can cultivate a bit of a community before embarking on a solo parenting journey, whatever that community may look like, then that could be really empowering in helping you to feel like you are not completely on your own. On my darkest days I do feel a bit overwhelmed by being alone, but I wouldn't want it any other way.

Leon Wenham – solo parent via adoption
Being a solo parent (via adoption), I've learned that anything is possible. Trust your gut and you will be fine.

David K. Smith
Knowing other parents whose children have additional needs has been hugely valuable and having some single-parent friends has also helped. They get it when you have run out of options and need someone to pick up your child from school in an emergency.

Talking Points

▶ Could you do it alone?

▶ Does the idea of being the sole decision-maker appeal to you?

▶ Are you aware of your own biases towards single parenthood and how can you continually challenge these in the language you use and assumptions you make about parents?

P

IS FOR PRESSURE AND PERFECTIONISM

The 1950s housewife. She devotes her life to her many, many children. She bakes, she cleans, she has a meal ready for her husband when he gets home from a long day at the office. She's there for her children day and night, without exception. She does this dressed to perfection with her hair perfectly set. She is perfect in every way. Sounds bloody exhausting! For generations this is the standard that women have been held to when it comes to parenting. From the moment they are given their first baby doll they are conditioned to be mothers. In the past few decades we've witnessed a long overdue backlash and the rise of joyfully imperfect motherhood. From the TV show *Motherland* to podcasts such as *Scummy Mummies* or the on-point and hilarious drawings from Katie Kirby's *Hurrah for Gin* series. Now, more popular than the highly curated, Instagram images of effortlessly *lovely*

and beautifully styled family setups are the countless TikTok videos of messy mums and memes celebrating their children going back to school. This kind of content has helped parents come together to agree, and acknowledge, that what we do is fucking hard, and the perfect mother does not exist.

Now, bearing this in mind, shall we grab the enormous suitcase filled with the complexities associated with queer perfection and start unpacking it? The pressure for gay men to be beautiful, fashionable, have abs of steel, be non-feminine and, dare I say, to have a cock the size of a large deodorant can, is, ummm, huge. I always remember being a young teen and discovering one of my all-time favourite books, *Tales of the City* by Armistead Maupin. Within his series of novels, which follows the lives of many queer San Franciscans, Maupin talks about a group of gay men who are 'The A-List'. These are affluent, well-connected, handsome gay men who live among high society. He goes on to describe B-List, C-List gays that get ranked depending on how rich, attractive or intelligent they are. I was young and insecure and felt I only belonged in the C-List. This thought stuck with me from then, until now. Queer women have to battle against what society expects them to be as a woman (and to define themselves as a perfect lesbian).

LOTTE'S VIEW

As I mentioned in 'B is for Better Late Than Never', I hate the term Gold Star Lesbian. There isn't such a thing as a 'purity' of the queer experience – come on, that's way too vanilla for us! I remember when I was younger and going out to lesbian venues, when they actually existed, being quizzed on the door about my sexuality. Apparently I didn't look like every other early 2000s lesbian and that made me less of one. As I've got older I feel my sexuality is changing along with my gender identity. I feel more fluid and 'queer' but identifying strongly as a lesbian was really important to me when I was younger. I feel we have to allow people the space to shift and evolve in life. Me feeling that my identity is something other than 'lesbian' now doesn't erase the existence of 'lesbians'. I feel like there's a real pressure for our individual journeys and experiences to conform and I'm not interested in that. People should be free to be who they want to be and that doesn't take anything from anyone else's identity. Isn't that the whole point of being queer?!

People who are multi-sex attracted, such as bisexual and pansexual, have to fight against the incorrect assumption that they are sexually 'loose' or just a stop on the road to full-blown gay-town. Then where do we even start for transgender queers who experience some of the most prejudice, and who surely have a deep sense of perfectionism to be role models for their community and to not 'let the side down'?

Do you sense where we are going with this? Same-sex marriage has been legal only since 2014, same-sex adoption from 2002, and it was only in 2009 that non-gestational mothers could be legally recognized as parents. 1950s perfect parenting mixed with the queer pressures we already have hanging over our heads equals an interesting set of emotions when it comes to being an LGBTQ+ parent. In the grand scheme of things, we are new to this whole socially acceptable parenting malarkey, so never have the words of RuPaul rung so true . . . 'Good luck and . . . don't fuck it up!' But back to those tributes to imperfection mentioned earlier. It's *Scummy Mummies* not *Scummy Parents*, *Hurrah for Gin* is based on the notion of 'mother's ruin', and the memes, TikToks and other social posts are made to make mothers, not parents in general, feel better about the trials and tribulations of parenting. They don't acknowledge the queer parenting experience, which has a whole other layer of pressure attached.

You might be reading this thinking, 'I'm a LGBTQ+ parent, or parent-to-be, and I've never given a shit what people think of me as a parent. I couldn't care less.' Well, good for you, but I'm not sure I 100 per cent believe you. Queer shame lives in us. We've grown up in a society that constantly made us feel like we are not normal. Section 28 made us a dirty subject that couldn't be talked about in schools and, guess what? It's happening again in America with the 'Don't Say Gay' bill in Florida (see page 87), which aims to silence the discussion around LGBTQ+ relationships, including families and identities, within schools (praying that this is a distant horrid memory and not still the current truth whenever you might be reading this!). The AIDS pandemic made us something to be feared. In films and TV shows we were always made the butt of the joke and portrayed as butch lesbians in dungarees with short hair, feminine jokey queens or 'trannies' who are sexual predators and to be feared, rather than seeing us for what we really are: diverse and individual in every way. However, on reflection, I may have just described Lotte and I quite well . . . we do nothing for anti-stereotypes!

The need to be perfect and to 'not let the side down' has played a huge part in my parenting and creeps up when I least expect it. For me this pressure comes in the form of not wanting to feel judged for being a gay parent, like, somehow, I am less than the other traditional parents. They can make mistakes, or not be perfect, because they are not being judged or held to a certain standard. In rational terms I know that no one in my circle thinks like this, but that doesn't change the internal, and often sub-conscious, feelings I have that dictate my day-to-day parenting. When my daughter started school, I became a deranged maniac trying to ensure I did her hair just right. I continually practised a plait to ensure it looked as perfect as it could be. I made attempt after attempt at a French plait, to no avail. I was a failure! In my eyes a simple ponytail was not good enough. I was fixated on it, as I genuinely felt if she walked into school with her hair being a mess I would be judged. There was a vision in my head of all the mums rolling their eyes and saying, 'Oh, that poor girl having no mum and two dads with no idea of how to do hair . . .' Looking back now I must laugh as I had clearly forgotten gay stereotype #28: 'Gays make great hairdressers', and no one would have thought that. Perhaps it was even the sub-conscious sense that people assume gays would be good at hair that was freaking me out; let me tell you it's a pressurized minefield! My practice eventually paid off: my daughter walked into school with a stunning plait and I felt so proud. As she turned around to wave goodbye, her gorgeous plait swinging as she turned her head, I realized she had a huge stain down her jumper and her shoes were caked in mud. 'SHIT!' I'd spent so long focused on her hair I had failed to realize the rest of her looked an utter mess. Today, after much reflection on the subject, I would turn and laugh, but I remember a feeling of utter devastation (did I mention I am a total drama queen?) and now in my head all the mums were having a kiki about the poor little girl with two dads who can't even put her in a clean jumper. Over the years this feeling has dimmed but it comes back to bite me every so often, like when I forget an important school date, party or collection for a teacher and can't help feeling that that particular parenting fail is down to me being a queer parent. What it takes me a little while to realize is that failings like this are universal parenting fails, we just don't have a character in *Motherland* to reflect our queer experience to make us feel better. We feel the pressure to be perfect parents to prove that us queers can parent just as well as School Gate Suze.

MEET . . .
Matthew Todd (he/him)

Matthew wrote the incredible book Straight Jacket: Overcoming Society's Legacy of Gay Shame,[20] about how this shame potentially creeps up on us as LGBTQ+ parents.

You wrote in **Straight Jacket** *about how our sense of shame leads to a life of control. Can you see how this then might affect parenting as a queer person? Does it fuel our insecurities as parents?*
I'm not a parent myself but I can absolutely see that, coming from a base of shame, that might express itself as perfectionism as parents. It's not exclusive to gay parents, of course. Straight people can feel pressure to be perfect parents too – that's what our society does – but with all the pressures put on us LGBTQ+ folk, those pressures can be exacerbated. I've heard gay friends who are parents express this idea that they feel extra-specially judged because they are same-sex.

Why do you think LGBTQ+ people have a desire to generally be seen as perfect?
When you don't feel safe, as most of us didn't as we were growing up, it can manifest as a desire to make up for it by being perfect. I remember having a very clear thought at school that I had to make up for being gay by excelling in other areas. So, we can sometimes strive to have the perfect education, perfect job, body, life. This can all be subconscious and not everyone feels it. But it's not surprising that that might come

out in gay parents as a desire to be perfect. But there's no such thing as perfect, so if you're chasing perfection, you're never going to feel satisfied.

When growing up, did you ever consider that one day you could become a parent?

No, I grew up in the 1980s and at that point there were so many laws that were unfair and homophobic. I never dreamed that we would even get partnership rights let alone parenting rights. I worked at Stonewall in the mid-1990s, and I regularly heard stories of lesbian women having their children taken away, gay men who had come out after being in a heterosexual relationship who weren't allowed to see their kids. I grew up in a very negative time, with Section 28 and HIV/AIDS raging, and that did real damage to my sense of whether I'd ever be able to have a family life. Gays were portrayed as being separate to family in itself, not part of families; the narrative was always of devastated parents casting their son or daughter out, never to be seen again, and that really did a huge amount of damage to my sense of being able to be part of a family. I love my niece and nephew and I love being part of that family unit now, but the time passed. I do have regrets that I don't have my own children, but I threw myself into my career during the time it might have been practical, which was a form of perfectionism for me, and I think that's not uncommon for lots of LGBTQ+ people. Also of course lots of queer people don't want to be parents. It's great now that it is an option for those that do.

Shocks, Shame and Being 'Good Enough'

The more time you spend as a parent the less you care what the outside world thinks, especially now being a parent of three I just care that they (and we) are surviving each day. The outside world, however, will continue to spin in its own heteronormative way and will every so often smack your queer face back to reality. Case in point: I was having a particularly difficult time on the street with my then two-year-old. There was screaming, tears, snot and feet stomping . . . and he was pretty upset too. I was doing my best to calm the situation while letting this tantrum run its course. A little old lady (it's always the little old ladies by the way . . . watch out for them) came up to us and stroked his head. 'Oh, bless him. I bet he just wants a cuddle with his mummy.' Cue my reaction akin to the camera effect in *Jaws* when Chief Brody spots the shark. I don't need to go into how I felt in that moment. If you've read the above, you'll know a little part of me died.

However, the biggest shock I've had so far in my parenting experience is my feelings towards my son's desire to wear dresses. From an early age he would always pick out the Snow White costume from our fancy-dress box. He looked super cute in it and it made him so happy. Then when our daughter started to outgrow some of her dresses, he would ask to wear them around the house. My husband and I didn't even discuss it. If that's what he wanted, then fine. Why would we, especially as a gay couple, have any concerns about our son wearing a dress? I then started realizing I'd been making some unconscious influences in relation to his outfit choices. We would be heading out to the shops or going to see friends and family and he would ask to wear his dress. I wasn't saying no to him, but I found myself suggesting other outfits. I've always been quite controlling about our kids' wardrobe choices as I used to have an aversion to the multiple clashing patterns they would pick. I found myself suggesting a pair of trousers or a T-shirt rather than the dress.

I realized I was deliberately steering him away from wearing a dress in public.

I use the word 'shock' as it unlocked something in me I never thought would happen. As a gay man, feeling this sense of shame that my son wanted to put on a dress in public was a very unexpected reaction. Was I worried for him? Worried that he would be bullied or teased? Potentially, but I've often thought that this reasoning is used by people to excuse forms of homophobia. I had to face what the real issue was. I was worried people would judge us as gay parents for dressing up our son in a dress. In my heart I assumed people would think we were pushing our 'gay agenda' on him, that we made him wear a dress or in some backwards version of mothers who say, 'Oh, I'd love to have a gay son', we were encouraging him to follow in our own pink footsteps. A straight dad gained internet fame after he stood by his son for wearing an Elsa dress. He wore one himself and sang 'Let It Go', which went viral and he was widely applauded. Would that video have been as viewed, shared and celebrated as many times as it was if it was a gay man? I think not. As my son grew older his desire to wear dresses and sparkly things only increased, and one day when we were due to go out with a friend and her family he asked me if he could wear his favourite pink flowery dress with strappy shoulders. Why would I say no to him? Why should I persuade him to wear something else? This was my issue, not his. In that moment I woke up to what was important and realized it was time I stopped caring what others thought or how I would be perceived. I couldn't be prouder of my son; he knows what he wants and wears his outfits with style. The first day he wore a dress to nursery I still had butterflies, but as he strolled in and his best friend went, 'Wow, I love your dress,' I couldn't have been happier. He recently went to a holiday club where I knew there would be children aged up to ten. He wanted to wear his dress so we put it on, but this time I asked him what he should say if anyone questioned why he was wearing a dress. 'People can wear whatever they like, and dresses are not just for girls. I love wearing my dress!' he told me. The lesson I've learned from my son is to not hold them back for fear of how they will be treated but to give them the tools and the strength to stand up for what they believe in. He will soon start school and I'm sure he is going to want to wear the summer dress uniform. And he can, and I'll be proud to drop him off at the gate wearing it.

Throughout the adoption process you are told to focus on being a 'good enough' parent, because you will tie yourself in knots trying to be the non-existent 'perfect parent'. No parent is perfect. Kids are unpredictable and life throws you curveballs that you will never expect. 'While we are not perfect, we are indeed good enough parents if most of the time we love our children and do our best to do well by them,' says Bruno Bettelheim in his book *A Good Enough Parent*. I remember throughout our adoption process focusing on 'fun and love' as the mantra we would use when asked by panels and social

workers what we thought we could bring to a child's life. I regret not carrying this through into my early days of parenting when I was so fixated on doing it 'right'. Today I repeat 'fun and love, fun and love' at any point I find myself overthinking plaits, my son wearing dresses or any other parenting challenge that is going to come our way. It doesn't matter what anyone thinks as long as we have fun together and love each other unconditionally – then the world can do and think what it likes.

Talking Points

▶ Why is control and perfection so prevalent within the LGBTQ+ community?

▶ Does the sense of queer shame fuel our insecurities as parents?

▶ Have you felt this sense of pressure as a queer parent?

▶ Have you noticed this in any of your LGBTQ+ friends who have children?

IS FOR QUEERIFICATION

Queerification is perhaps (along with blasto-cyst) one of our new favourite words. Defined as the process of making something queer and (our favourite bit) not conforming to main-stream heteronormative identity or behaviour.

Once upon a time there was a mum, a dad and two perfect children. They could be kings and queens, rabbits in burrows or a suburban family who happened to have had a tiger pop in for tea and drink, shock horror, Daddy's beer, but they had to be straight. There has been some progress, but we are still very much living within this straight fairy tale, with countless story books, animated films, toys and TV shows all still projecting the nuclear family dream. Therefore, as an LGBTQ+ family, it is sadly sometimes on us to queer it up and create our own twists on the classics till the world catches up.

Growing up, I was obsessed with Sylvanian Families. God, I loved those little furry families, but let us face facts: you won't

see Mrs Rabbit on the back of an officially endorsed Sylvanian Families low-loader at London Pride any time soon. It seems their values are as buttoned up as Mrs Hedgehog's Victorian blouse. For those not familiar with the classic 1980s toys that still delight little children, and some grown adults, today, they are little humanized animal characters that live in the idyllic land of Sylvania. You buy them in pre-packaged family sets with a mum, a dad and, generally, two children. The Panda Family and the Labrador Family are my favourites and my God, they are ridiculously cute, but crikey they are just so straight! I mean it's the twenty-first century and they don't even have a single-parent set; divorce obviously doesn't exist in Sylvania. I bet they are also anti-abortion.

LOTTE'S VIEW

It was my lesbian friends' son Alfie's third birthday and I had a genius idea. I bought two identical Sylvanian bear families, carefully opened the boxes and extracted the Daddy Bear from one and the Mummy Bear from the other. I put the mum in the box with the other mum and the dad with the other dad – lo and behold, the world's first unofficial gay Sylvanian Families! I gave Alfie the mums and I gave Stu's daughter the dads. It so often falls on us to 'correct' kids' stuff in this way. I've also had to draw longer hair on one of the dads in a book, which is all about diverse families and shockingly doesn't feature any same-sex parents, because my daughter actually asked why all the kids in the book had a mum and a dad.

Is this all just a massive smokescreen to help Lotte and I create a huge LGBTQ+ Sylvanian Family swap-shop network to form an army of queer squirrels, badgers and rabbits living in Victorian realness across the globe? Busted! We may even start a new product range of Pride outfits so Mr Bear can literally be the bear we want him to be.

This is of course just one example of how as an LGBTQ+ family we sometimes need to go above and beyond to ensure our children can see their own family reflected back at them. We have made incredible, yet at times very slow, strides in LGBTQ+ representation, however the notion of queer families is still incredibly under-represented. It is 2023 and yet we still do not have a fully formed queer family on any of the primetime soaps, even though gay characters have been represented on screen since 1985, with Michael Cashman (now Lord Cashman) making history in *Eastenders* by playing the first gay character in a soap. When four years later Michael made further history by being part of the first ever same-sex kiss on a British soap, the tabloids created an ugly furore about it. Piers Morgan called them 'yuppie poofs' and wrote up an MP's comments calling the kiss a 'perverted practice' and the scene 'revolting'. Almost thirty-five years later and why no representation? I connected with Lord Cashman (he/him) on Twitter on this subject. 'Given how our soaps often accurately reflect the lives around us it is high time for us to see a picture of same-sex families facing the same problems, often misunderstandings and discrimination, but battling to have their place in our communities. I hope one of our major soaps will lead the way!' he told me.

We proposed the question of why there are no queer families on a primetime soap to screenwriter James McDermott (he/him). James is a queer writer who previously worked on BBC One's *Eastenders*.

As a queer man and writer, and not from my experience of working on *Eastenders*, I think the representation of a fully formed LGBTQ family in soap opera is long overdue, to reflect the modern world, the people who live in it and the change in LGBTQ rights in the UK in recent times. Perhaps this is yet to happen as characters settling down, starting a family and going about their daily lives simply doesn't seem sensational or dramatic enough for a soap storyline. However, I think that such fresh representation would be quietly sensational and intriguing for audiences. Perhaps many mainstream shows feel they have to represent stereotypical LGBTQ characters and storylines so as not to distress or alienate mainstream audiences. For example, viewers in the UK are now comfortable with, or at least familiar with, seeing on screen the camp or promiscuous single gay man who has become a stalwart of British soap operas and TV dramas since the 90s. Audiences aren't used to seeing a gay man with his loving husband searching for a house to raise children. I believe in time, this will change, but in order for change to happen in the world, culture has to assert the change we want to see to show people other ways of being, thinking and living are possible.

In our fight for equality and understanding in the queer parenting space it's clear that literature plays a huge role in making children feel represented. Until incredibly recently there has been almost zero queer family representation in major children's books. The tide is changing with books, like Lotte's own *My Magic Family* (available at all good booksellers – had we mentioned she had another book out?!), *My Daddies* by Gareth Peters,[21] which was the first LGBTQ+ family book to be published by a major publisher, and Benjamin Dean's tween-focused *Me, My Dad and the End of the Rainbow*[22] all getting recognition for representing LGBTQ+ families in their stories. We love these books because, reading them to our children, we feel represented, and they can see themselves in the characters and stories. The problem potentially with these books is they are at risk of becoming echo chambers. Nothing will change if we produce LGBTQ+-focused books solely for LGBTQ+ folk. We need our allies to be buying and reading these stories to their children; we need our kids' school friends to be picking these books up in the library to help them open their minds beyond their own families. We need to be in the mainstream. I found an ingenious way to push our gay agenda on my daughters' friends. I bulk-bought copies of Todd Parr's fabulous *The Family Book*,[23] which celebrates every shape and size of family, and it became my go-to present for birthday parties. We got great feedback from the parents, with many saying how it created a great space to have the conversation about other families. Give the gift of gay!

While the publishing world does seem to be one step ahead in terms of representation, why has it still taken so long for this representation to happen? Before 2021 the only representation we've had has been in independently published books as far back as the 70s. I wonder if the introduction of recent education policies (as mentioned in the chapter 'E is for Education', see page 87) has changed the game. After all, these books can now actually be placed in schools without facing a national hullabaloo. In recent years we've had some amazing LGBTQ+ books independently published, such as Carolyn Robertson's *Two Dads,* but I wanted to take a look into our (fairly recent!) history and explore some of the earliest queer family stories. In the 1980s one of the most famous LGBTQ+ children's books in the UK was *Jenny Lives with Eric and Martin*. The book was published by the Gay Men's Press, an independent publishing house that was founded by Aubrey Walter and David Fernbach, who were part of the Gay Liberation Front. I spoke to David about *Jenny Lives with Eric and Martin*.

INSIGHT:
Pioneering Publishers and Writers of
LGBTQ+ Books for Kids

We spoke to three people who have played an important part in bringing queer family stories to children.

David Fernbach, founder of the Gay Men's Press
We published *Jenny Lives with Eric and Martin* in 1983; though never reaching very high sales figures, it brought by far the greatest publicity we would ever receive. The book was written by the Danish children's author Susanne Bösche. It innocuously tells the story of a child of six or seven who lives with her father and his boyfriend, while her mother comes to visit at weekends. Published just before the AIDS pandemic struck Britain, this was a time when progressive education

authorities were responding to lesbian and gay pressure to present positive images to schoolchildren.

We anticipated some hostility, despite the book's harmless character. But for a couple of years all was quiet, while a few thousand copies percolated through to progressive educationalists and parents. Such feedback as we received suggested that the book was popular with young children, particularly girls. But the AIDS pandemic gave new fuel to homophobia, while the Thatcher government was waging war against left-wing local authorities. Our book was suddenly in the news, with banner headlines in the gutter press like 'Vile Book in Schools'. This reached a peak when Thatcher denounced the book at the 1987 Tory Party conference, and the cover of *Jenny* was displayed on the national news.

The notorious Section 28 of the 1988 Local Government Act, which prohibited the 'promotion of homosexuality' by local authorities, was more a sop to the homophobe lobby than a serious policy of repression. However, it created a climate of fear, leading teachers to avoid discussing homosexuality in the classroom. As a sign that the precarious rights our community had achieved were under attack, it galvanized massive opposition. The very year it was passed, it was called 'one of the greatest promotions of homosexuality we have ever seen'. Combining with the wave of community activity in response to AIDS, the liberation movement emerged in the 1990s with unprecedented strength. Section 28 seemed an archaic anomaly, although it was not repealed until 2003.

Though Gay Men's Press did not publish more children's books, we distributed without further controversy Alyson Wonderland, the children's list built up by our sister publisher in the USA.

Sasha Alyson (he/him), founder of American LGBTQ+ publisher Alyson Wonderland

Our first three books [that focused on LGBTQ+ families in children's books] were *Daddy's Roommate*, *Heather Has Two Mommies* and *The Duke Who Outlawed Jelly Beans*. The inspiration came when I was talking to the owners of Category Six, a gay bookshop in Denver in the late 1980s. I asked what books their customers were looking for, and they said they were starting to have same-sex couples with small children looking for books that showed families like theirs, so I talked with Michael Willhoite about it.

Daddy's Roommate

Michael Willhoite (he/him) is an American author and illustrator. He wrote and illustrated the book *Daddy's Roommate*. Released in 1990, the book was the first book in the US to feature a male same-sex couple in a parenting role and address the subject of homosexuality in a children's book. The story focuses on a young boy who has divorced parents. He finds out his dad is now living with a man called Frank. He enjoys spending time with them both and his mother explains to him that Frank and his dad are gay and enjoying life as a couple. She tells him that being gay is just another form of love. Since his dad, and mum, are happy, so is he. 'I always wanted to write and illustrate children's books', Michael tells me. 'I mentioned this to the publisher Sasha Alyson, who produced LGBTQ+ literature, and he proposed the idea of creating a line of children's books with a gay theme.' Sasha created Alyson Wonderland, an offshoot of his gay publishing brand. 'I thought of the title, *Daddy's Roommate*', says Michael. 'No ideas came to me though.

One day I was sitting in a cafe, eating lunch, when the whole thing flashed into my mind. I hurriedly wrote it on a napkin, with notes for illustrations. That night I made a few adjustments, and the next day took it to Sasha, who said, 'Let's run with it.' The reaction from the LGBTQ+ community was overwhelmingly positive, and its success was immediate. This surprised me; I assumed it would be a book of a season and then fade from view. It became a cause célèbre, in large part because of homophobia, which aroused the bluenoses, and efforts to suppress it ironically made it a success.'

As Michael notes, the book of course created controversy. *Daddy's Roommate* became one of the most-challenged books in the country. Even in 2008 it was rumoured that Republican politician Sarah Palin had tried to remove the book from her local library. It was used by another politician as evidence of 'militant homosexual agenda' (insert Ryan Gosling giggling gif here). 'I never expected controversy,' says Michael. 'Which indicates how laughably naive I was. To be truthful, I am guardedly grateful to the people who attempted to ban it, since they were instrumental in ensuring its success. The nation's librarians, whom I now call the foot soldiers of the First Amendment, overwhelmingly supported the book in libraries, and fought valiantly to keep it in libraries. I have spoken to many librarian groups: most gratifying. A library in Wichita Falls, Texas was forced to remove my book, and the case went to the Supreme Court. The library won.'

Has all this controversy led to a reduced focus on queer family representation? While Michael Cashman believes we are just not being thought about in TV writer's rooms, Michael Willhoite actually believes there is more to it. 'The reason is fear and ignorance. The media are cowed in large part by conservatives. The public is, as you know, much more supportive of gay unions, but politicians have not caught up with them. That also suggests that the public at large quickly grew used to the idea that we could sustain happy marriages. Thus, no controversy. However, the Trump years have put us on guard again, and Christian nationalism is on the rise – a scary thought.'

I asked Michael Willhoite about how right-wing society seems to only focus on the sexual part of being LGBTQ+, and that they can't see beyond that, and he responded: 'America is still in many ways steeped in puritanism. Sex scares many people, and these people need a bugbear to scare their children with. African Americans, women and other groups are convenient scapegoats. If people would just fucking stop and think, they would see us as we are.'

In Lotte's picture book *My Magic Family*, while the first focus is on a girl with two mums, the book features all different types of families with the narrative not being particularly queer or focused on a subject that directly speaks to only LGBTQ+ audiences. Surely this is natural progression to true representation. Gay characters featuring in family books alongside seemingly straight characters. They are there and present but not part of the story. I'd like to imagine a world where *The Tiger Who Came to Tea* is retold with two dads and the tiger drinks Daddy's bottle of rosé rather than 'Daddy's beer', and the focus of the story is still about a rude tiger that steals all the food but the parents just happen to be queer. I do think the continued sexualization of the queer community by the far-right media is one reason it's taking so much time. We are families. Yes, my husband and I have sex, but so does every straight couple. We even conform to the traditional straight notion that once married you end up having sex about once a month (and that's if you are lucky!). Unless you are some form of nymphomaniac, one does not think of sex the moment you see any couple on screen, in a book or in a toy set (fun fact: someone who has sexual attractions to a toy has 'agalmatophilia' – just in case it helps you on *The Chase* one day). So why do the anti-gay brigade always throw sex in our faces? In an article in *The New Yorker,* journalist Jessica Winter gives the great example that 'straight adults do not instantly think of straight sex when they see straight characters. When my kids watch *Bluey*, I don't keep one finger on the remote just in case Mum and Dad suddenly start going at it atop their kitchen counter. Introduce a gay character into your children's entertainment, though, and you become a "groomer": the buzzword that's now omnipresent in right-wing media.' Wouldn't it be incredibly radical if the ever-growing number of queer families actually became the catalyst for finally breaking down the stigma attached to sexualizing the LGBTQ+ community? What if this minority within a minority becomes the way we can finally knock down this stereotype? In short, we need Alice Oseman to write a sequel to *Heartstopper* where Nick and Charlie settle down, start a family and all the homophobes' heads implode.

MEET . . .
Jane Severance (she/her)

Jane wrote what is considered the first ever picture book that features a lesbian parent. *When Megan Went Away,* **which tells the story of a young girl who has to deal with the absence of her Mum's now ex-partner, was written by Jane when she was only twenty-one and was released by indie LGBTQ+ publisher Lollipop Power.**

When I decided I wanted to write a children's book featuring a lesbian mother I was very young – only a few years out of high school. I was heavily involved in the women's/lesbian movement, mostly concentrated on working at Woman to Woman Bookstore in Denver.

This was a time period where suddenly a number of women's/lesbian presses sprung up and began putting out books such as *Rubyfruit Jungle* and *The Cook and the Carpenter*. Some were adult presses, but there were also a few small presses printing books for children.

We were at the height of great change and parents were looking for books showing children with different families, children making non-traditional choices and being supported for making those choices, and even books showing adults in unexpected roles. For example, one of Lollipop's books, which were really more like pamphlets, was the story of a farmer who cared for a sheep, sheared it and then knitted a warm sweater from the wool. The twist? The farmer was a woman. This probably doesn't seem like such a big deal to you, but at the time I had never seen a picture book in which a woman was called a farmer. As opposed to a farm woman. I had seen plenty of women in aprons feeding the chickens and hanging up wash. They were always secondary characters and always the real farmer's wife.

You must understand the time in which I was living. Now it is common for a lesbian or lesbians to choose to have children – at the time I wrote *Megan* I did not know one single lesbian who had a planned child. Everyone who I knew who had children, and there weren't a lot, had them from a previous marriage to a man. I worked with kids and liked kids in the work setting, but I couldn't imagine anything worse than having one. It would have totally cramped my style. I wanted to have lots of sex with lots of women and I avoided women with children like the plague. Neither my book, nor *Heather Has Two Mummies* (which was written by Lesléa Newman and published a decade after but is often misclaimed as the first lesbian picture book), even mentioned the word lesbian. I don't remember why not. I think it was just because I couldn't figure out a way to do it without seeming awkward and pedantic. I don't think it was an issue with Lollipop – I'm pretty sure we never even discussed it. The timing of the book was just off. I'm not the first person this has happened to in history for both writers and inventors. The press was too small. The distribution was too small. The illustrations weren't that great.

LOTTE'S VIEW

I wrote the picture book *My Magic Family*[24] because when I was looking for books for my daughter that might give her some representation of her own family, I struggled to find any that resonated for us. The books I did find were somehow lacking the joy that I wanted to share with her, so I wrote my own book to really answer a gap on our bookshelves. I wanted to write something that felt warm and loving and joyful and magical and not 'issues'-based. You'll notice in the book, the character says, 'I wonder if the other children have two mums like me?' She's not worried about it, she's not anxious, she's just interested, and I think that spirit of curiosity is something wonderful to encourage in children. While of course, as we address throughout *this* book, there is still discrimination and prejudice, I really wanted *My Magic*

Family to reflect more of the positivity around being a different kind of family. It's not a niche book, and within its pages it explores all different kinds of families, so even the most conventional family in the world will find something in it for them. But there's also something that, if you are from a different kind of family, it's going to make you feel seen and make you feel understood in a way that perhaps you haven't before. As I write in my book: 'Families are interesting, each different from the rest. There isn't one that's perfect, not one kind that's best. But a family is magic, no matter who is who, real and fantastical, they're full of love for you.'

Talking Points

▶ Do you actively seek out books that feature queer characters?

▶ Have you ever had to change a character's gender or identity to help it reflect your own family?

▶ What can we do to help create change?

R

IS FOR RACE

As discussed in the chapter 'A is for Adoption' (see page 11), the selection process when adopting a child is complex. We had to clearly define the type of child we were looking for. Having those early conversations with my husband was key to us being able to narrow down what we thought we wanted and what we felt we could take on from a health, disability and background point of view. However, one of the key areas that we had to discuss early on was also ethnicity and race, and my reaction to it took me by surprise. I think it's important that I offer full transparency and honesty here. Whenever I imagined us with a child, I had never pictured us with a child being anything other than white. It was another conversation that John and I had to have that we had not been expecting. Did I find it uncomfortable? Absolutely. For the first time I was questioning my own views on race and what my views would be on having a child with a different race to my own. I'm very aware that my white privilege plays a major part here and the fact that, up until the age of thirty-two, I'd never had to give any real thought to the subject of race says it all. We spent time discussing it and looking at the varying factors, including our predominantly white neighbourhood. Ultimately, we decided to only look at the profiles of children of white ethnicity and explained to our social worker that we felt that, as same-sex parents, we would already be a minority within the school and community and having a child of different ethnicity could create further complications for the child. Was this just an excuse? Was the fundamental fact that we just wanted to have a child that looked like us? Perhaps. When you look at surrogacy and donor conception, it's common for people to explore donors that share similarities with themselves, including their skin colour and heritage. It feels like the same applies to adoption. Perhaps this is heightened by being queer? We know that we can't biologically create a child that is genetically linked to both parents, so therefore we do everything we can to at least have a child that displays some of the characteristics we see looking back in the mirror.

If we had made the decision to adopt a child of a different ethnicity to our own, this would be called transracial adoption. I wasn't even aware of the term at the time we were making our decision, but I've since learned that there are a lot of mixed feelings on the subject, which perhaps would have further influenced our decision. Given that children of Black and minority ethnic backgrounds spend the longest time in care awaiting adoption, some think that colour and ethnicity shouldn't be factored in when deciding on placements. However, if there is one thing that my – fairly recent – education on systemic racism has taught me, it is that there is no such thing as being colour-blind. By attempting to be 'colour-blind', you ultimately erase several fundamental factors, such as heritage, history and the life experience that a Black child has. With identity being such a gigantic and important part of growing up as an adoptee, if you can't see yourself reflected back via your parents, are you going to feel even more isolated than you potentially already do? If we had adopted a black child, would John and I even be equipped to support, or even understand, what that child would face in terms of everyday white supremacy and racial bias?

MEET . . .
Nathan Yungerberg (he/him)

Nathan has the rare experience of seeing transracial adoption from both sides . . .

I identify as a gay male African American and I grew up as a transracial adoptee. I am now a single father to two fostered children that I'm in the process of adopting. They are of different heritage to me as they are half Puerto Rican and half Italian.

My adoptive parents are white and I was raised in a small town in the very white American Midwest alongside two adoptive sisters, one whom was of Korean heritage and another that was multi-racial. It was traumatic for me growing up and feeling so uniquely different to everyone. We would go to the store and everyone would stare. I was a kid and I didn't want to stand out, yet I had the spotlight on me the whole time. My parents were just not equipped to help me understand and celebrate my heritage. Kids at school would be fascinated with my hair and made me uncomfortable with all their questions, while they poked their pencil into my curls. My parents did not have the experience nor knowledge to support me through that. It was when I was about eight years old I realized I was completely on my own. I was introverted and I just wouldn't let people get close to me.

My history has made me extra conscious in how I parent my children. For one it's slightly easier as even though we are of different background we share a darker skin so people immediately connect them as my children. That said I want to ensure I have a community surrounding us that means they can stay rooted within their culture. It's even small things like making sure I am cooking Puerto Rican food, so they are growing up experiencing parts of their heritage. From my childhood I feel there are things my parents could have done differently and if anyone is going down the route of transracial parenting then I suggest you make sure they can see people like themselves. Although where we lived was 99 per cent white, we did have ten to fifteen black people in our town and I feel my parents could have made the effort to seek out Black families for us to spend time with. Books would have also helped, but ultimately it was the lack of understanding and acknowledgment of the pain I brought to the table as a Black child with two white parents that was the true dismissal. I needed them to hear me, which they did eventually, but by then the damage was done. I don't want that for my children.

There were many conversations that took place over the years, but one day my dad finally wrote me a letter. He was admitting his failures in not giving me the attention I deserved in regards to my cultural needs. His explanation made sense to me. He wrote about how he had come from a small farm in Minnesota, from parents who had survived the Great Depression, growing up with no heat in the house and very little food on the table. He had anxieties in his own parenting style connected to that. His focus was just to give us the things he didn't have. But being a white man and not going through that extra layer of oppression and struggle evaded his perception. I think for a long time he was in denial and didn't want to face that he had failed me. This healed me within an instant. It repaired so many of the holes that had grown over the years.

INSIGHT:
Race and Adoption

Grace Gomez is an Adopter Diversity Recruitment Officer for PACT, an adoption charity and family support provider.

Black children and those of mixed Black/white ethnicity are over-represented in the care system and also historically wait longer for an adoptive family. Black boys of Black African heritage in particular wait the longest. Yet there is a shortage of approved adopters with Black ethnic backgrounds. Adoption guidance states that adoption agencies should not seek to match all aspects of ethnicity and cultural background where this could lead to a delay in a child being placed but instead should look at what is needed to support the child and their family.

We are looking for parents who can understand and celebrate their child's identity, ethnicity and culture. If their child's ethnicity is different to their own, prospective parents will need to demonstrate how they can positively promote their child's culture and support their identity needs as well as preparing themselves and their child for the challenges of racism and prejudice.

Children who have been in the care system are more likely to have attachment issues as a result of loss, abuse or neglect suffered prior to being adopted. This must be recognized alongside the additional challenges that a child may face while trying to find their own identity within a family that doesn't represent their own ethnicity.

Race/Ethnicity and Donor Conception

And transracial parenting isn't just an adoptive issue. As mentioned, it's also as important for those going via donor conception to ensure they are creating children who they feel are part of them, part of their heritage. This is especially true for couples who themselves come from different ethnicities. I spoke to Bola and Bex on this very subject and about some of the challenges and complexities involved when looking for Black donors.

INSIGHT:
Black Donors

Bola (she/her/they/them) **and Bex** (she/her) **are lesbian mixed-race parents via donor conception.**

Bex: We are Mummy and Mam to T, who is three years old. Bola is the oldest, so we decided that it would be best if she was the first to carry.

Bola: We also felt it was potentially going to be easier for us to find a donor match because I'm Black Nigerian and Bex is white, and we wanted a white European donor that shared characteristics with her.

Bex: Before we decided on this path, we had looked at some of the donors out there and quickly realized it would be challenging to find someone that matches Bola's genetics. At the time the London Sperm Bank only had one Black donor. The focus was always for us to have a mixed-race child. If we could conceive naturally then that's what we would have. We knew our child could of course be a lighter or darker shade, but regardless he would always be our child.

Bola: We don't know why but it seems there is a very small pool of Black donors, so it makes the process incredibly difficult. You've also got to keep your standards, as with little choice you want to still be choosing a donor, for more than just heritage. It's about matching personalities; you don't just settle with the Black donor because that's the only one available. Therefore, if we do go down the donor route for a second time round, with Bex carrying this time, we might have to look further afield, like America. I think they get paid for donations in the US so that means there is more choice.

Bex: For us this raises a moral question though, as in an ideal world we want someone who has chosen to donate because of an altruistic intention, not a money-orientated incentive. We would always be questioning their motive. There is also the question of the UK standards that come with sperm donation, and we know they do a lot of regulating. Because of this we are exploring all different options to extend our family.

The one donor from the London Sperm Bank, at the time, was also of Nigerian heritage. This opened an interesting conversation about if we would use a black donor from another region or country, such as the Caribbean. Would we feel fraudulent raising a non-Nigerian with our Nigerian influence? We both actually got DNA tests and Bola found out she could actually trace her heritage to multiple places.

Bola: If you think about it, there is no race 'gene', only genes that might make your skin darker, or your hair curly. When you break it down and unpack it your culture is created socially; one is not genetically Nigerian. It does become a bit of a wormhole!

The only thing we knew for sure was that if and when Bex tries to conceive, we didn't want to use the same donor that we used for T. It's funny, as people ask us if we are going to use the same donor and we are like, 'Ummm, no.' If Bex used her egg and the same donor the child would be white. Our son is mixed race, and we wouldn't want him to have a different social experience to his sibling. For us that is far more important than any genetic connection.

Talking Points

▶ If you were to adopt a child from a different race
to your own, what would you need to do to show
a deep understanding of their race and
background and how different it is from your
own? Do you even think that is possible if you
have no experience of living life as a person of
colour?

S

IS FOR SURROGACY

We've spoken to lots of people who have experienced surrogacy for this chapter, and we've had plenty of myths and unconscious biases busted along the way. Overwhelmingly what we've found is people build incredible relationships with their children's surrogate and their families. It's a potentially extremely complex dynamic – here is someone who may have been a stranger a matter of months ago, gestating your child in her body. Unlike family, friendships or romantic partnerships, negotiating the relationship between intended parents and surrogates is still uncharted. There's no rulebook, and so it demands a great amount of empathy and emotional intelligence (something we queers excel at, if we do say so ourselves). Of all the couples we spoke to, the overwhelming love and gratitude they felt towards the woman who had carried their child was palpable, and it's lovely to see how they have integrated her and her partner and children into their extended family. As Alex Wood Morton and his husband Freddy put it on the eve of the birth of their first child: 'It takes a village, hope and a lot of prayers to make surrogacy possible. This miracle is testament to the incredible love and kindness humans can create, no matter the barriers or borders.'

As the process of surrogacy can be complicated, particularly legally, this chapter is designed to give you an overview and to share the experiences of people who have used surrogacy to start their family.

Dads by Surrogacy and Adoption

Brian Rosenberg and Ferd van Gameren were already in their forties by the time they began thinking about having kids. Their early years together focused on keeping Brian, who is HIV-positive, healthy and Ferd negative. But once protease inhibitors emerged and Brian's health was stable, the couple decided to focus on enjoying life. After several years of having fun, 'We started thinking that life had to be more meaningful for us than the next party, the next fabulous vacation,' says Ferd. They wanted a family, and all the responsibility, love and exhaustion that went with it. They tried adoption first, but when one birth mother backed away, their hearts were broken – so they discussed surrogacy, but stayed on the adoption register.

Given his HIV status, Brian assumed it would be impossible to biologically father a child. But in 2009 Ferd discovered the Special Program for Assisted Reproduction in the US, dedicated to helping HIV-positive men father children safely, and the couple pivoted from adopting to pursuing surrogacy as their route to parenthood.

HIV/AIDS and Parenting

This feels as good a place as any to discuss HIV/AIDS and parenting. Until we started work on this book, we had no idea that gay men who are living positively with HIV or AIDS could biologically father children. Like Brian, we thought this would have been impossible. It's not the first time we've learned new facts and details about HIV. As 1980s babies, we feel part of a generation that didn't live it first-hand but were surrounded by misinformation, or no information at all. Raised by parents who were living through the traumatic narrative that was spun at the time, our generation has had very little access to true information about what living with HIV or AIDS means. Learning that people with HIV or AIDS can biologically have children was another reminder that we still have a lot to learn about something that affects our community.

However, while Brian and Ferd could legally have children via surrogacy in the US, the current law in the UK means many people living with HIV are barred from accessing fertility treatment. The National AIDS Trust are calling on the government to end this ban and ensure equality for people living with HIV. And here is the massive homophobic twist in the tale.

LEGAL EAGLE:
The National AIDS Trust

Despite science showing that there is no risk of HIV transmission, existing laws mean many people living with HIV are not allowed to use their eggs or sperm for fertility treatments. People in mixed-sex couples where one or both partners is living with HIV are allowed to undergo fertility treatment such as IVF, as they are viewed as consenting adults in an intimate relationship.

But whenever an egg is transferred from one woman to another, and whenever a man gives sperm to someone who is not their partner, they are legally seen as a donor and different rules apply. Because the law is different for people having children using donated eggs or sperm than it is for mixed-sex couples having a child, it currently discriminates against LGBTQ+ people living with HIV who want to start a family. For example, the law treats a woman living with HIV who wishes to implant her egg in her female partner as a donor rather than a partner and currently prohibits her from doing so.

Outrageous, right? We are hoping that this section of the book quickly becomes outdated and that the new policy that the National AIDS Trust is campaigning for, that will allow people with HIV/AIDS to start their families safely and within the law, comes into effect soon.

How can HIV-positive men safely father children?

Experts agree that it *can* be done safely. According to Dr Brian Berger of Boston IVF, over the past fifteen years fertility centres in the US have helped conceive thousands of babies fathered by HIV-positive men – and not a single woman or child has been infected as a result. HIV cannot attach to or infect spermatozoa – the single-cell swimmers that deliver chromosomes to an egg. Sometimes the surrounding fluid – the semen, the ejaculate that carries the sperm along, and which is made separately – does include HIV. But sperm is made only in the testes, which are walled off from the rest of the body, heavily fortified against the illnesses or infections that might affect the rest of the body, for obvious evolutionary reasons. Because sperm doesn't get mixed with semen until the very last moment, at ejaculation, it remains safe. And after decades of research, the medical profession has figured out how to use only the uninfected sperm to fertilize an egg.

For those who go through the process, there are a couple of particular steps you will face specifically because you are HIV-positive. First: will you tell the egg donor? And second: you must tell the gestational carrier, to ensure informed consent. Depending on the route you pick, the agency, lab or centre you are working with will have its own protocol. If you would like more information about becoming a biological parent if you are HIV-positive, the website Gays With Kids[25] is a great resource.

Dr Tristan Barber, Consultant in HIV Medicine at the Royal Free Hospital, London and Honorary Associate Professor at University College London, adds:

> Starting a family through fertility treatment is completely safe for people living with HIV. HIV medication is now so effective that people on treatment cannot pass the virus on, and can have babies born without HIV.

Deborah Gold, CEO of the National AIDS Trust, says:

> This law completely overlooks the fact that most mixed-sex couples living with HIV are freely able to start a family using fertility treatment and denies others on the basis of their HIV status and sexuality. Not only is this law homophobic, but it also fuels HIV stigma by incorrectly reinforcing the idea that people living with HIV can't safely have a child when the science says they can. This is about equal access to fertility options, but also about challenging discrimination towards LGBT people, getting the government to listen to the science, and stamping out HIV stigma which has existed for decades.

MEET . . .
Noel Watson-Doig (he/him)

Noel has been living positively with HIV from a young age. He is currently working with the National AIDS Trust to help get the law changed.

I got involved with this campaign as I am a gay man with HIV who may, or may not, want to have a family, and under British law we are prohibited from doing so. At the moment it is treated, in the eyes of the law, the same as an organ transplant, which you can't do if you have HIV. It means anyone with HIV can never be involved in surrogacies. They could never be an egg donor or a sperm donor.

Antiviral therapies mean that when you are undetectable you cannot transmit HIV. It's madness, as the UK government is promoting this fact themselves, but then when it comes to the law they won't repeal or review it.

How does it work?
The antiviral medication literally locks the HIV into reservoirs in your body. It's locked into your lymph nodes that are spread around your body, particularly under your arms and in your groin. The HIV is trapped there; that's what the antiviral medication does, and essentially it is confined to these areas, so it doesn't spread to the blood. That's why it's undetected and why we call it undetectable. If you're undetectable, you can't transmit.

Do you think the current law is connected to the prejudices around HIV/AIDS?

The fact that there is no engagement with the science at all is what I've got a massive problem with because obviously it's really easy to say, 'Well, we're just going to forbid something and have a blanket ban.' Essentially criminalize it. But what about the people? What about the people that it impacts? I don't think anyone has really cared enough, which I find extraordinary, and I think it's down to neglect rather than prejudice.

Do you feel that queer people who have HIV or AIDS are aware that being able to parent safely biologically is even possible?

No, I think no one is aware about anything. I think we're often all fairly ignorant about anything except what's right in front of our noses, and I'm sure that very few people have any comprehension of this. Very few people who have HIV perhaps even thought it would be possible for them to use surrogates or donate. The trauma of an HIV diagnosis means a lot of people want to just ignore the consequences or shy away from them and by engaging in questions about surrogacy you are pretty much confronting it all head on. I can't really speak for other people, though; I can only speculate.

If the law was to change, would it mean that HIV-positive people would also be able to make anonymous donations via sperm clinics, etc.?

That's an interesting question, and that's not something that I believe has yet been raised or thought about. You'd think that in theory the answer should be yes. I would expect that they'd have to test that sperm and the clinics might feel that that's a cost they don't want to cover, but in theory that doesn't sound unreasonable.

It will be another interesting step in this development for sure. From a personal side, is having children something you would like to do?
Oh, definitely. I'm very keen. I haven't decided but I'd love to do it. I was diagnosed with HIV when I was very young, so I grew up with HIV as part of my life and in a way I've always confronted the world as an HIV-positive person. I didn't think parenting could be part of my life and it was only later on as my life evolved and I thought, 'Oh, I'd like to have a family.' It just never occurred to me when I first thought of it that there would be this block with the HIV. I could go abroad to start a family but doing things within your own country is so much more appealing. I'd be much more inclined to think more about it if this law was changed.

You can't pretend that HIV isn't highly emotive. There is an extraordinary amount of historical prejudice and it's interesting where policy, science and prejudice are mixing.

So where did all this leave HIV-positive Brian and Ferd, who we met at the beginning of the chapter? Back to their story . . .

Once Brian's sperm had been washed and cleared for use by a lab, the couple put down a sizable financial deposit with the surrogacy agency. Then they went off to Fire Island for Memorial Day weekend (oh, the joy of pre-kids life!). On Tuesday morning they got a call from their adoption agency – which, unbeknown to them, had bumped them to the front of the queue after their previous adoption possibility had fallen through. A baby had been born in Brooklyn. Did they want him?

The answer was easy: Of course! Within two days, Brian and Ferd were exhausted, delighted fathers of a newborn.

But they didn't want him to be an only child. And they had already put down that huge non-refundable deposit. So they decided to continue with the surrogacy process and went ahead with meeting Andrea, a surrogate in West Virginia, who preferred to work with gay men because, according to her, there was no woman involved to be potentially jealous that Andrea could do what she could not. The two couples – Andrea and her husband, Ferd and Brian – got along well and, crucially, Andrea was aware of Brian's HIV status but understood the infinitesimal risk this posed given how the sperm had been treated and the extra precautions that had been included in the process of fertilizing the egg. They agreed to start the process.

The couple's adopted son soon had twin sisters – seventeen months younger than him. 'People ask if I feel differently towards my adopted and my biological children,' Brian said. 'I've heard people say, "Oh, adoption's great but nothing is the same as having your own biological children." We have the experience of becoming parents through adoption and through surrogacy and I absolutely don't support this. The bond between us and our adopted son is just as strong as the bond between me and my biological children.'

MEET . . .
Zara, a three-time surrogate based in the UK

Why did you decide to be a surrogate?
I had my first child fifteen years ago. At that time I wasn't particularly 'maternal', so I wasn't sure if I wanted

any more, but I really enjoyed being pregnant and giving birth to him. The experience changed my life. It was just like the most amazing, incredible feeling ever. And I thought, well, if I can give that to somebody else, you know, then why not? I had quite a straightforward pregnancy, so it just seemed like an easy thing to do. I went on to have three surrogate children, one with one couple, and then two with another. The first two pregnancies were through an agency and the third one was independent. I had my last child of my own three years ago.

Did the experience of being pregnant feel different when you were carrying for an intended parent or for yourself?
It didn't really feel different. Even with my own son, during the pregnancy I was quite detached – you can't imagine there being a baby at the end of it. I think it became easier for me to accept that I was giving a baby over to its intended parents. It actually seemed more normal for me to have a baby and give it away than have a baby and keep it because surrogacy was the majority of my experiences of pregnancy.

Did you have any concerns about attachment post birth?
Not really. I mean, even while I was pregnant, I dared to explore the scenario where I would want to keep the baby, but it just didn't make sense in my head because it wasn't conceived by me. It was like I was babysitting a baby for my friends. It was never my baby; I was just looking after it. And I had the

excitement of the parents looking forward to meeting their baby. Maybe if I hadn't had such a close bond with the parents and they were a bit more distant, I'd have felt a bit more maternal towards it.

What do you think is the biggest misconception about surrogacy you've encountered?

People think that you do it for money or that you will want to keep the baby and that you're going to bond with it.

When you first told your friends or your family that you were going to be a surrogate, did you encounter much resistance from them?

No. I think quite a lot of people are aware of it now. I mean, there's a lot in soaps and that always tends to be quite controversial, not very realistic, but people are more used to the idea. I'm quite a strong-willed person anyway, so I don't think anyone was particularly worried about me.

What has been the hardest thing about being a surrogate?

Sometimes the logistics of all the appointments can be complicated. But being with a partner is probably the most challenging aspect. I suppose it's hard for him, particularly when it comes to being intimate. When I'm pregnant and it's more visible but it's somebody else's child, that can throw the sexual dynamic a bit off. And obviously you have to abstain before you go through the IVF, just to make sure that it is their baby and not your male partner's. And then when you're really heavily pregnant, you don't want to be intimate particularly. So that relationship is probably the hardest to manage.

And what's the most joyful thing?
I think just seeing how happy the parents are when you give them a baby. For them it's even harder to imagine that they're ever going to have a child. And I suppose there's always that worry as well, that as a result of being pregnant, you will have bonded with their child and you are going to try and keep it. They're so in love with this child, they can't imagine why you would want to part with it.

Can you describe the best kind of relationship with intended parents?
It varies. I'm in a lot of surrogacy groups and there're polls all the time about what people want from their intended parents. Some people want phone calls daily and messages. But I don't want all that. So I think it's important to make sure that you find people who are on the same wavelength as you. All my intended parents have been in London and I'm up north. That was good for me. I didn't want somebody who lived in the next town or that I might keep bumping into all the time. I can visit as and when, and they can visit me when they feel like it. But we're quite distant. We can go months without speaking to each other.

What would be your advice about finding a surrogate?
I would always say take your time. A lot of people seem to be going more independent now and avoiding the agencies, and there's so much going wrong because

surrogates are matching with somebody that they've met like a week before. You wouldn't have a child with someone under normal circumstances within a week and then expect it all to go well. As a surrogate, I think if things sound too good to be true – if somebody's agreeing with absolutely everything you're saying – I'd be wary of that. There are a lot of people who are let down, especially by the relationship that's promised after the baby's born.

What advice would you give to the parents in terms of things that they can do to make their surrogate feel like this is a good experience for them?

Every surrogate is different. You've got some that are really excited that they're getting sent gifts every week and they're being thought about, and then others who are just happy to meet up for a brew. Find out about the personality of your surrogate and remember there is always somebody out there for you. So don't be tempted to just go with the first person that offers to help. The surrogacy community is quite small, and there are sub-groups where they do discuss intended parents and they will promote couples that they think seem really nice, but they will also blacklist people if they do come across as a bit fake.

How have you found negotiating the legal aspect of surrogacy?

Well, the surrogacy contract that you write while you're pregnant is more of a guideline and it's not legally enforced. So basically if anything goes wrong, you've got that to show as a statement of intention, but it doesn't actually have any legal standing. Then afterwards, you've got the parental order, and that varies. If you're married, then the surrogate's husband has to go on the birth certificate. It doesn't make it any more difficult for the parents to apply for a parental order, but it still just seems a bit weird, really. I'm not married, so immediately it made life a lot easier.

LEGAL EAGLE:
UK Law and Surrogacy

UK law supports same-sex parents conceiving through surrogacy in the same way it does different-sex couples. There are different types of surrogacy, and they are outlined here:

Gestational Surrogacy

You create embryos with eggs from a donor and sperm from one of you, which are then transferred to your surrogate (who is therefore not the biological mother). Many UK fertility clinics offer egg donation treatment and can match you with a suitable egg donor; however they are not allowed to match you with a surrogate, who you will have to find yourselves. If one or both of you is transgender, you may be able to use any eggs you have in storage instead of your sperm.

Traditional Surrogacy

Your surrogate donates her egg to you as well as carrying your child, and so is the biological mother of your child. She might conceive through IVF or IUI (intrauterine insemination) with your sperm at a clinic or at home.

Surrogacy in the UK

Surrogacy is legal in the UK. However, the law prohibits third parties arranging surrogacy for profit and outlaws advertising for surrogates, so finding a surrogate can be challenging. Once you have found a surrogate, any agreement you enter into is unenforceable under UK law (although arrangements rarely go wrong in practice).

International Surrogacy

Increasing numbers of UK parents conceive through international surrogacy arrangements, particularly in the USA where in many states both fathers can be named on the birth certificate, and in Canada. India was previously a common destination, but legal changes in India mean this is no longer possible; Thailand, one of the newer destinations which emerged to replace it, has now also been shut down, as have Mexico, Nepal and Cambodia. Take care if you are offered surrogacy services involving these countries as it may be illegal.

UK law does not automatically recognize your status as the parents even if you are named on a foreign birth certificate or court order. You need to check what nationality status your child has at birth (particularly if you are in a multi-national relationship), and what you need to do to bring your child home. Your choices about who is the biological father and where you conceive might be significant, so careful planning is sensible.

Legal Parenthood and Parental Orders

Your surrogate is your child's legal mother under UK law, regardless of where in the world your child is born. Who is treated as your child's father is complicated, and depends on the circumstances, including biology, your surrogate's relationship status and where conception takes place. The solution under UK law is a parental order, which reassigns parenthood fully and permanently to you both, and extinguishes the legal status and responsibilities of your surrogate (and her husband or wife). It also leads to the re-issue of your child's birth certificate (or the issue of a first British birth certificate if your child is born abroad) naming you both as the parents. Same-sex parents have been able to apply for a parental order since 6 April 2010.

Alex and Freddy, who worked with a Canadian surrogate, told us that, 'We had a legally enforceable contract, protecting both our rights and our surrogate's under Canadian (Alberta) law, as well as being legally recognized as parents on his Canadian birth certificate. This gave us a major sense of security. We see the UK parental order as a formality to recognize what has already been agreed under Canadian law.' As well as the legal benefits, it was the fact that surrogacy was so established as a process in Canada that meant the couple chose to do international surrogacy. Alex says:

Our egg donor agency, IVF clinic, local lawyers and even the ultrasound clinics had decades of experience of working with LGBTQ+ couples and surrogacy as a process. We felt properly welcome at all times. One particularly nice moment was at the hospital where L was born, the team kept referring to a folder of policies on surrogacy to make sure they were conducting everything in the correct way for our situation (for example what to do with L's ankle tags as his surrogate would be discharged before he was). These things may sound small, but as nervous first time parents, it meant a lot to us and we do not feel the UK is yet at the same level of broad acceptance and knowledge of surrogacy compared to Canada and the United States.

INSIGHT:
Surrogacy Support

Michael Johnson-Ellis (he/him) is co-founder with his husband Wes of My Surrogacy Journey, a non-profit surrogacy organization designed to offer plenty of professional, emotional and clinical support to intended parents, surrogates and known egg donors through every aspect of a surrogacy journey.

What's the main reason that surrogacy might feel like the right route to parenthood for someone?
Most gay men who first approach surrogacy do so because of wanting a genetic link to their child. Quite often when the journey has completed, and usually when you've had more than one child, you definitely understand that the genetics are less important. But for some people, adoption is never on their radar and surrogacy has always been their go-to way to build a family.

For trans and non-binary people, surrogacy might be an option for quite varied reasons, but one might be that it could be triggering to carry a child. If a trans man has a good egg reserve, then they can still donate those eggs to be part of the journey. And if a trans or non-binary person wants to use their own sperm, they may also need a surrogate in that instance.

What kind of anxieties and biases or internalized prejudices do some people come to surrogacy with?

For a lot of heterosexual people, when they first arrive at surrogacy it's usually coming from a place of loss, and therefore surrogacy was never how they wanted to build their family. So there tends to be a lot of grief and counselling required. But this isn't the case with gay couples – it starts from a happier place.

There's often confusion or concern around 'What if the surrogate wants to keep my baby? I always like to flip that and inform people that the surrogate has a very similar anxiety, and that's 'What if the intended parents don't want this baby anymore?' It's important to show both sides of that. Another of the big fears at the start of the process can be: 'What if I never find a surrogate?' Along with 'How much is this going to cost?' and 'How long is this journey going to take?' Surrogacy really requires a lot of patience. And if you're working with an organization then you'll be putting a lot of trust in them too, because they will essentially be helping manage that process.

So how much does surrogacy cost?

It varies depending on whether you do traditional surrogacy or gestational surrogacy. The difference between the two is traditional surrogacy is when the surrogate uses her own eggs. And you usually conceive by home insemination. So therefore you negate IVF, which is the costly part. If you're using a gestational surrogate, usually then you have IVF to create the embryos you transfer into that particular surrogate.

At the time of publication, in the UK, you cannot pay a surrogate, but you do pay her expenses, and these may vary from zero to £25,000, with the average being around about £12,000 to £15,000. So if you're doing traditional surrogacy, you'll just have that one element. If you are doing gestational surrogacy, then depending on if you're creating two sets of embryos with two separate sperm, then that will obviously impact the cost too. For IVF with donor eggs, you are looking at anything between £16,000 to £20,000 for that element. And then a further, let's say, £15,000 for your surrogate's expenses. And if you're working with an organization, there's their management fees as well. Then you'll want to hire a lawyer, so allocate anything between £1,000 and £3,500 for that.

How do you find a surrogate?

You can go down one of two routes to match. There are organizations such as Brilliant Beginnings or my own, My Surrogacy Journey, that can help you meet or match with a surrogate. Or there is an organization called SurrogacyUK. They don't match, but facilitate regular meetings around the UK; these are mainly attended by other intended parents. Then there is the independent space, and that predominantly sits on Facebook. My advice regarding the latter is to seek out well known groups and safe spaces – choose those Facebook groups really, really carefully.

We always recommend that you spend at least twelve weeks getting to know your surrogate and understanding whether you are all on the same page with every aspect, particularly your legal positioning and your parental responsibility. You want to ensure that when the time comes to send your parental order to the family courts that it's going to be done without any issues from the surrogate or her spouse.

How should you decide whose sperm to use? Is it possible to use both?

This is often a question that can cause difficulty as the journey begins, because what you don't want is any resentment and you definitely both want to agree about who goes first. You can't mix sperm, but what you can do is both still create embryos and then choose to implant the best ones. We recommend that when your eggs are retrieved, if you do have the option to split that egg retrieval and then fertilize 50 per cent with one intended father and the other 50 per cent with the other; that then hopefully ensures that you have enough embryos, meaning that all your future children will have a genetic link. In the UK, you can only transfer one embryo from one genetic father. You can't mix those embryos or do a double embryo transfer, with two separate embryos from each father.

What kind of support can you offer your surrogate once she's pregnant?

Be aware of what stage your pregnancy is at by using a really good pregnancy tracking app and just understand how she may be feeling as the weeks go by. It's also really good for your baby to be hearing your voices, so sending voice notes that your surrogate can play with special adapted earbuds to your baby is a good plan. And obviously meet regularly, check on how she's doing, support her by attending any appointments that she's happy for you to attend. And post birth and during recovery it's important to still offer your support, even if the 'contract' has ended. Your surrogate can sometimes be left feeling quite isolated and alone. So still keep in touch with your surrogate in that fourth trimester, because it is a crucial part for them and their body as they're healing after pregnancy.

What should your role be at the birth?

You'll need to have had a few conversations in advance about this so you can prepare a plan together and discuss whether they would prefer a vaginal birth or an abdominal birth. Is your surrogate prepared to pump and offer colostrum for the baby's first feed?

You'll need to agree whether you'll be present at the birth, as the surrogate may want their partner or someone else with them. Things to consider are: Where will you be when your baby is born? Will you have your own room? Has the hospital factored that in? Have you seen the hospital's surrogacy policy and does it meet the national guidelines that were updated in 2019?

You are a parent and, like any new parent, you ideally want to see your baby being born, but that's not always possible. Your role thereafter is to be there immediately for any skin-on-skin contact.

MEET . . .
V and B (both he/him)

V and B are UK-based dads via surrogacy.

We had a calm and enriching experience with surrogacy. Our surrogate was awesome. J is such an easy-going human being that we were able to discuss all the options and possible eventualities openly with her and her partner. We talked about everything up front and never felt awkward about any of the questions.

I had anxieties of 'she is going to keep the baby' or 'will she eat healthy while pregnant?'. These anxieties were so far from the truth; J was amazing throughout the process! All of these were stupid for us but I'm sure are valid in other cases. I had friends who have been through the process and not had as great an experience.

Then came the birth! It was a snowy day in Calgary. We just changed all of our flights and rushed to get to Canada from the UK within twenty-four hours. We arrived at the airport not knowing whether our visas would be accepted in time after last-minute flight changes. B burst into tears at the check-in desk after receiving his visa moments after saying goodbye to V, assuming that he was going to be the only one allowed to travel. We landed and twenty-four hours later, after doing a final scan with our surrogate, J was being induced! We knew baby D was going to be over four weeks early at that point and so would need to go into the neonatal care unit. While J was being induced we got a few hours' sleep in the local motel by the hospital. Then the phone call came, 4 a.m.! J was in labour!

We rushed to the hospital and only four hours later the OB broke her waters and she gave birth in eight minutes. It all happened so fast, V had only just got back from extending the car parking. The birth was such an exciting moment, but nothing went according to our birthing plan – we were meant to be at home in a birthing pool. D was immediately put on J's chest as normal with a birth, when he was supposed to have been passed straight to us, but in that moment we didn't really mind. We were just so happy to have a wonderful baby. From that moment on we rushed into the NICU and D's first feed was traumatic. D wasn't able to coordinate sucking, swallowing and breathing and ended up choking and going blue in the first feed. Both V and I were holding hands, tears in our eyes, worried that we were going to lose D. We were reassured that this was very normal, but it was still very distressing when all of the staff gathered around D's bed ready for resuscitation. The first time we were able to hold D was later that day when we both did skin-to-skin. It was such a magical moment.

It was something that had taken years of planning, saving, hard work and fostering a very close relationship with our surrogate. But in that moment, all of the effort was more than worthwhile. We knew we would love D forever.

There's no denying that surrogacy can be one of the most expensive routes to parenthood for LGBTQ+ people. And money is far from the only hurdle that might be encountered if pursuing this route. As with all of our options for starting a family, a huge number of conversations and a really deep interrogation of our motivations is necessary at the start, and these complex discussions continue throughout the journey. Finding a surrogate and then building a relationship with her is not necessarily easy. But with sensitivity, understanding and an open heart and mind, it can be one of the most beautiful and deep friendships life has to offer.

Talking Points

▶ If you were to consider surrogacy, how would you decide whose sperm to use?

▶ What would you be looking for from an egg donor?

▶ Are you prepared to welcome a surrogate into your family?

▶ What kind of contact would you be happy for them to have with you and your child after the pregnancy?

IS FOR TRANS

Until 2013, trans people in Sweden had to undergo sterilization before they would be allowed gender-confirming surgery. This barbaric practice has thankfully since been outlawed (although is still legal elsewhere in the world), but to think that even one of the most progressive and ostensibly queer-friendly countries in the world (er, hello, ABBA) could have condoned it for so long gives a shocking insight into how 'normal' it is for trans people to be ostracized from parenthood.

In terms of societal acceptance and support, trans parents and parents-to-be are probably where gay and lesbians were in the 1980s – seen as problematic, a threat, and unworthy. It's important that as we celebrate our wins as gay, bi and lesbian people, we acknowledge that until our trans friends are treated fairly, particularly when it comes to healthcare and family planning, there is still a long way for us to go. And for us to go together.

When we spoke to Dr Sam Hall, a trans man and father who works as a GP in Brighton and specializes in trans healthcare, he said, 'The pressures are from all angles for trans people to not even think about having a baby, let alone try. There are so many deep and unpleasant nuances around trans people having children. It's only as trans rights have become a bit more mainstream, and we've become more vocal, that people are coming out of the shadows and losing their shame and fear to talk about their lives.'

And thank goodness they are. We love following trans couple Jake and Hannah Graf, who beautifully documented the birth of their first child via surrogacy (during the pandemic) in a show called *Our Baby: A Modern Miracle*. And someone we have a huge amount of respect for is single dad Freddy McConnell, who has been campaigning to be legally recognized as his children's father. (Find out more about Freddy on pages 121 and 191.) Freddy also made a must-watch documentary called *Seahorse* about giving birth (in the UK if a trans man gives birth he is automatically recorded as 'mother' on the birth certificate, even if he has legally changed his gender). There are more and more high-profile trans people proving that becoming a parent is not just possible, but joyful.

Amid all of the transphobia permeating politics and the media, it could be easy to think of the 'transgender issue' (as Shon Faye's book of the same name so brilliantly satirizes[26]), as something simply to debate, rather than a lived experience. It's why it's so important to follow trans and non-binary parents on social media or engage with their stories however you can, because alongside the campaigning and the calling-out of injustices and sharing of resources, it allows us an insight into the reality of day-to-day life with kids. And we don't know about you, but we are here for all the cute kid content you can throw at us! Because being a trans parent is mainly just about being a parent (while having to deal with a ton of extra shit alongside the regular dirty nappies).

Parenting: It's a Privilege

It's really no surprise that because of the stifling gender binary we have constructed, many people are driven to transitioning as a last resort – a way to survive in the cishet hegemony. According to a 2018 Stonewall report[27] (unfortunately at the time of writing there are no more up-to-date statistics available), it was found that almost half of the people who identified as transgender (46 per cent) had thought about taking their own life in the past year; 60 per cent thought their life was not worth living; and 12 per cent had made a suicide attempt. In addition, the survey found that 41 per cent of non-binary people and 35 per cent of transgender people had self-harmed in the past year. Furthermore, 67 per cent of transgender people and 70 per cent of non-binary people had experienced depression in the past year.

The need to preserve one's own life of course takes precedence over the desire to have children, and these sobering statistics remind us of what a privilege it is to be able to envision a future and a family and strive for it in a way that feels happy and safe and supported. This is what everyone deserves, but at the moment it's far from everyone's reality.

Same But Different

Just like there is no single homogenized gay parenting experience, within the trans community, routes to parenthood are many and varied. A young trans woman contemplating storing sperm pre-transition to allow her the possibility of becoming a biological parent one day is in a very different position to a trans woman with teenage kids who has come out and begun a transition in her fifties. Some trans men want to give birth; others might have stored their eggs and started a family with the help of a surrogate or partner. All trans people have the potential to be approved as adopters or foster carers.

Dr Hall told us that in his work at a gender clinic, he's seeing people who don't regret their transition, 'but do regret that they didn't have children or weren't given the opportunity to find a way'.

Coming Out as Trans When You Have Kids

As we discuss elsewhere in this book, taking care of tiny people, even as they get bigger and bigger and start throwing us serious shade, involves putting ourselves second. For this reason, many people wait until their children are fully grown before giving themselves permission to explore their identity and potentially come out as trans or non-binary. We've spoken to people whose partnerships and relationships with their kids have continued to thrive after coming out, and some people who had to make a horrible choice between their family and their own ability to keep existing in this world. Everyone we spoke to cited honesty, communication, love and understanding as the key ingredients for navigating a parent's transition as a family.

MEET . . .
Dr Sam Hall (he/him)

Sam, pre-transition, was married to a man and gave birth to three children.

My transition was the most extraordinary moment of self-liberation I could have possibly taken. It was immense. It ruined my life. Nearly ruined my career, ruined a lot of relationships. But for me personally, it was absolutely the best thing I could have done. And my kids are starting to see that now ten years later.

I married my ex-husband because he was a nice guy and a Catholic and that was important to my parents. But it wasn't a good marriage. I always wanted kids and so this felt like the best way to fulfil that dream at the time. I was thirty-five, working as a consultant at a hospital and I had three kids. And then my world just fell apart once I accepted I was trans. It hit like a volcano. At first I told him [my husband] I was in love with a woman and he was sort of okay with that – we stayed together. Then I realized, this isn't gay, this is something much worse, bigger or harder to deal with.

When I separated from their dad, my kids were four, seven and nine years old. I've been on my own with them since then.

Before my social transition, when I changed my name on my passport and just went for it, I was presenting as a butch dyke, and six years earlier I had long hair and was trying to be uber feminine. The change for the kids was really gradual. So they would've just absorbed that, like kids absorb everything. The big thing was really then changing my name and taking male pronouns – that was crossing the divide. And they all took it differently. But none of them was distressed. I remember my son, who was about seven at the time, walking up the hill from school, with me and his friend one day. And I overheard him say to his mate, 'My mum's changed his name to Sam because he's a bloke.' And I just thought, oh, that's perfect.

There was a time when my kids were like, 'Do you want us to call you Dad?' And I said, 'You've got one of those. That's not really fair.' For a long time, actually still now, they call me by my first name or initials and there were all sorts of combinations: 'Sam Jam', 'Sammy Jammy', 'Daddy penguin'.

There were just some beautiful moments of break-throughs in understanding. I remember when my eldest was about twelve and we were camping. She was in the shower and I was standing outside the shower, waiting for her to get out, holding her towel and stuff.

And she suddenly shouts: 'Men can have babies because you did!' That was her seeing the truth of a trans nature, which is – I haven't become a man. I'm just becoming who I always was.

Now, my kids are in their late teens and early twenties. They each talk about their family in a different way. And dependent on context. At my daughter's graduation she introduced me and her bio father as her dads. She tends to say that and then it's like, 'End of. I'm not gonna explain anything. I don't owe you an explanation.' But her closest friends know I'm trans and that I gave birth to her. My eldest was nine or ten when I transitioned so she really remembers it and was able to observe the breakdown of gender and I think she's felt it in herself. She doesn't identify as trans or non-binary, but she lives outside of gender.

I had my children before I transitioned, and I think what I loved most about the experience was breast-feeding. Absolutely loved it. It was just a monumental experience. I felt really Zen and really connected to my animal self. I was feeding this creature that kept growing through nothing else than what my body created. I just found that extraordinary. Despite my dysphoria, I fully appreciated what my machine could do. And I'm so glad I did it. When I see trans guys now most of them will not have made it to pregnancy with their breasts intact. If you need a masculine chest and you have top surgery, it is totally liberating. I've never met a single person who's regretted it, but I can see that if you go through pregnancy and childbirth, you might be thinking, I wish I could breastfeed my baby. More and more research is being done into chest feeding and inducing lactation so there may still be a way if you have had top surgery that you can look into [see Insight: Fertility in Trans Men and Trans Women, page 304].

If you let trans doctors like me look after trans kids, we can [save] their organs and save their bodies. For example, we can give drugs to stop breast development but allow them to develop later, when they need to, if you want. The fact is, trans people need choices.

Preserving Your Fertility Before a Medical Transition

Speaking to Dr Sam about his work with young trans people, he stressed the difficulty of asking teenagers to consider that they may want biological children one day when there are so many more immediately pressing issues for them. He told us, 'Their potential for biological parenthood is really poor if they need to transition in their teens, because they won't have sexually developed enough to make adequate sperm. So there is an issue there, and I do try to encourage the young people who I look after to really preserve their bodies as best they can, and to think about coming off hormones, to see if they can produce gametes for their own sake in the future. When they're seventeen, they're absolutely sure they need the hormones – and they're right, they do. But they also recognize that they don't know how they're going to feel in twenty years. And I'm like,

'Okay. So right now we have to face what's in front of us, and your future fertility, which you're not particularly worried about because what's right in front of you is insurmountable unless we ease the pain of your dysphoria.'

INSIGHT:
Fertility in Trans Men and Trans Women

Within the trans community there is frustration that men are told repeatedly that hormone treatments will over time make them infertile. There is not enough evidence to prove this, and there are lots of examples of men who have stopped taking testosterone and have had no problem becoming pregnant. There are also cases of accidental pregnancy because of the misinformation around fertility and hormone treatments. It's hard to find any data on the fertility of transgender women (historically and consistently this demographic has been woefully overlooked in healthcare and, well, everywhere thanks to the double whammy of misogyny and transmisogyny), so no one really knows the impacts of oestrogen and androgen-blockers on their reproductive systems.

The HFEA provides this advice:
If you think you would like biological children at some point and you haven't started medical treatment or had surgery, you may wish to preserve your fertility by having your sperm, eggs or gametes frozen and stored for later use in fertility treatment.

The law now permits you to store eggs, sperm or embryos for use in treatment for any period up to a maximum of fifty-five years.

Depending on your situation, you, your partner or a surrogate may undergo fertility treatment (such as IVF) using your stored sperm, eggs or embryos.

Egg freezing involves taking fertility drugs to stimulate your ovaries and then collecting the eggs by a surgical procedure while you're sedated. [Lotte talks about her experience of this on page 150.]

Sperm freezing involves masturbating or undergoing vibratory stimulation to produce a sperm sample, which is then frozen and stored. If you do not feel comfortable producing sperm in this way, it is possible to extract the sperm in different ways (such as through surgical sperm extraction), although these involve more invasive surgical procedures.

Having genital reconstructive surgery will prevent you from having biological children without the use of a surrogate or interventional fertility treatments.

If you've already started hormone therapy or you're taking puberty-supressing medication, you should speak to a fertility specialist. They will probably recommend that you stop taking your medication to increase your chance of having a family through assisted family treatment. This means your ovaries may start to ovulate again or your body may start producing sperm, generally over a few months.

The HFEA points out that 'Some trans and non-binary people find it distressing to come off their hormone therapy and may consider other options for having a family, such as using donated sperm or eggs in treatment or adoption.' Which is true. But we would like to add that many trans people feel the temporary adjustment to their hormones and potential for body dysphoria is worth it for a chance to carry or create a biological child.

MEET . . .
Dee Humphries (she/her) and her ex-partner Alexandra (she/her)

Dee and Alex, whom we speak to more in 'X is for Ex-Partners, Divorce, Separation and Step Parents' (see page 347), co-parent a five-year-old. Dee began her transition when her child was six months old.

Dee: Our son has always known that some families have two mums, two dads, a mum and a dad and so on. We've always read him books about that. In regards to transgender, I don't think he understands fully what that means but he doesn't feel uncomfortable about it. Soon, it's going to feel important for me to talk to my kid about it in terms of oppression, which is where we are at the moment with the discourse. I'll also need to think about how I represent the trans experience positively. Questions come up, but it's very calm and he is unfazed by it. We have told him that I was a boy and I'm not a boy anymore. He doesn't seem that interested at all – he just wants the love, silliness and security.

Alexandra: I say we're a two-mum family now even though Dee uses the word parent for herself more often. Up until five years ago, I was sailing through life as a cishet woman. Now if we go out to eat we'll seek out places that are queer-friendly and where we know the loo situation, and I'm hyper attuned to people's reactions or mutterings about us. Really, it has illustrated all my past privilege and assumptions and has opened my eyes. I realized the degree to which I'd been coasting. It was like I had a secret window into a world that I wasn't being asked to necessarily live in, but I was adjacent to it.

Dee: I had a lot of privilege before transitioning too, unhappiness with myself and dysphoria aside. The way I moved through the world was entirely different. So it was new and we were learning together.

Transitioning has made me a happier and more confident parent, and I feel I am able to be a parent now which I didn't before. I think that's why I felt I needed to transition when our son was born. The timing was critical. Because I knew, I can't be a parent as I am. Parenting is so gendered and it started to push those buttons again for me, so I was like 'Okay, hold on a minute. I need to recalibrate here. This isn't me.' We went through IVF. And a lot of the time it was like an out-of-body experience, literally.

Misinformation and Transphobia

Many trans people will arrive at their own, a partner's or surrogate's pregnancy with personal stories of being treated badly by healthcare professionals who may not have given them the support they needed. As an example, some young people are still waiting three years (or longer) to get their first appointment with a gender identity clinic. The NHS has not historically made it easy for trans people to access healthcare. So walking into a GP's or midwife's office for the first time comes with baggage. The important thing to remember is that *everyone has the right to individualized and humanizing care* as part of the Nursing and Midwifery Code of Conduct. Because there is so little data on the trans experience and fertility, people may be presented with information as fact when the reality is that further research is necessary.

Here are some of the things the Queer Birth Club[28] (an invaluable resource!) suggests you may want to know:

- A lactation 2022 study called Drugs and Lactation states that 'breastfed infants appear not to be adversely affected by transgender paternal testosterone therapy'.[29]
- It may still be possible to lactate after top surgery depending on the type of surgery you had.[30]

There's so much more we could say in this chapter, from more details on preserving fertility, inducing lactation and talking to children about what it means to be trans, but we can hear our editors shouting WORD COUNT at us, so we'd better let Dr Sam have the last word:

> The number of times I've sat with my therapist and said, 'Oh God, this has happened with one of my kids and it's my fault for being trans.' And without fail my therapist will say, 'Hey, Sam, these are just normal parenting problems.'
>
> If you are trans, that's just an aspect of who you are. It doesn't stop you from being a parent. It doesn't stop you from being a good parent. It doesn't stop you from being a shitty parent either. It doesn't mean that you should or could be denied parenting. So if you want children, find a way to have them and, you know, it's the biggest ride of your life.
>
> It's horrendous and joyous all at the same time. But . . . the job of parenting – that is a universal one that we all need to learn, and nobody should be excluded.

Talking Points

▶ During your transition have you explored the options available to you to parent in the future?

▶ Would you consider freezing your eggs or sperm for potential future use?

▶ Do you follow enough trans parents on social media?

▶ How can you be a better trans ally?

▶ Try to identify some of the language you use around parenting and pregnancy that might be unintentionally excluding to trans people.

U

IS FOR UNDERSTANDING
(. . . OR LACK THEREOF)

It's unlikely you'll have found this book on the shelves of a bookshop in Bulgaria, Russia or Poland. Why? Because the 'promotion' of families like ours is illegal. The reality that outside of our own echo chamber people do still have a problem with LGBTQ+ parenting never stops being sad and shocking. A few years ago a bookshop in Bulgaria was fined £6,000 for stocking a picture book for children about a little girl with two dads. Today in certain US states what is known as the Don't Say Gay bill is prohibiting schools from including LGBTQ+ people in discussions about families or relationships. The Republican authors of the Parental Rights in Education bill, to use its proper name, have forbidden any 'instruction' on sexual orientation or gender identity in kindergarten through to third grade, as well as any instruction characterized as 'inappropriate'. The deliberately vague wording of this means the bill could be used to suppress and intimidate anyone even thinking about acknowledging the existence of the LGBTQ+ community in public schools. How are we back here, battling for our right to simply *be* the people and the families we are proud to be?

MEET . . .

Dr Matt Cook, a professor of modern history at Birkbeck University

Matt gives us some context about how far the fight for LGBTQ+ equality has come over the past century and why our rights, particularly as parents, continue to be challenged. He's also a gay dad – first co-parenting with his boyfriend and a lesbian couple and twenty years later via adoption with his new partner.

Historically, kids have always been brought up in unconventional configurations. If we expand our definition of queer beyond LGBTQ, then a queer family could be anything other than the mum, dad, two kids norm. There were as many single-parent families in the 1890s as there are today – though in that era it was more often because of death than divorce or separation. The idea of eccentric family relationships and family forms is pretty long-standing. One of the case studies I've come across from the 1920s was a queer guy who lived with his male working-class lover and his wife and their kids. Queer men and queer women have been parents for a very long time, including those that were within apparently conventional marriages. So the idea of a queer person being a parent is not a new one. It's just articulated and thought about in new and different ways. And it's more on the social cultural agenda.

When I had my two kids in the late 1990s, it felt very new. It felt like the idea of being gay and being a dad were not compatible identities. I co-parent my two eldest children with a lesbian couple and my ex-boyfriend and more recently I have an adopted child with my current partner. When adoption legislation changed to allow same-sex couples to adopt in 2002, it was at least as important and significant as the civil partnership act. It completely shifted the possibilities for parenting

In a way, the most important legal milestone for queer parents was the introduction of Section 28. And I say that because obviously it was a negative piece of legislation, but it made the idea of lesbian and gay families visible for the first time. I don't think people had realized that queer people had families and made families and had been doing so for quite some time. That moment was very important as it also galvanized gays and lesbians to come together in campaigning. It really mobilized the debate about parenting.

What became very apparent in the 1970s and 80s, is that though lesbians might be able to divorce their husbands more easily following divorce law reform in the 60s, they were likely to lose custody of their children. So you see how the law changes, but actually the culture of implementation and the surrounding rhetoric and ideas affect the way the law works and is put into force.

In one case from 1978, a gay man was disputing his former wife's new partner becoming the adopted dad of his kids. That would've necessitated the gay guy disclaiming parental responsibility, and he refused to do that. It went through the courts and he was forced to in the end and on the basis that the judge said that he, as a gay man, had nothing to offer his child now or in the future. The child was explicitly forbidden from going to his biological father's house as there was a quite entrenched assumption that even the space gay men occupied was corrupting.

In the 1980s and into the 90s, queer men and women were losing custody of their kids, but it was seen to be the obvious and right thing to do.

A particular model of family is very entrenched and can inform the way people think about their own suitability to adopt or judge the suitability of others. Some potential adopters feel cautious about disclosing their open relationships for fear it might prejudice their case.

When I first told my mum that my partner and I were having a child and co-parenting with our lesbian friends, her immediate response to there being four parents was, 'Well, that was how I was brought up.' She was raised in the late 1930s and 40s by her parents, but also grandparents and uncles and aunts and so on. She always believed you needed more than two people to raise a child. So her model of family was oddly accommodating of ideas of queer parenting, while the more stereotypical model of two parents, two kids didn't fit with what we were doing. From that perspective it seemed odd and controversial.

How does a big shift in societal attitudes happen?

Well, I think the first thing to say is that change is uneven. Many of those homophobic ideas are still in full swing. According to a 2020 IPSOS survey, a quarter of the almost 3,000 people interviewed believe LGBTQ+ rights have 'gone as far as they should'. There's a substantial chunk of the population that think homosexuality is wrong and there's a substantial chunk beyond that, probably more people, that think that parenting among queer people isn't appropriate.

Is now the best time in history to be gay?

The culture war that is being mobilized against trans people now, and the way you can see the government using it, is so reminiscent of the late 80s and the way in which single mothers and gay men and lesbians were seen to be the enemies of common sense and society. And that is what's happening again. So I suppose there's that slightly depressing sense of little progress.

When I look back to my first experience of parenting, I think I had a much tighter sense of queer community and a much tighter sense of bringing up my children with their mums and my former partner in a queer network. And I think those networks have dissipated over the last ten, fifteen years, partly because of bars closing, partly because of apps and the internet and partly because of the Equalities Act. Previously there was more to bond you to each other because there was some sense of a common enemy or fight. That sense of solidarity doesn't exist for me in quite the same way anymore – probably because I'm older and also because attitudes and cultures have changed.

How Gay-Friendly is the UK?

In 2022 the UK suffered a significant drop in ranking on the IGLA's list of the most LGBTQ+-friendly countries in Europe, going from tenth to fourteenth place[31] as evidence was brought forward that the Equality and Human Rights Commission is not protecting on the grounds of sexual orientation and gender identity. This comes at a time of widespread political and media anti-trans sentiment, while the British government is – at the time of writing – not moving on long-promised reforms on gender recognition and banning so-called 'conversion therapy' for all.

But, on the whole, we feel very lucky to live in a country that supports our families and offers us legal protections.

Queer Parenting Around the World

I find it hard to reconcile my own positive personal experience of being queer and raising a child with some of the harrowing accounts of living in less progressive countries. It's so important to engage with the experiences of our wider LGBTQ+ community across the world; until we are *all* equal, none of us is equal. It's an absolute privilege to have been able to create a little sanctuary full of fabulous queer people and supportive allies, to have my daughter at a school that champions LGBTQ+ rights and to feel a level of safety and comfort in my day-to-day life. I know this isn't the case for everyone. I wanted to get a sense of what life is like for a queer family who live in a country where culturally and legally it's harder to thrive, so I talked to Sandeep in Hong Kong.

MEET . . .
Sandeep (she/her)

Sandeep and her wife live in Hong Kong. They both fell pregnant at the same time via donor conception and gave birth on the same day. Their marriage is not legally recognized in Hong Kong.

How were you treated as a couple when you explained your relationship to doctors during the pregnancy?

We didn't get a chance to explain our situation to a doctor in the public healthcare system due to appointment scheduling. We didn't explain our family to the nurses who did our check-ups in the public hospital because I was a little nervous of what they would say if they knew our 'trying to conceive' story. Our marriage is not legal here, nor is it possible for us to get fertility treatment here, so I was anxious of what to tell them. We are in a very fortunate situation that we were able to get pregnant via services and facilities in London, but I can only imagine how hard it must be for a local same-sex Hong Kong couple to try to get pregnant here.

Once we left the public system and went to the private sector, our doctor there was very understanding. She was familiar with the different ways people can get pregnant. I felt she just treated us the same as any other person who would've walked into her room.

Are you able to be 'out' as your children's parents in day-to-day life?

Yes and no. We share what we want to share with others. We know we are in a highly privileged position to be able to disclose what we want when we want. Overall, I am happy with how much I am 'out' as a parent in my children's lives. Also, the language barrier makes it difficult for people to understand that we are two mums. Even if I want them to know that both my wife and I are parents to our sons, if English isn't their first language they won't know. Maybe here I need to brush up on my Cantonese and have that in my toolbox to use when explaining.

What's the most challenging aspect of being a queer family in Hong Kong?

The lack of normality around our family. So, when we explain to people our family unit, some are a little confused. Maybe one-fifth of people would understand, ask questions and be interested. Two-fifths may understand but may not know what to ask or even how to respond because it isn't something they are familiar with, and the ones who don't understand are not rude or impolite to us, it kind of just goes over their head.

The Legacy of Prejudice

The legacy of prejudice is something that most LGBTQ+ people carry to a greater or lesser extent. However wonderful our own life is now, the knowledge that if we were living in a different time – or even the same time but in a different place – we may have been subjected to horrific discrimination, is a psychological burden. Add to this our own personal experiences of bullying and homophobia, even if we've only experienced the kind of microaggressions we explore in a later chapter on awful questions we've been asked (see page 334), and there's no denying that trauma runs deep.

Dr Julia Samuel is an eminent psychotherapist. In her book *Every Family Has a Story*[32] she explores how we inherit love and loss and the main takeaway is that when pain isn't dealt with, avoidance is then passed down to the next generation and the next until someone is prepared to feel the pain. Often the coping mechanisms that people develop do them and subsequent generations much greater harm than the trauma itself, she suggests. I mention this as a way of stressing the importance of understanding ourselves and what we have overcome (or may still be in the process of overcoming). Having therapy has without a doubt been one of the most important and positive acts of self-care in my life and I'm convinced I am a happier parent for it. Those who adopt or foster are forced to confront themselves and their relationships with therapy in order to be approved as potential parents. Wouldn't it be brilliant if the same applied for everyone considering having children?

I don't even think it needs to be an expensive session with a therapist: understanding ourselves better in order to address the many factors that influence how we parent and what we may be passing on to our children is something that can equally be done over a cup of tea with a friend. Talking, sharing experiences, writing, reading, thinking – these things are all free but their impact is invaluable.

Because once we come to know, and like, ourselves, we become more resilient and able to deal with the irrational demands and wild emotions of a child. We have also created a sturdy base for ourselves and our family from which to confront other people's lack of understanding. Whether it's a government or a great aunt with an unwanted opinion – we should try to face prejudice with the strength and compassion of proud individuals who are secure in the love that surrounds us.

Understanding why someone is bigoted or homophobic, understanding what unhappiness someone faced in their own family life to have a problem with yours, and understanding that hurt people hurt people is a hugely generous response to prejudice, but ultimately it is one of self-preservation. Taking anger out of a situation means a confrontation takes less from you emotionally. We know it's not easy when you're put under pressure, but making the time to listen to someone with different views to your own, even when those views are negative and harmful, can be the surest way to change someone's mind. And if, in the end, these damaging opinions are too deeply ingrained to be challenged, meeting hatred with kindness can at the very least diminish its power.

Hopefully, with each generation of children born or brought into queer families, we erase a layer of inherited pain. And if we live somewhere that protects our human rights and grants us equality, then we can – and we will – flourish.

Talking Points

▶ Would you consider having therapy if you haven't already?

▶ How have you experienced the trauma of growing up queer in a heterosexual world?

▶ Do you think of yourself as resilient?

▶ Does understanding why you might react a certain way or where a particular feeling comes from make you a better parent?

▶ How can you confront prejudice while protecting yourself and your family?

IS FOR VACATIONS

 Excuse us if we go all American on you for a second (oh and hey y'all to our American readers!), as this chapter is all about holidays and the experience of heading abroad on 'vacay' as a queer family. After approximately five big trips away as a family, I can tell you that travelling with kids is no easy feat. I always thought *Home Alone* was so incredibly farfetched, yet it wasn't until we were running round the house like lunatics trying to get everything, and everyone, in the car at 5 a.m. that I suddenly felt I could relate to the McAllister family. While I'm 99.9999 per cent sure that we wouldn't leave an actual child at home, the reality of leaving something behind in among the chaos is a very real possibility! If I were to rewrite *Home Alone* with a queer family at its centre – which, let's be honest, wouldn't happen just yet as we are too busy trying to appear to be perfect parents to society to ever let a film be released with the essential plot focusing on queer parental neglect! – however, IF we were to rewrite *Home Alone* with a queer family, there would have to be a whole bunch of additional scenes added to the plot. Firstly, one parent would be seen frantically googling destinations to check they hadn't booked a family ticket to a country where being a gay family would mean the death penalty (fun fact: there are still eleven countries where it's not just illegal to be gay, but you could actually face the death penalty), as let's face it, that would be a bit of a holiday downer. Meanwhile, the other parent would be cross-checking lists for known homophobia, anti-LGBTQ+ discrimination laws (fun fact #2: seventy-one counties criminalize LGBTQ+ people) or anything else that might suddenly rear its ugly head in another country. The parents would then run out to the car bundling the children into their seats, frantically strapping them in before unstrapping them again so they can run back in and go for a wee before finally heading off. They check passports, snacks, activities for the plane, make sure the iPads are charged, double-check the time it takes to get to the airport, that the Calpol is packed, and that each child has their favourite cuddly toy. 'Do you have the adoption paperwork?' asks one parent of the other as the car finally gets switched on. The engine cuts out as the other dashes back into the house to grab said paperwork. 'Adoption paperwork?' I hear you ask.

When we first travelled with our children, we had not yet received their new passports. They did not yet have 'Oakley' as names on their passports. We were effectively two men travelling with two children that didn't seem (on paper) to be connected to us. Heading to America, we imagined all sorts of questions or potential issues aka 'Sir, are you trafficking these children?' Let's be honest, they ask you on your ESTA to confirm if you plan to commit genocide on your trip to Florida so this question wouldn't seem too unbelievable. We made sure we had a letter from the local authority where we had adopted our first two children, plus copies of their adoption order. When we travelled with our youngest son, who again didn't have Oakley at first on his passport, we again made sure we had all this paperwork. To date we've never been questioned or asked about our family situation but that doesn't change the fact that every time we head abroad, we have this sense of dread that we are going to be asked, and we would rather be prepared, even when the children all share our name. It's these things that add an extra element of stress and worry when travelling as an LGBTQ+ family. We shouldn't have to, but having that documentation with us makes us feel more secure and gives us one less thing to stress about . . . unless we leave it at home!

Choosing a Destination

Pre-kids, we never used to worry too much about where we travelled, although we obviously avoided heading out to the death penalty locations! As any queer traveller knows, there is a certain amount of caution you take when in a location that you don't feel 100 per cent comfortable in. I remember John and I travelling back from a holiday in Bali. Our connecting flight got delayed by twelve hours so they decided to put us up in a hotel in Malaysia, where it is a criminal offence to be a gay man, and twenty years' imprisonment with a spot of whipping is implemented. We smiled, nodded and complied as the receptionist told us they had a twin bedroom for us. We didn't correct them or even dare to ask for a double bed. I remember feeling sad as I lay in my single bed that night while John snored across the other side of the room. I snuck out of bed and snuggled into him, squeezing myself up to him. I feel fortunate that we've not yet had to experience anything like that while abroad as a family. Because it doesn't matter how much you plan, you could, like our Malaysia experience, find yourself in a situation beyond your control that leaves you feeling uncomfortable or even potentially in danger. We travelled to Cuba recently, and while we had checked the LGBTQ+ rights situation in the country, what we hadn't counted on was the fact that it's a very popular destination for Russians. Making it clear that I know that each individual Russian does not share Putin's viewpoint, as the country is not known for its pro-queer stance, it's safe to say that not every Russian tourist is wearing a #LoveIsLove badge. We experienced this in Cuba in an encounter that both shocked and slightly amused me. The kids and I left John sunbathing on the sand and headed to the BBQ area for lunch. We enjoyed a meal together and they were all in a great and light-hearted mood. Next to us, a group of Russian ladies sat eating their lunch. They kept smiling at us and waving at the kids. One turned to me and said, 'Oh, they are so cute! Lovely kids.' I felt a wave of pride and smiled back saying, 'Thank you.' Then the other lady said, 'You and your wife must be very proud. Where is their mum?' Oh lordy, here we go. Now sometimes I decide to just move on, ignore or skirt round questions like this. It makes life easier and eliminates any uncomfortable moments. Anything for an easy queer life, hey? This time, and the lunch-time drink may have helped, I decided to just be a bit more direct. 'Oh yes, my husband and I are very proud of them. They are great kids.' All three ladies just stared at me, and I'm not exaggerating when I say their mouths dropped open slightly and a look of disgust washed over their face. They then just blanked us completely and quickly got up from the table and marched off, leaving some of their food behind. So, let this be a lesson that it doesn't matter how hard you research the actual country you are going to, you can't do anything about the homophobes who might be making a trip there at the same time as you.

The Awkwardness Travels

Just because you are abroad doesn't mean you will get to escape semi-ignorant questions from strangers. Leon Wenham, a single gay dad from London, told us about the experience he had when he and his son were on a beach in Dubai:

We had seen this couple hanging around the pool and beach quite a bit and they had clearly seen me on my own with him. My son is a massive chatterbox, so while I was having my time doing some sun-worshipping, he started chatting to this couple. They were mid-chat and I was listening in when she suddenly asked him where his mum was. He told her he didn't have one, to which she then asked him, 'Aww, why not?' Who does that? Regardless of sexuality or how you've come into this world, it still baffles me that someone can just make a child potentially feel bad and push them to ask why they don't have a parent? I was so proud of him as he shut it down quickly but was really not expecting that as we lay relaxing in the sun!

Bola Ajayi-Walmsley shares her experience of travelling with her wife and their young son and her experience as a Black woman.

We recently went to Tenerife. It's very family-orientated which was nice, but people were giving us curious looks, we felt that. One woman even came up to us and asked if we were friends. It was done in a friendly way, and she turned out to be a single parent who said she gets people asking her all the time where the father is and she'd have to explain there isn't one. As a Black woman I feel I do stand out a lot more on certain holidays already.[33] When you are on your own it's one thing, but when I'm with a child and my family it feels a lot more exposing. I feel very protective, but I try and be as open and friendly as possible. The destination is obviously important too, especially as two women travelling. For example, we wouldn't go to anywhere where we would constantly feel on high alert, like Egypt or Dubai. We just wouldn't do that as a family.

MEET . . .

Sanjay (he/him) and Doug (he/him), known as 'The Travelling Gays'

Sanjay and Doug have built a huge following on social media after travelling the world and sharing their experience as an LGBTQ+ couple abroad, but in 2021 another member of the family came along: baby Arya. We chat to the guys about how life has changed for them since she arrived and how she has changed their approach to travel.

You have both been travelling and documenting your adventures for some time. Now you have a little person to join you. What are the main changes you've noticed in the way you travel?

There's a lot more planning involved! No more throwing everything into a suitcase the night before; we have to make sure we have everything that our daughter needs and think through all the little logistical things, like does the place we are staying at have a cot? Do we need to bring one? Have we packed all her food and milk? Do we have clothes for every eventuality? Can we take formula through security? Do we have enough nappies? There is so much more to think about!

What's the biggest challenge in travelling with a child? Was it a bit of a culture shock the first time?

As we did surrogacy in the USA, the first time we travelled with our daughter was on a flight back from Atlanta when she was four weeks old! So that was a bit of a shock as we were still working out what to do let alone get on a ten-hour flight. We were still in that worrying-about-everything phase and we made sure that one of us was awake the entire flight to make sure she was okay in her bassinet. She just slept the entire time and was pretty unphased while we were dropping milk all over the place and working out how to change nappies in the tiny plane toilet. The biggest change has probably been that we used to treat the flight as an extension of the holiday – have a few drinks, watch a movie, read a book. Now it's all about keeping our daughter entertained!

I specifically want to ask about the plane. We talk a lot about the pressure we sometimes put ourselves under as LGBTQ+ parents to be perceived as a perfect parent. Taking a flight with kids feels like the perfect environment for 'judgy' eyes. Have you ever felt this?

Yes, 100 per cent – we actively try to sit at the back of the plane to avoid this. In any kind of public space, you feel you are on display, you feel like you could be getting judged. Babies draw attention anyway because they are cute and loud and then when they have two dads the curiosity grows. We were in a row of three once with a guy sat next to us and his wife was sat across the aisle from him and said loudly to him, 'I want to know everything about that baby by the end of this flight' – I don't think she would have said it like that if we were a straight couple. Fortunately, there was an empty row that we managed to escape to!

You can feel eyes on you in any situation, and there is definitely the pressure to feel that people will be judging to see if we live up to a stereotype, or using us to justify their confirmation bias. But we just have to remember that we are good parents giving our child love and that the only people's opinions that matter on our parenting is ours and our daughter's. That doesn't stop the discomfort that we sometimes feel so we will still hide in the back row if we can!

Do you find that you are more cautious in where you travel? How do you research places to go?
LGBTQ+ people have to think much more carefully about the places that we travel to anyway due to different laws and customs that might be in various countries around the world. We have to take a risk-based view on every destination about whether we will be safe here. Will we feel uncomfortable? Will we have to edit our behaviour?

Boycotting countries isn't always helpful because many countries, cultures have moved on even if anti-quated laws exist. We also have to remember that LGBTQ+ people live in those countries, and often will work in the tourism industry, so hurting the tourism industry in a particular country may have a dispropor-tionate impact on their LGBTQ+ population.

That being said, we have to take a different view now that we have a child because we are thinking not just about our own safety but about hers too. Previously, where we might have been perceived as two 'friends', that perception is less likely now we have a child and we are much more visible. Where we have previously visited countries that have anti-LGBTQ+ laws as a couple, we are less likely to do that now. We use the ILGA country map to research places to go to under-stand the laws and attitudes towards LGBTQ+ people to help inform where we travel as a family.

Have you yet experienced any prejudice as a two-dad family when travelling?

Oh, definitely. There's smaller things like distasteful looks or people making assumptions. We were away with some straight friends recently whose baby is eight days younger than ours. People kept on asking our friend Hannah if they were twins – they got a right shock when she said, 'No, but they are eight days apart.' You could practically see the cogs turning in their heads trying to figure out how this could work with three men and a woman.

There have been more overt things too. Our daughter is very fair-skinned, and Sanjay is half Indian so has brown skin. We got off a bus in Tenerife once and Sanjay was carrying Arya and a man came up to him and said, 'Why is your baby so white?' He asked what they meant and the man poked Sanjay in the arm and said, 'Well, look at the colour of you, and look at the colour of her. Why is she so white?' Needless to say he got an earful!

It's important to point out we have also experienced so much positivity too! People often go out of their way to show how accepting they are, and we have also had our own prejudices challenged. We were worried about being in South Carolina for four weeks, which is where Arya was born, as we weren't sure how people would react to us, and people could not have been nicer!

Do you miss travelling alone (as in together as a couple)? Do you try to make time to go away with one another?

We're only ten months in, so we haven't missed that yet as we are enjoying creating memories together as a family, but we are sure that time will come. We have also managed to get some time separately with our friends on short trips. We've found that going on holiday with the grannies has also allowed us the best of both worlds where we have got to have a family holiday, while also getting a couple of evenings where we can go to dinner just the two of us!

Travelling As a Queer Family

So, what can one actively do when planning a queer family 'vacay'? Well, Mrs Jeffs, aka Jenny Southan (she/her), is a travel journalist and founder of travel trend forecasting agency Globetrender. She's shared some top things to think about when travelling as a queer family:

- Be aware that kids 'out' you all the time, so when you previously might have been able to travel the world freely as a member of the LGBTQ+ community, now you are a parent you will have to be more discerning about where you go.
- Speak to other LGBTQ+ parents about their holiday experiences and ask for recommendations. As any parent knows, the way you travel and the places you go to change as your priorities shift. Don't feel the need to always be 'adventurous' and do a long-haul flight. Often a short flight or road trip to somewhere tried and tested is the best approach.
- Focus on countries where gay marriage is legal – these will be the most progressive destinations to go to, although remember that big countries such as the US have less open-minded attitudes depending on the state you go to.
- At the moment there are thirty-two countries where gay marriage is legal – these are: Argentina, Australia, Austria, Belgium, Brazil, Canada, Chile, Colombia, Costa Rica,

Denmark, Ecuador, Finland, France, Germany, Iceland, Ireland, Luxembourg, Malta, Mexico, the Netherlands, New Zealand, Norway, Portugal, Slovenia, South Africa, Spain, Sweden, Switzerland, Taiwan, the UK, the US and Uruguay. (Note that the legislation of same-sex marriage in South Africa and Taiwan occurred after courts mandated them to do so, so these countries may not be so relaxed in reality.) In the US, the ten most progressive states, in no particular order, are: New York, Connecticut, Massachusetts, Maine, Vermont, New Jersey, Oregon, Rhode Island, California and Colorado.

- If you are looking for a city break, travel to destinations that have big Pride festivals – although do not necessarily go there during Pride. According to Airbnb,[34] the top ten cities for bookings during Pride are: London, Paris, Rome, Los Angeles, Lisbon, Barcelona, Toronto, New York, Milan and Madrid. Do think carefully about how old your children are as some cities aren't so good for younger kids.

- Beyond Pride, head for LGBTQ+-friendly hotspots with established queer scenes. Places I would recommend for families include: Mykonos (Greece), Ibiza and Sitges (Spain), Vancouver (Canada), Miami, Key West and Palm Springs (USA), French Polynesia, Thailand, Los Cabos (Mexico), Tel Aviv (Israel), Berlin (Germany) and Manchester (UK). Asher and Lyric[35] (professional travel journalists who focus on family safety and travel) has evaluated the world's safest countries for LGBTQ+ people. The top ten are: Canada, Sweden, the Netherlands, Malta, Portugal, the UK, Belgium, Norway, Spain and France.

- As Stu mentioned above, there are seventy-one countries where being LGBTQ+ is still criminalized. Included in this list are the following (in no particular order) holiday destinations that could prove problematic for travelling as an LGBTQ+ family: Barbados, Jamaica, Saint Lucia, Indonesia, Malaysia, the Maldives, Mauritius, Singapore, Qatar, Morocco, Ghana, Dominica, Papua New Guinea and Samoa.

Words of Wisdom from the Travelling Gays, aka Doug and Sanjay

- Don't feel the need to have to explain yourself all the time. People can be nosey and intrusive sometimes, and at times it can feel good to use it as an opportunity to educate or broaden someone else's horizons. But at the same time, you go on holiday to relax and enjoy yourself, so don't feel this burden – have a few stock responses prepared for the different questions you get asked that will easily and politely shut the conversation down.

- Don't feel the pressure to be 'the perfect parent' in other people's eyes. Firstly, 'the perfect parent' doesn't exist, and secondly you are an LGBTQ+ parent but you do not represent all LGBTQ+ parents. Your child is going to scream their head off on the plane or make a scene in the middle of the all-inclusive buffet, but these things happen to all parents. Give yourself a literal and metaphorical break and just carry on doing what you do. After all, you're on holiday, and you're never going to see any of these people ever again!

And a Top Tip from Stu . . .

We have now travelled to a few places with the kids and have stayed in both self-catering accommodation and hotels. I think anyone who travels with young children will agree that having a pad to yourself can be so much more relaxing, especially when it comes to food prep or even getting them to bed and being able to go outside and enjoy the evening together. I also feel incredibly more relaxed in our own place. I don't feel on guard or conscious of eyes watching us. We can just be us and enjoy our own space without worrying about awkward questions. It can be a little more expensive, but we've found it worth it for the peace of mind that comes with it. It's a price worth paying, and after all, we are on holiday for a reason.

Talking Points

▶ Would you take your family to a destination with a dubious record on gay rights such as Dubai or the Maldives?

▶ What are your biggest fears about being in a foreign country with your family?

IS FOR WHO'S THE REAL MUM?
(AND OTHER AWFUL QUESTIONS)

You know the feeling – some smiling stranger asks you a question about your family, your gender or sexuality, or offers a 'harmless' comment or observation, and instead of delivering a smart and witty put-down in return, tossing your hair and striding off with your head held high, you mutter a short, friendly enough answer in order to avoid any further confrontation. The likelihood is, this encounter and all the myriad ways you could, or should, have responded will play on loop in your head for the next week.

For some reason, it's deemed acceptable to interrogate queer and trans people about their past and personal lives in a way that would be considered outrageously rude were it applied to heterosexuals. From the classic 'When did you know you were gay?' (Err, when did you know you were straight, Karen?!) to 'Who wears the trousers in your relationship?' (as if queer partnerships are fancy-dress versions of straight ones – sigh!) And worst of all: 'Hey, trans person, can we have a casual chat about your genitals?' A lifetime of protecting our safety at any given moment has resulted in us having learned to smile politely and not make the other person feel awkward or bad, as if *their* feelings in this scenario are more important than our own.

Most LGBTQ+ parents will have faced obtuse questions from well-meaning strangers, and let's face it – there are bound to be more to come. But next time this happens, we'd like to gently encourage you to challenge the offending person and use it as an opportunity to teach them something. Perhaps they'll change their behaviour in future. Of course, if your children are present during such an encounter you may need to think carefully about what you say and how you say it. We've both had moments where we've been forced to correct people when we might have otherwise just ignored them because we've had little people staring up at us and we've had to model a response that they could use in future.

The woman at the library who asked E if she was taking the books home to 'read with Daddy', for example, is something I might have shrugged off when E was younger and less attuned to every single thing people say or do like a tiny Sherlock Holmes. 'You'll share them with Mummy, won't you, sweetie?' I interjected, looking at my daughter and then back at the librarian, who was making that face people make when they're trying to recalibrate their expectations. In case she was thinking, 'Okay, so this person isn't her parent,' I went one step further than I might normally and clarified, 'My daughter has two mums.' We didn't stay for any follow-up chat, but I was proud of myself for leaning into the social awkwardness in order to set the librarian straight, so to speak!

I do try to live life by the saying 'No question is a stupid question.' Truth be told, it's a mantra that stands up better in the workplace, but if you've not been through adoption yourself, there is a huge amount of curiosity from outsiders. Everyone has skeletons in their family closets, yet for some reason learning a child is adopted seems to give the green light for people (aka strangers) to delve into that child's past.

So here is one rule if you have indeed picked up this book to understand more about queer families: when you are informed by someone that their child is adopted, do not use this as a springboard to dig into the neglect and trauma that child has most likely experienced. Do not ask about the birth family. Do not ask what 'happened', do not make assumptions, and do not try to vilify the birth parents. 'Oh, why do they let them keep having children?' and 'How could anyone do that to a child'?' are not okay things to say especially if you have no idea about the circumstances.

For the record, we have an incredible amount of empathy for our children's birth family and it's not up to anyone else to make judgements. Note that even if the other person offers up a little bit of information, then leave it at that. I cannot tell you how hard it is as an adoptive parent to avoid certain questions without coming off as rude. I am constantly put into situations where I'm being pressed for information and at the end of the day it's just not fair on my children. Their story is theirs to tell, if and when they want to.

INSIGHT:

How to Answer

We asked some of the Gay–Ze community to share with us the most unintentionally offensive things people have said to them. If you can bear to read through this cringe-inducing list, what follows is our thoughts on things to say in response.

'Who's the real dad/mum?'
'Was it an artificial pregnancy, then?'
'Where did you "get" your baby?'
'Do you know much about the father?'
'Such a shame the mum couldn't look after them.'
'What, so you can just "buy" a baby daddy now?'
'Oh, it must be so hard for the surrogate to
give up her baby.'

Here are some lines to have up your sleeve in response:

'You may not have meant it to come across this way, but the tone of your question is quite offensive.'

'Just so you know for future – that's not the kind of question adoptive parents are comfortable answering.'

'In case you ever meet another two-mum family, a nice question to ask might be, "What does your child call you both?" instead of "Which of you is the mum?"'

'Our daughter has two mums and a donor; we don't use the word father to describe him.'

'If what you meant to ask is, are we both this child's parents, the answer is yes.'

'If what you meant to ask was, which of us carried the baby, the answer is my wife did, but obviously that doesn't make me any less of her mum.'

'If by "Who's the real dad?" what you meant to ask was, which of us is the biological father – we don't feel that's necessary information to share with anyone other than our paediatrician.'

'You chose your partner based on their looks and personality, right? Well, choosing an egg/sperm donor is no different.'

'I wouldn't call it "shopping for a baby daddy" as much as making a hugely nuanced and meaningful decision.'

'Our surrogate is still a huge part of our life, we love her and are grateful for what she did for us but she entered into this contract of surrogacy knowing the child she was carrying wouldn't be legally or biologically hers and that's the reason she did it. She's a mother to her own children. This was very different.'

'One in ten young women in the UK now identify as LGBTQ+, so it's probably a good idea to get your head around queer people having children because in another decade there will be even more LGBTQ+ families.'

'The answer to that question is actually long and complicated. If you're seriously interested in learning more about LGBTQ+ families, I'd happily chat to you at another time.'

There is a fine line between genuine curiosity, a well-intentioned desire to learn or open one's mind and the clawing entitlement that comes from being a cis heterosexual person who believes anyone outside of their idea of 'normal' owes them an explanation. There might be a time to engage, but don't forget, there also might be a time to simply heed the advice of Mama Ru and sashay away.

Talking Points

▶ Is confrontation ever a good thing?

▶ When does curiosity veer into inappropriate?

▶ Why do we so often feel the need to make it okay for the other person?

▶ What's the most offensive thing anyone's ever asked you about your family, identity or sexuality and how did you respond?

X

IS FOR EX-PARTNERS, DIVORCE, SEPARATION AND STEP PARENTS

I remember the day my mum called to tell me my dad had 'gone' as if it was yesterday. I was getting ready for work, I'd just graduated from university and my future felt like this twinkling universe of possibility. 'Gone where?' I asked, thinking she must mean he'd gone to Waitrose or something like that, but her tears suggested otherwise. As she told me the details, nothing seemed real. My world as I knew it came crashing down. I thought my parents had a great relationship. I loved my dad – he was one of my best friends. I had no idea they were having marital problems, and while I tried to make sense of the news, I was also having to accept that my father was not the person I thought he was. I was a typically self-obsessed twenty-three-year-old. I was happy. I didn't want this but there was nothing I could do to fix it. I matured about a decade overnight and as I supported my mum through the devastating next few months while keeping my own feelings of betrayal on the backburner, I learned that my parents had protected me from so much. They were people; complicated, flawed, fallible, just like everyone else. They weren't simply this unit of caregivers devoted entirely to me anymore. It was a revelation, but one which, in retrospect, I'm very happy to have come to so young.

In the decades that followed I came to forgive my dad and build a new kind of relationship with him that, over time, allowed me to welcome his new family into my life. I've also become extremely close to my mum and have come to know her as a multifaceted individual more than just a parent. I learned that I was stronger and more resilient than I ever knew.

Dealing with my parents' divorce in my early twenties forced me to have an open mind and to be understanding and empathetic in a way that has, I believe, made me a better person and a better parent.

Divorce and separation is never easy, particularly if you share parental responsibilities, but through communication, kindness and reserves of forgiveness you may not have realized you had, it can enrich and expand your family.

Since same-sex marriage was made legal in 2014, LGBTQ+ divorce rates have been rising accordingly.[36] There were 822 divorces among same-sex couples in 2019, nearly twice the number in 2018 (428 divorces); of these, nearly three-quarters (72 per cent) were between female couples. There's no doubt a sense of shame associated with the breakdown of queer relationships – because we had to fight for the right to marry, we then feel an extra pressure to make those marriages work when maybe they just aren't meant to be. Likewise with parenting – we've internalized the sense that we're *lucky* to be able to have children as queer couples, so we can't possibly be seen to fail. But please, try as best you can not to carry these burdens. Children benefit from happy, calm and self-actualized parents. If you are not happy in your relationship, staying together for the sake of the children may not actually be the best thing for them in the long run.

LEGAL EAGLE:
The Law and Divorce in Same-Sex Partnerships

Our friends at NGA Law give us the lowdown on where queer couples and parents stand.

If you are same-sex parents (whether cis or trans) and you are both registered as parents on your child's UK birth or adoption certificate, then you will share legal parenthood and parental responsibility. Like any other parents, if you cannot agree living and contact arrangements after separation, the family court will need to make a decision.

If you are not your child's legal parent, a great deal depends on the particular circumstances. Generally speaking, the court will look first at the child's welfare and if the child has an established attachment with a parent, the fact that the parent is not a biological/ legal parent should be irrelevant. However, in practice, biology can be important.

Child support issues depend purely on a parent's legal status. This can have unexpected outcomes in cases involving female same-sex parents, since a non-birth mother who is not a legal parent might have no financial responsibility for her child following a separation.

Separation During or After Surrogacy
After a parental order has been granted by the UK family court, you will be the legal parents of your children and you will share parental responsibility for them. If you separate or divorce, the law is just the same for you as it is for any other parents breaking up.

The surrogacy background and who is a biological parent should be irrelevant, although in reality we know that it is something that may need to be explained to the court, and can be attempted to be used as a weapon where a separation is acrimonious, so care and specialist help may be needed.

What happens if we separate without a parental order?

This is a much more complicated position, but the court may allow you to seek a parental order before you formally divorce or separate, even if you have missed the usual six-month deadline for applying. Otherwise, one or both of you will not legally be a parent of your children.

What happens when only one partner has adopted?

Until 2002 it was not possible for same-sex couples to adopt children jointly, and in practice some couples got around the rules by having only one partner formally adopt, although the child was cared for by both partners. If you separate, that may mean that there are complex issues to resolve, particularly around financial responsibilities and parental responsibility.

MEET . . .
Franklin (he/him)

He and his now ex-husband were foster carers when their relationship broke down.

We had fostered a seventeen-year-old before, and we'd had time to prepare for that. But even that was a kind of scramble. In the case of the six- and four-year-olds, when they came to us it was an emergency placement. We had a few hours' notice and we were only supposed to be getting them for the weekend. I was going through a really rough patch in my relationship at that time. I wanted to divorce my husband, but I was worried about losing the kids. I instantly fell in love with them and wanted to provide them with a forever home, but my ex had other ideas. I had to find a way to end our relationship without jeopardizing the foster placement.

What do you wish you'd known when you first went into fostering with your ex that you know now?

You mean apart from the fact that my ex was a complete nightmare? Okay. So one very practical thing, I suppose, is that I wish I had known about special guardianships. And thank God I got told about it at a crucial stage because when the shit was hitting the fan between me and my ex, I was told by the head of fostering at social services that we wouldn't be able to keep the kids because my partner didn't want them to stay. And I did. She even said if we divorce, she could foresee no circumstances under which I would be able to keep the kids. I said to her, 'Well, I'll leave no stone unturned in my attempt to keep the kids, because I think it would be catastrophic for them to be moved on at this stage. And even if they do get moved on, at least in years to come, they will be able to look back at their file and see that I left no stone unturned, which hopefully will go some way towards undoing the tremendous damage.'

Thankfully this unhelpful social worker left, and her very good deputy said to me, 'You can get a special guardianship. You can do that in a relationship, but you can also just do it yourself.' And so I could become the special guardian for the kids and my then-husband wouldn't have had to worry about it.

That gave me so much more power and freedom. And ultimately that was the path I went down, although with some further complications, but it's just a great way of managing the end of a relationship without the kids having to go through a massive upheaval.

Going back to my first flippant point about what else I wish I'd known when I first went into fostering with my ex. I guess I wish I'd known him better. I think it's very specific to our relationship, but he was a different person after the kids came along. I saw a very different side of him. I guess a lot of people have that experience even in traditional heterosexual marriages with biological children. People change. But I think in our case, it was more that he very much presented one face for the first part of our relationship. And then when he realized he wasn't going to have everything his way, I saw the real him.

***What advice would you give someone who is
having doubts about their relationship, but has
started an adoption or fostering journey with that
partner?***

I think the most important thing that I would say is:
don't think you have to be in a relationship to adopt
or foster. I thought I did have to. I mean, not legally,
but I thought I needed the support. Because my relationship wasn't great, I actually spent a lot of the time
single parenting anyway, and that is what I do now,
and in many ways it's much easier because you're not
having to try and manage a relationship at the same
time. And you're not trying to manage a relationship
with someone who is resentful of you doing things a
different way or having a different parenting style or
someone who's resentful of you giving your attention
to the kids rather than giving your attention to them.

So if you're having doubts about the relationship,
maybe ask yourself if you really need this relationship,
and be confident that fostering or adopting is going
to give you this ultimately far more rewarding, although
very different, kind of relationship. And remember –
intimate relationships *will* become possible again after
you've become a parent.

You never know what's going to happen in a relationship anyway. It's very hard, especially in the modern
age, to have a relationship last forever. So even if your
relationship is brilliant and rock solid, there's still a
chance it might end.

MEET . . .
Alexandra (she/her) and Dee (she/her)

As you'll recall (see page 306), Dee came out as trans and began her transition when their son was a young baby. The couple separated but remain great friends and co-parents.

Dee: I suppose my greatest fears around my transition and our relationship ending were that it would somehow mean I'd no longer have contact with Alex or with L or even have a home. I went to worst-case scenario because everything I'd seen, heard or was told was that I'd be rejected by family and friends. I'd been carrying a not-unfounded understanding that there were lines I couldn't cross in regards to my gender and I'd be punished if I did. It was a very deep-rooted emotional response but it was a fleeting moment in terms of mine and Alex's relationship, because we quickly agreed to be supportive of each other even though we didn't know how things were going to pan out.

Alexandra: I felt really worried that Dee's personality would change if she was prescribed hormones and that she would become some sort of parody of a mother, meaning I would feel like my place was being taken. I'm not proud of this reaction these days, but now I know that that was really based on what I had read online when I'd dared to look, which was always a worst-case scenario. There was no one saying anywhere that there might be a positive path through. I'm vocal about how damaging those stereotypes are now, because I've lived the visceral emotional moment, and I've also lived that just not being true.

Dee: After separating, we continued to share a home because we couldn't afford not to. And L was six months at the time . . .

Alexandra: . . . so getting him in a sleeping and eating routine where he knew where he stood was the priority. For the two of us, we were just white-knuckling it for the first few months, living day-to-day, sometimes hour-to-hour emotionally. But we had the baby there as the focus – he took up most of the day. And then in the evening we were exhausted. We weren't at each other at all by that point.

Dee: Before agreeing to separate, tension had been building within our relationship and I was becoming more and more distant – going through the motions of being a husband and father but never connecting to those experiences as mine. I didn't yet know what transition meant for me. It was an often-painful route to understanding myself but once I was honest with Alex about what I needed to do by way of transition we felt a real sense of calmness. I don't think it was a huge surprise but it did feel incredibly sad in terms of our relationship, and neither of us wanted to feel that sadness, so we had to make a conscious decision to centre L in our decisions and develop a route to happiness through that new dynamic in our relationship.

Alexandra: Yeah, definitely. I'd stopped trying to please. I'd stopped thinking, 'What's she gonna do? Who is this person? And why aren't I enough to make them happy?' Then once I knew why and that it was nothing to do with me, it did feel calm.

Dee: And children that age are ridiculous. You can't really continue to be a serious person around someone who's learning to walk.

Alexandra: We always really agreed that we didn't want L to be going back and forth between places when he was still the age when he was trying to get into a sleep routine. So we knew that if people were going to be moving around, it would be us. Dee slept in the living room for what was supposed to be a few months but turned into years due to the pandemic. Now she lives with friends nearby. One of the great things about our arrangement is that we never need to pay for a babysitter. Even when L was a baby, I was able to go and see my friends and come home at whatever hour I wanted, which most parents of a nine-month-old probably don't feel they can. Whereas I knew that Dee would actually really relish doing the late-night feeds and having that bonding time with L alone.

Dee: It was just about striking a balance. Like, okay, if we're still living together, we need to look out for each other in different ways or allow each other to do what each person needs to do on their own. After the pandemic when I actually moved out it was a bit more miserable. We'd do that classic separated-parents thing of handing over in the playground, and I think there was a feeling that we were following tracks that had already been laid for us, but they weren't our reality. It was like, hold on a minute, we don't need to do this. There was a realization that we could do things our own way. So I could still sleep at the house, or we could still hang out as a family even though Alex and I weren't partners anymore.

Alexandra: For the years between L being one and three, people identified me as a single mum. I got lumped in with a straight, divorced narrative that I wasn't feeling. It was only through the combination of writing my memoir *Somebody to Love*,[37] and then us living together during the pandemic, that I understood why I didn't like being part of a gang that I didn't feel like I belonged in. Dee hadn't cheated. We didn't just fall out of love. It was really complicated. And there was so much closeness and funness. And if you on any level understand and empathize with the intractable nature of any form of queerness, then there can be no real blame to be apportioned. But people didn't want to really hear that from me. They thought that meant I wasn't getting better. It took writing the book for me to own the fact that I didn't want to be in that gang even if it sent shock waves through the divorced ladies. The problem was I also felt that because I'm straight and cis that I couldn't take L to a rainbow family coffee morning by myself, as I was so aware it wasn't my space. So it was hard to find where I belonged. I do feel more welcomed by the queer community now, but there was certainly a period of adjustment for me to feel allowed in those spaces.

Dee: We were always very supportive of each other. We understood and we were very sympathetic because we knew that we were both trying to find ourselves. So that helped us give each other space. Lots of the things that we had in our marriage remained, like how well we knew each other. I think, when a trans person comes out later in life and decides to transition or seek medical interventions, whatever it may be – if their partner is the first person they talk to about it, that says a lot about the amount of trust they have. Even though we were coming apart, I felt closer to Alex than ever because that honesty was there then.

Dee: We haven't divorced yet as it hasn't been a priority. Through seeking greater legal recognition of my identity or new relationships developing, I'm sure it will happen in time, but right now I think we'd prefer to spend money on other things rather than the formal dissolution of our marriage.

What advice would you give parents separating after one person has come out as trans?

Dee and Alexandra: Centre the child. We think everything that was really emotionally difficult for us became easier when we did that.

Look for local or national support around managing transition as a parent within a family. Look for trans peer support groups locally.

Look out for each other in public and be mindful of seemingly everyday places and interactions that may prove challenging to a trans parent and the co-parent as well. These things will change as your relationship changes. Shout for each other!

There are rainbow family groups – few and far between – but they can provide that informal social space to be yourself. If there isn't one, maybe create one!

The biggest thing that held us together is silliness. Find and celebrate the moments of silliness to lift the weight of separation and transition.

We've got a shared calendar. And we have pre-agreed times of pick-up and childcare, though we're very flexible.

We do all the important stuff together. Like all the school meetings and the doctor's appointments, even when it might be easier for just one of us to go, we both go so no one can harbour resentment.

Alexandra: For me, it was very valuable when I worked with FFLAG [a national organization and charity dedicated to supporting families and their LGBT+ loved ones][38] a little when *Somebody to Love* came out and they told me how reassuring people had found it to read in the book about the moments when I felt rage or grief, while also reading in the same place that I had come through it. So often families just read the blog or column or social media post when the someone is in pain, and there's no follow-up. I learned that it was okay for me to be distraught about what happened, but at times in the beginning I was so worried that that in itself would be somewhat disrespectful or even transphobic – of course it wasn't!

INSIGHT:
Step Parenting

Katie L. Acosta (she/her) is Associate Professor of Sociology at Georgia State University. She is also the author of *Queer Stepfamilies*,[39] which is the result of her seven years of research into the subject. We asked her about the challenges and joys of step parenting.

Could you start by telling us a bit about your research and what you discovered?
My book *Queer Stepfamilies: The Path to Social and Legal Recognition* is an exploration into the lives of forty-three step-parent families that are led by lesbian,

bisexual, transgender and/or queer parents. The families all included children from at least one parent's previous relationships. Some of the children were originally conceived or adopted in a same-sex relationship. Others were originally conceived or adopted in a heterosexual union. Most of the children were being parented by three or more parents (of varying gender and or sexual identities) in two homes. I find that these families create what I call plural parenting arrangements – where origin parents and step parents take on roles in their children's lives based on their individual skills, availability or emotional bandwidth. Rather than taking on roles based on societal prescriptions of appropriate parenting.

Many of the families I interview had also expanded their families to include additional children. I found that while the families de-emphasized the importance of biology when describing their parenting roles, they still privileged biology when making decisions about how to conceive future children. For instance, the step parents described wanting to use the same donors that original parents used in previous relationships to conceive their children in order to ensure that the future children would be biologically related to the existing children. These families wanted to preserve a biological sibling tie because they hoped it would facilitate more closeness for the children.

Does being a step parent in a queer relationship when the ex parenting partnership was heterosexual bring unique challenges?

Yes. In particular, families that included a heterosexual father, a mother and her lesbian, bisexual, queer or transgender partner described the most tension in their plural parenting relationships. Some reported the children's heterosexual father being unsupportive of their queer step-parent union, using homo-, bi- or transphobic language to describe the queer step-parent union, or engaging the family court system in an effort to keep the children from being raised in a queer step-parent household.

As a step parent, is it important to have a good relationship with your partner's ex? Any tips for doing this?

It certainly helps when a step parent can develop a healthy relationship with their partner's ex, but it is not required. Step parents who do have good relationships with their partner's ex can serve as mediators, diffuse tension, or keep the plural parenting arrangement running smoothly when there are disagreements between the original parents. I found that step parents sometimes served as co-ordinators. They organized information from all the other parents in order to create opportunities for the children. Because they were often removed from the original parent's conflict, they could serve as a buffer or a less emotionally invested individual who could stay focused on resolving the conflict. It is, however, a delicate balance and a relationship that takes a great deal of work. I would caution step parents away from wanting to serve in these roles too soon. In more established step-parent families, step parents gradually became a resource in times of conflict.

How best should you deal with rejection from a step child?

It's important to remember that a child's rejection isn't about the step parent as an individual. Children need to process the changing family dynamics. In particular, the children who are going from having been raised in a heterosexual household to being raised in a lesbian-, bisexual-, transgender- or queer-parented household have their own adjusting to do. It's important to give the kids time, to remain consistent in their life and let them (in their own time) determine that the step parent is safe to let in.

Because we already exist out of the hetero 'norm' of what a family is, as LGBTQ+ people there is a chance to embrace big, blended families in a way that straight people might struggle with. The white-hot centre of a divorce or separation might be painful, but if you can find a way through it then there's a lifetime of expanding and evolving as a family to look forward to.

Talking Points

▸ What steps should you take when thinking about separation?

▸ What do you need to have in place before you become parents to protect you legally as a family?

Y

IS FOR YOU DO YOU

'I want to get back to the fun person I was before I became a parent,' I confessed to my best friend Joe. He looked at me kindly and said, 'Babe, you've never been a fun person.'

Oh, the outrage! But, he wasn't wrong. I was the kid at sleepovers who actually wanted to go to sleep. I was the teenager at parties who filled beer cans with water and the student at Freshers' Week who preferred to binge-watch *Will and Grace* than get wasted. I always wanted to be a parent; it would be an excellent outlet for my naturally responsible nature, I thought.

To prove that I am footloose and fancy free *actually*, I went on a boys' weekend minibreak with Joe and another friend. They went out to a gay club and I lay in bed looking at photos of my daughter.

The next morning we went for brunch and I ordered a marga-rita to prove that I can be a fun person, thank you very much, and because I suddenly felt GREAT without a three-year-old screaming at me for snacks.

By the afternoon I had drunk a number of cocktails and was relaxing into the dynamic of being on my own with friends. It felt unfamiliar, having such prolonged adult conversation. I somehow located the 'me' I was before I was a parent, but there was a disconnect. Even without my kid tugging at my sleeve, she was there. My little family surrounds me like a force field, however far away I am from them. As hard as I've tried to maintain my sense of myself since becoming a mum, I've been changed by it, and I can't deny that.

We ended up in a fabulous Euro gay club. We watched a drag show and danced and drank espresso martinis. I was ready to tell the many women who would throw themselves at me that I was married and HAVE A CHILD SORRY, but there were A) three women in the entire venue and B) two of them were a couple and the other one barely noticed that I was noticing that she was not noticing me. Eurgh, I don't miss being single.

Forever Friends?

I have some parent friends who have completely given up their social life for their kids, and I have other parent friends who valued their social life so much that they made finding a nanny a priority when their first was born so they could maintain it. There's no right or wrong way to be a parent in this respect, and personally I think I fall somewhere in between the two extremes.

As queer people, we may have found our community and forged a big part of our identity on 'the scene', so still going to gay spaces has a deeper resonance than it does for the straight parents who just want to go to Wetherspoons on a cheeky date night or whatever it is straight people do.

Spending forty-eight hours with my two gay besties felt like a fabulous escape from my normal parent life and it was good, and I think important, to have to be present entirely in my adult self.

I find that I'm so used to always thinking about my daughter, I don't put as much effort in with friends as I should and sometimes I worry that they might be annoyed with me for not being as available as I once was.

INSIGHT:

Queer Identities as Parents

We met Lucy and Paul before in 'G is for Gender' (see page 119) and 'L is for Labour' (see page 186), but a reminder that they are a bisexual couple from Oxford who have a three-year-old.

How do you both stay in touch with your queer identity within an ostensibly hetero relationship?

Paul: For me, as our relationship has progressed and I have grown older and more comfortable in myself and my sexuality, I have taken on more visible symbols of my bisexuality, dressing with items with the bi flag on for example. This has also coincided with having our child and coming out of lockdown and reengaging with the world more generally. We both talk openly about our experience as queer people and how we have both navigated our sexualities through teens, university and as adults, which I think helps us to stay connected to our identity as broader than that which is visible on the surface to the casual observer.

Lucy: Right now, with difficulty. This is something I always used to do through nightlife – I hosted a queer cabaret night, and I used to go out with friends to queer spaces. My work as a performance poet offered a lot of opportunities to express and explore my identity in all kinds of ways. Since pregnancy, the pandemic, and new motherhood, my options feel very limited.

The fact is, most of my best mates are gay men who don't want to have children. I've been at parties with them when I've got my phone out and started showing pictures of my daughter, or I've realized I've been talking about the TV show *Bluey* for ten minutes, and I've kicked myself. Be cool, Lotte! But it's tough because if someone asks what I've been up to – at least 80 per cent of what I've been up to involves my daughter. And not admitting that feels strange. By my age, most straight people's friendship groups probably mainly comprise other parents. I love that my queer mates are different, and their sex lives and general antics keep me entertained and part of a fun adult world. But sometimes when they've been talking to me about their gym routines and glamorous holidays, I've felt very aware of the contrasts in our lives.

When E was first born, I remember struggling to think of anything interesting to say to anyone at all – I didn't feel like I had a view on politics or popular culture, I hadn't read anything or listened to any podcasts. Actually, the summer E was born, we just lay on the sofa completely sleep-deprived watching *Love Island* and were barely able to keep up with that most of the time. Thankfully my friends hung around while I pulled myself through this catatonic phase and they were there waiting for me on the other side.

MEET . . .
Tommy (he/they)

Tommy is a dad by surrogacy to a three-year-old and a six-year-old.

Growing up I used to DJ a lot of the Manchester gay clubs. It was a huge part of my life. It's where I made my best friends, and where I met my husband. I had a crew of about ten queer people who I went around with. We were like a family, with all the usual bickering as well as that unconditional love. After I met my husband and we started talking about wanting kids, I remember being out for drinks with these friends and they'd roll their eyes or do these big fake yawns whenever we started talking about finding a surrogate. Their lives were all about the scene, who was going to what party, who hooked up with whom . . . they weren't interested. As we got further into becoming parents, our lives drifted apart. I always got the feeling they thought we had let the side down by becoming dads, like we had done something really 'straight'. Now our closest friends are all fellow parents, as we just have so much more in common. But there's still this part of me that wants to go out and have a big night on Canal Street once in a while. I've not done it since the kids were born and I lost touch with that crew I came up with. But maybe I should.

Take Yourself on a Date

You'd be forgiven for thinking the only time a parent gets to enjoy some time away from the kids has to be at night and has to involve socializing. I'm all for this, and now we have a great local babysitter, and a child who understands that if we go out, we will most likely come back, it's easy enough to plan fun evenings as a couple or with friends. But what I think we do neglect as parents is that time in the day to just *be*. Granted, it can be hard if not impossible to carve out this time, particularly as a single parent, but if by hook or by crook you can make it work, it'll change your life.

There's always a reason not to do something for yourself, whether it's work you need to finish or chores around the house, but why not try sorting childcare in advance and taking an afternoon off to just do you. If once a month feels unachievable, aim for once every two months: where there's a will, there's a way. Take yourself on a date – you deserve it! Go for lunch on your own somewhere nice, see a movie in the day, visit a gallery or museum, explore a new area near you or book a spa treatment. I know most parents feel guilty about prioritizing themselves once in a while, but I wonder if as LGBTQ+ parents we feel it even more acutely. We had to work so hard to have our children, we had to prove how much we wanted them and fight even for the right to have them at all – once we do have kids we must be devoted to them 24/7!

Well, yes, but also . . . no. Remember how it's important to put your own mask on before helping others if there's an emergency on an aeroplane? The same goes here: you will be better able to care for your family if you allow yourself the occasional opportunity to look after yourself. Parenting is so physically exhausting and can involve every last iota of resilience and patience – these are finite resources that we need to recharge. When we start running on empty, nobody's happy.

STU'S VIEW

The saying 'Happy Mum, Happy Baby' might be super heteronormative, but it's at least correct in its meaning. In order to be 'good enough' parents, it's important we look after ourselves and remember to enjoy the things we used to enjoy before nappies, weaning, plaits and gymnastic classes took over our lives. Every weekend John and I alternate lie-ins until 11 a.m. I'll open the blinds, put on the radio and have a coffee while reading magazines. Bliss! I also really try to make time for myself in the week. I'll take myself off somewhere for an hour or two just to have some headspace and be with my own thoughts. That might involve reading a book in a cafe, getting my nails done, going for a long walk. I do have to battle the sense that if I am having time away from family I need to be catching up with friends or having masses of 'fun'. Because actually, sometimes, what I really need more than anything is a bit of peace and quiet. I do try and see friends one on one and I love socializing, but I'm also getting better at recognizing that 'me time' isn't frivolous – it's vital!

Who Am I?

Becoming a parent can cause a bit of an identity crisis for many of us. It's an identity that threatens to negate all others as it is so overwhelming. But as an LGBTQ+ person, our sexuality and or gender identity may have been hard-won. We may have spent decades reckoning with it, and hopefully, eventually, embracing it. I don't know about you, but I'm not going to become any less queer because I'm now a mum. Quite the opposite. The heteronormative connotations of motherhood make me keen to push against what's expected as much as possible. In fact, embracing parenthood and all the gendered paraphernalia that comes with it has made me more motivated to explore the shadowy corners of myself and my queerness. It's only since approaching forty that I've dared entertain the idea that 'non-binary' might be an identity that better expresses how I see myself and how I like to show up in the world. And I know Stu also has leaned into being his most gay now he's also a dad. There's no way either of us are letting parenthood quash this hugely important part of who we are as people.

MEET . . .
Brian Rosenberg, founder of Gays With Kids

We first met Brian in the chapter 'S is for Surrogacy' (see page 274). He shares his thoughts on being extra _extra_ gay now he lives in the very straight suburbs!

When we were younger we lived in gay ghettos in Boston and New York City. So even though we weren't available to go out to the bars on Friday or dancing on Saturday because we chose to have other priorities in our life, we still felt part of a queer community. And what's hard now is, we don't live in those communities anymore. We're in the suburbs, and so that means we hang out 90 per cent of the time with straight people. And so that makes me want to be really gay. When I'm with straight people, in every conversation I'll just bring up something gay. I feel like I want to be extra gay – I guess it's my way of staying in touch with that part of myself. We've taken the kids to P Town [a gay mecca in the US], and they love it. One of my kids is obsessed with drag queens so she has the best time there.

Since having a child, attending Pride has felt more important than ever. Going with my family is a chance to bring these two strands of 'queer' and 'parent' together and there's nothing more affirming. We are people, we are parents, we have gender and sexual identities that aren't etched in stone but that can shift and evolve throughout our lives, and it's so important we allow ourselves to *be*, fully, because in the visceral moment of caregiving it's easy to lose track. We contain multitudes – and we are better parents when we realize this.

Talking Points

▶ Have you spoken to your friends about your desire to start a family?

▶ Are they supportive?

▶ What do you stand to lose in terms of your social life and what do you stand to gain from having children?

IS FOR GEN Z AND THE FUTURE

Maybe you are part of the cool crowd who knows what 'Ze' means. Alas, as usual I was not in the cool club and it was Lotte who brought Ze to the table when we were discussing the *Gay to Ze* element of our subtitle.

So here is an education. Ze is a gender-neutral pronoun. While discovering what Ze meant myself, I was looking on Pronouns.org, a really useful website in educating oneself on pronoun use. I stumbled across this quote, which I love:

> If someone shares their pronouns with you, it's meant to disrupt the culture of making assumptions, and to provide you with the information you need in order to refer to them appropriately. Just as we generally have names we go by, we also tend to have pronouns that we want to be

referred to by. The name or pronouns someone goes by do not necessarily indicate anything about the person's gender or other identities.

Cool, right? This generation has taken the old-fashioned 'Mr and Mrs' and thrown it into the air. This is the generation that fucks shit up. I'm here for it. Generation z – today's twelve- to twenty-six-year-olds – will be (some already are) the next generation to start having children. They are growing up in a world of multiple pronouns and gender fluidity; they live in society that has queer parents that they can look up to. For those that want children – and not everyone does – it's an empowering and exciting generation to be part of, unless the world burns to death because of climate change of course! The Future Lab, the trends and forecasting agency, told me that 'families are no longer nuclear, nor does one size fit all when it comes to parenting. The family will be in flux in the years ahead. No longer the epitome of youth culture, members of Generation Z are having kids of their own, with the eldest of this generation turning thirty in just two years' time, driving the parenting sector in unexpected new directions.'

But are we entering a new generation where the LGBTQ+ community starts to feel the pressure that straight people have endured for years, to have a family and 'settle down'. Gone are the days of your dear old mum crying into her teacup as you come out because 'she always wanted grandkids'. Enter your aunt coming up at a wedding to ask when you and your beau are going to start having kids. 'You'd make such a lovely dad, dear.' I for one am not some militant pro-queer parenting advocate, as surprised as you might be by that. I can't think of anything worse than a world where every gay settles down as a family. We need our hedonistic, free and fabulous LGBTQ+ folk across the world leaving a trail of poppers and leather chaps in their wake and living their best life, with or without children.

Zes and Zirs . . . This Is the Next Generation

TOBIE DONOVAN (he/him)

Tobie (twenty) is an actor who stars as Isaac in the Netflix LGBTQ+ teen drama phenomenon *Heartstopper*.

When I was growing up there wasn't any representation of queer parenting anywhere, or at least not that I could find. As a child I never read books, watched TV shows or saw movies with queer parents in them, so I think I just assumed that to live out the 'mums and dads' fantasy I used to play with my friends on the playground I would have to marry a woman. Which was honestly never going to happen!

Although it is still really stigmatized, it's great that kids today can find representation of all different types of families in a lot of media. Going to the cinema and watching Pixar's *Lightyear,* I felt so much joy at seeing a child being brought up by two mums. And while this was only a short moment in the story, which managed to get the film banned in however many countries, it was so refreshing to see these massive studios taking note and realizing the impact they have in shaping the mind of the future.

I am definitely aware that if I were to ever have children, my partner and I would probably still face a lot of hate and have to answer a lot of uncomfortable questions at the school gate when talking to the other mums and dads. Therefore, I can really understand why some queer people would be put off the idea of having children. But I'd hope that if they really wanted to be parents, they could push past it and try to focus on the opinions of people who love them.

I would love to see a world where queer people are treated equally on all fronts around the whole world and I think a great way to work towards that goal is to look within our own community. We are not successful in our activism if we end the conversation at, 'Me and my husband can now have a baby.' We are not free from oppression until we ALL are. Particularly for our trans siblings, now more than ever, it is important we remember that. I hope that the future of the queer community is one with more internal acceptance, for the asexual communities, for the non-binary communities, for the intersex communities, for everyone. When we are united and stand together, we are unstoppable.

CALUM McSWIGGAN (he/him)
Calum (thirty-two) is a YouTuber and author.

I'm among the first generation of LGBTQ+ people who entered adulthood knowing that having children was now an option to me. This put me in the unique position of having grown up accepting that I would never have children, and now being confronted with the fact that I could if I wanted to. It came as a surprise to me that my parents just assumed that I would have children and make them grandparents one day, and a few years ago, I had to sit down and explain to them why I'd decided that I didn't want children and that it was unlikely I'd ever change my mind.

I think there's an enormous pressure on all people to have children – the typical nuclear family is drilled into us, and we're taught that *get married, buy a house and have children* are some of the major, most crucial milestones in life. I think luckily we're now starting to move away from that fact – we're starting to see more single parents adopting, queer parents having children, and heterosexual couples choosing not to. In some ways, I think advancing the rights of LGBTQ+ people has had a knock-on effect on emphasizing the individual choice we all have when it comes to having children, regardless of our identity.

Sometimes I do wonder if my desire to want children has been affected by growing up in a world with unequal rights for LGBTQ+ parents. Had I known that it would be possible for me to have children, I may have grown up wanting them. But for me now, I've long since come to terms with the fact that I *can't* have kids – and it's difficult to undo that. Who knows – maybe one day that will change – but for right now at least, it's very difficult to imagine children as being part of my future because most of my life I was told that they wouldn't.

My hope for the future is that everyone grows up knowing that whether they have children is their own personal choice and has nothing to do with their identity or relationship status. Only then will we truly have parental equality.

YASMIN BENOIT (she/her)

Yasmin (twenty-six) is an asexual activist, model and writer.

I feel like I grew up in a world where the possibility of being a parent was a real thing – regardless of how you have the child – namely because of my own family and the media, I assumed. Both of my parents were adopted by their grandparents.

My favourite characters in the films I watched usually ended up being raised by someone who wasn't their biological parents – take Matilda being adopted by Miss Honey, Annie being adopted by Oliver Warbucks and his secretary was her surrogate mother, Madeline is raised in a boarding school, Becky in *A Little Princess* was adopted by her friend's father, and chosen family was the whole point of series like *Tracy Beaker* and *Harry Potter*. If anything, I feel like the idea of chosen families was always portrayed as being very romantic and freeing, especially in media aimed at kids.

The main thing that would put me off [having a child] is literally not being able to afford to support a child. That would be my concern, because as someone who is asexual and aromantic, the chances are that the adoption process would be complicated, IVF would be very expensive for a lone person to afford, and my job is unconventional and irregular. I'd worry that I wasn't able to give a child absolutely everything they needed – and more – long-term.

I've paid attention to the issues that lesbian couples, for example, have had acquiring IVF on the NHS. Even though those laws are changing, they haven't included asexual or aromantic people. I have considered that if I wanted a kid and wasn't able to adopt – or decided not to for some reason – that I might just have to force myself to have sex with someone for the sake of pregnancy, which wouldn't be great.

My hope for the future would be that less traditional families are valued the same way as traditional ones. I'd love to see queerplatonic relationships, platonic marriages, third parents, poly-families, same-gender parents, friends raising kids together or having kids together, childless families and every other variation of the family structure be perceived as being equally loving, committed and important to our society. There's more than one way to have a family, especially in the queer community, but I think that straight communities could benefit from that way of thinking as well.

CALLUM SCOTT HOWELLS (he/him)

Callum (twenty-three) is an actor, best known for playing Colin in Russell T. Davies' series *It's a Sin*.

Honestly, I didn't really think a lot about the possibility of being a parent growing up, until I was around sixteen when I started to see (for the first time I guess) LGBTQIA+ parents. There was a boy at my school who had two dads and it was such a big moment for me, particularly growing up in the Welsh Valleys. Seeing that made me understand and realize that I would be able to maybe raise a little human one day within a queer relationship.

I guess like many queer parents, the fear of them maybe being bullied is a horrible thought. I'm bad enough when another dog barks at my little Dewi (my dog).

However, having nieces and nephews and chatting to them regularly, kids are so cool nowadays, a lot more accepting and understanding even from when I left comprehensive school five years ago. So, I hope that continues to develop and grow and that soon LGBTQIA+ parenthood, and the concept of it being a 'new thing', is a thing of the past and it is just accepted universally.

I'm aware of surrogacy as I know a handful of couples who have gone down that route (and are the most amazing parents), but other than that I don't know an awful lot about what the other options are. I would love to know more, however I'm not in a position right now where I'm actively pursuing parenthood in any capacity. I haven't really got a great understanding of what the options are.

When my grandparents were alive, they would always ask me about maybe, one day, having kids. My mother does it a bit too. I'm always very honest though and I just say it's not really something I'm thinking about right now. One day, I'm sure I will want kids. But right now, I'm happy just having the occasional little thought about it.

My hope for the future is for every queer person to find their superpower. And use it.

CHAR ELLESSE (she/her)

Char (thirty) is the founder and director of Girls Will Be Boys, an online platform that blurs the lines between gender roles.

I definitely want children! I grew up dating only men, until the age of twenty-four, and even though the option of 'naturally' conceiving was a possibility, I was always super open to adoption. I always knew I wanted to be a parent, and that I just wanted at least a child to call mine and to love unconditionally. I wasn't dead set on that being biological. So yes, being a parent has always felt like a real thing, by any means.

I'm very aware of the layers of marginalization I have as a queer Black woman and being in a relationship with someone who is also a Black woman, we have our struggles as is, let alone then being responsible for the life of another marginalized person in the current state of the world. But we want to create our own family, it's super important to us, and especially my fiancée, who's wanted to carry since she can remember. So that desire to create a family and create something so special together trumps all.

My fiancée knows EVERYTHING about our options. I'm less in the know, but the news of IVF being free for LGBTQ+ people on the NHS was definitely something that made me really emotional. Due to our age, and the process taking a while, we knew it would be something that we'd have to save for and plan years ahead. So having the cost removed gave us an overwhelming sense of joy and even more excitement that we're closer to starting a family than we'd previously anticipated.

When I told my family I had started dating women, it was as though I'd told them what I had for breakfast; it really wasn't major news and they've been so supportive of me. My mum never put any pressure on me or my sister to 'give her grandchildren' (my sister is also gay). So, with the news that I had found the love of my life, and we do want children, was like an added bonus that she didn't expect as a given.

My hope for the future is support, community, and liberation for all!

JAMIE WINDUST (they/them)
Jamie (twenty-six) is a non-binary writer, public speaker and model from London.

In my experience, I grew up in a time where conversations around being an LGBTQ+ parent were just beginning to surface in the media, but not into everyday life. Personally, it felt like that was something that wasn't going to be an option and that it would either be being single permanently, or in a relationship with another person without any children. There never felt like a strong sense of 'oh, creating a family is a viable option for you'.

Much like for a lot of LGBTQ+ people, often doing everyday tasks such as working, living, going to the gym, theatre or the hospital for example can have another layer of complexity added to them. In my life, a lot of negative experiences I've had have been because of unwanted and unsolicited opinions from people who aren't happy with my trans or queer identity. I would worry that if I were to be a parent, I would face that same hostility but in a more vociferous and amplified way.

I am aware of the options available [to create a family], however I feel aware that as a single twenty-six-year-old, I am less informed about the ever growing options that are out there.

With my family there tends to be almost a feeling of complacency or disregard for me ever being in a long-term relationship or having that path that many non-LGBTQ+ people have. It's not that they don't think I can have that necessarily, but I believe it's the narratives that are played out around LGBTQ+ couples and children as being something taboo or rare that means often people don't think that LGBTQ+ people, like myself, can have families, or even have the desire to want them.

My hope for the future is that we are able to tell our own stories in ways that empower and enrich, rather than embroil us in scandal or hate.

A Last Word

Whoa. We did it. We hope we've taken you on a journey, an odyssey, full of twists and turns and highs and lows across the landscape of LGBTQ+ parenting today. We've learned so much from writing this book and meeting people whose experiences of becoming and being queer parents are so different to our own. But what we've found so heart-warming is that however radically unlike our own route to parenthood other people's journeys have been, there is something deep, and true, that we share with every single person we've spoken to: an abundance of love and unwavering desire to raise happy, confident and bloody fabulous humans.

But allow us to reveal our biggest secret right now, yes, right at the end of the book – if you've made it this far you deserve the truth. Our title *'Everything You Need to Know'* is a falsehood. Why? Well, there's no way we could have covered everything or shared every kind of LGBTQ+ parenting story. Maybe you've read the book and thought, 'But what about this?!' or 'What about that?!' or 'What about parents like me?!' We'd love to hear from you and share your story as part of the ongoing work we are doing with our other platforms, so please do get in touch (you can find out how on page 381).

We hope we've given a fun, yet informative and supportive snapshot, and that it has demystified at least some things for you, whatever your identity.

The beauty of queer parenting is that it's endless and amorphous. There is no right way, no wrong way, no formula, no standard. To be queer in the twenty-first century means you find

an identity that matches you, and if you can't find one, make one up or joyfully reject them all. As much as that annoys Piers Morgan, it means that we are now free to define ourselves and feel comfortable, and confident, in our true selves. And what this means is that our idea of 'family' can also take many shapes, forms and dynamics.

And What About Us? What Does the Future Hold for Our Families?

When John and I first adopted, we thought that was that. A family of four. A boy and a girl. We didn't know that just around the corner our littlest was about to make his dramatic debut into our lives. And how happy we are that he did. It taught us to expect the unexpected. What's next for us? We have no plans to adopt again but if for some reason another sibling came along, they, like our son, would feel immediately part of the family, regardless of if they came to live with us and be part of our Oakley clan. A lot of people ask us, 'What if there is another one? Would you adopt them?' In our hearts the answer is yes, but we don't know what the circumstances would be. Living such an unknown could really mess with our heads if we thought about it too much. Instead, we crack on and just enjoy every day that we have with our family. That family includes our children's older siblings, who, as time goes by, we get closer and closer to, which is such a joy.

In terms of everything else, well, we are really at the very start of our parenting journey still. We have a long, long road ahead of us and I'm sure there will be bumps along the way as we navigate all sorts of issues. Some we can predict and some we can't. Being connected to queer families everywhere and understanding the challenges and joys they navigate has enriched my parenting experience in ways I could never fully explain. And the future? What I know is that whatever happens we will continue to practise the mantra we repeated during the initial adoption process. And that is to love and have fun. It's all we can do.

I'm loving 'the school years'. It feels like the kind of parenting I was built for. Volunteering on trips, reading mornings, drama club, recorder lessons (okay, I might be regretting that one a bit); I'm in my organizational element. I enjoy the social aspect of meeting other parents and watching my daughter build the friendships that will hopefully last her a lifetime, and of course I'm championing the LGBTQ+ community at every opportunity. We'd love to expand our family, and if it wasn't for the insane expense of doing so, we would be trying every month. But in the current financial climate we have to be strategic about when and how we do so. It's not easy. In the meantime, I am now the reluctant owner of two kittens. These little fur babies have found their way into my heart and despite my better judgement have brought so much joy into our household and it feels as if our family has actually grown in a way I never could have imagined!

Roll the Credits

This feels like such an exciting and important time to be a queer parent. We're at the vanguard of the next movement in LGBTQ+ history where more and more of us become parents and we raise a new generation of humans who, whether or not they end up being LGBTQ+ themselves, deeply understand the queer experience. And a world with more queer allies is, without a doubt, a better and a happier world.

REFERENCES

1   New Family Social https://newfamilysocial.org.uk/Statistics-adoption/
2   https://explore-education-statistics.service.gov.uk/find-statistics/children-looked-after-in-england-including-adoptions
3   https://statswales.gov.wales/Catalogue/Health-and-Social-Care/Social-Services/Childrens-Services/Children-Looked-After/Adoptions/AdoptionsOfLookedAfterChildrenDuringYearEnding31March-by-Gender-MaritalStatusOfAdopters
4   https://www.nrscotland.gov.uk/statistics-and-data/statistics/statistics-by-theme/vital-events/adoptions
5   Equality Act 2010 https://www.legislation.gov.uk/ukpga/2010/15/contents
6   *My Magic Family*, Lotte Jeffs and Sharon Davey, Puffin, 2022
7   cryosinternational.com/en-gb/dk-shop/professional/research/our-scientific-research/donor-motivation/
8   https://www.legislation.gov.uk/ukpga/2008/22/contents
9   https://www.legislation.gov.uk/ukpga/1988/9/enacted
10 https://www.gov.uk/government/publications/relationships-education-relationships-and-sex-education-rse-and-health-education
11 https://assets.publishing.service.gov.uk/government/uploads/system/uploads/attachment_data/file/1101454/Keeping_children_safe_in_education_2022.pdf
12 https://dictionary.cambridge.org/dictionary/english/mother
13 *Mama you got this*, Emma Bunton, Ebury Press, 2021
14 *Young Gums*, Beth Bentley, Ebury Press, 2018
15 https://www.hks.harvard.edu/publications/summary-mueller-report-those-too-busy-read-it-all
16 https://www.gov.uk/government/publications/womens-health-strategy-for-england
17 https://www.ons.gov.uk/employmentandlabourmarket/peopleinwork/earningsandworkinghours/articles/womenshouldertheresponsibilityofunpaidwork/2016-11-10

18 *Drag: The Complete Story*, Simon Doonan, Laurence King Publishing, 2019

19 *tw-eat together: big feelings and short recipes for those who cook & eat with love*, David K. Smith, Scarcroft Publishing, 2021

20 *Straight Jacket: Overcoming Society's Legacy of Gay Shame*, Matthew Todd, Bantam Press, 2016

21 *My Daddies,* Gareth Peters, Puffin, 2021

22 *Me, My Dad and the End of the Rainbow*, Benjamin Dean, Simon & Schuster Children's UK, 2021

23 *The Family Book*, Todd Parr, Little, Brown Young Readers, 2010

24 *My Magic Family*, Lotte Jeffs and Sharon Davey, Puffin, 2022

25 https://gayswithkids.com

26 *The Transgender Issue*, Shon Faye, Penguin 2022

27 https://www.stonewall.org.uk/system/files/lgbt_in_britain_health.pdf

28 https://queerbirthclub.co.uk

29 https://www.ncbi.nlm.nih.gov/books/NBK501922/

30 https://pubmed.ncbi.nlm.nih.gov/31861638/

31 https://www.ilga-europe.org/

32 *Every Family Has a Story: How We Inherit Love and Loss*, Julia Samuel, Penguin Life, 2022

33 https://travelnoire.com/safest-countries-for-black-lgbtqia-travelers

34 https://news.airbnb.com/let-your-rainbow-flag-fly-the-top-50-pride-celebrations-around-the-world/

35 https://www.asherfergusson.com/lgbtq-travel-safety/

36 https://www.ons.gov.uk/peoplepopulationandcommunity/birthsdeathsandmarriages/divorce/bulletins/divorcesinenglandandwales/2019

37 *Somebody to Love: A Family Story*, Alexandra Heminsley, Vintage 2022

38 https://www.fflag.org.uk

39 *Queer Stepfamilies: The Path to Social and Legal Recognition,* Katie L. Acosta, NYU Press, 2021

ACKNOWLEDGEMENTS

A huge thank you to Abigail Bergstrom at Bergstrom Studio and Martin Redfern at Northbank for seeing the potential in our idea and helping us shape it. Thank you to Carole Tonkinson, Jodie Lancet-Grant, Martha Burley and all at Bluebird for your enthusiasm and absolute belief in the necessity of this book. Thank you to all at StoryHunter for the *Some Families* podcast adventure.

Thanks to our partners John and Jenny for their patience and support while we wrote this book, and to our kids for bringing us so much joy (and stories!). A huge thank you to all the wonderful LGBTQ+ people, friends and allies who we spoke to while researching each chapter. We are so grateful for your honesty and openness and it's so special to us to share your stories of queer parenting. And finally, thanks to anyone who has read to the end of this book – go forth and spread the word!

Keep in Touch

Lotte Jeffs and **Stu Oakley** are the hosts of the UK's first LGBTQ+ parenting podcast, *From Gay to Ze* (previously called *Some Families*).

If you want to get in touch with us, you can do so here:

Instagram: @FromGaytoZe
Twitter: @FromGaytoZe

Listen to the podcast: *From Gay to Ze*
fromgaytoze.substack.com

GLOSSARY

2WW: Two-week wait. During IVF treatment, this is the waiting period between fertility treatment and a pregnancy test.

Adoption order: This is a legal ruling giving full parental responsibility for a child to approved adopters, made on their application to the court.

Blastocyst: Five or six days after fertilization, a fertilized egg is known as a blastocyst – a rapidly dividing ball of cells. The inner group of cells will become the embryo. During IVF, a blastocyst is implanted into the uterus.

Cisgender or cis: A term used to describe a person whose gender identity corresponds to their sex assigned at birth.

Cishet: A short way of describing someone who is cis (see above) and also heterosexual.

Egg sharing (IVF): When someone undergoing IVF treatment donates their eggs to the clinic where they're having treatment, often in return for discounted treatment.

Gametes: Reproductive cells (eggs and sperm).

Gender dysphoria: The sense of distress that a person may experience because of a mismatch between their biological sex and their gender identity.

Heteronormativity: Denoting or relating to a world view that promotes heterosexuality as the normal or preferred sexual orientation.

Intersex: An umbrella term for people with differences in sex traits or reproductive anatomy.

IUI: Intrauterine insemination – when sperm is inserted via a catheter into the uterus on the day of ovulation. The closest thing to 'natural' conception.

IVF: In vitro fertilization – fertility treatment, explained at length in chapter 'I is for IVF' (page 145).

Non-binary: Relating to a gender identity that does not conform to traditional binary beliefs about gender, which indicate that all individuals are exclusively either male or female.

Non-biological parent: A parent who is not genetically connected to their child.

Non-gestational parent: A parent who did not physically birth their child.

Pansexuality: A sexual, romantic or emotional attraction towards people regardless of their sex or gender identity.

Parental order (surrogacy): This is a legal ruling that assigns parenthood permanently and extinguishes the legal status and responsibilities of a surrogate. It also leads to the re-issue of the child's birth certificate naming the parents.

Placement order (adoption): This is the legal ruling which authorizes a local authority to place a child with approved prospective adoptive parents. A placement order will last until an adoption order is made (see opposite).

Polyamory: The practice of romantic relationships with more than one partner at the same time, with the informed consent of all partners involved.

Reciprocal IVF: During IVF, one person's egg is used to create an embryo which is then transferred into another person's womb.

Section 28: This clause from The Local Government Act 1988 banned the 'promotion of homosexuality' by local authorities and schools. It was finally abolished in 2003.

TTC: This stands for Trying to Conceive – an acronym popular on fertility forums.

Therapeutic parenting: A highly nurturing, empathetic parenting approach, which uses firm but fair boundaries and routines to aid the development of new neural pathways in the brain so children may gain trust in adults.

Trauma-informed: A framework in social care and health care for working with and supporting children and adults who have experienced exposure to trauma.

Ze/Zir: A gender-neutral pronoun.

Visit https://www.panmacmillan.com/thequeerparent-resources for a comprehensive list of resources that should answer any remaining questions you have.

INDEX